"No one who has known Dr. Goodwin in Williamsburg can ever walk the streets of that dream city without sensing his presence in all that he sees, as well as the touch of his loving hand and the inspiration of his spirit. In the fullest meaning of the word, Dr. Goodwin is the spirit of the Restoration. He conceived the idea and made it reality. For all time his name will be connected with the enterprise as its originator, for everyone knows that without his vital, courageous, impelling personality, the Restoration would never have been other than a dream.

"These years of my association with Dr. Goodwin have been very happy years. I shall miss him profoundly and shall always be grateful that I have had a part with him in the realization of his great vision."

John D. Rockefeller, Jr.
The Eyrie
Seal Harbor, Maine
September, 14, 1939

The Dietz Press
Richmond, Virginia

A LINK AMONG THE DAYS

THE LIFE AND TIMES OF
THE REVEREND DOCTOR W. A. R. GOODWIN,
THE FATHER OF COLONIAL WILLIAMSBURG

BY DENNIS MONTGOMERY

Dietz Press
Richmond, Virginia

Contents

Introduction

Toward the end of his life, William Archer Rutherfoord Goodwin didn't remember when or where he got the idea. He wasn't sure it was his to begin with. But Goodwin could say for certain that he had persuaded one of the wealthiest men in the world to invest a fortune in phantasms—the once glorious ghosts of a decaying Virginia village.

The restless rector of an antique Episcopal church, he was formally addressed as the Reverend Doctor W. A. R. Goodwin, but most people, to his mild annoyance, called him "the Doctor." Besides tending his parish, the Doctor did double duty at the town's troubled college—teaching religion and raising money. He had taken for his part-time occupation the primary responsibility for the full-scale restoration of 18th-century Williamsburg, Virginia.

Goodwin began to promote his dream in 1924—a dream so daft it was at first ridiculed. No one had before suggested, let alone attempted, the restoration of an entire town. The president of the college told him he would be run out of town. The *Baltimore Sun* said that even if it could be done, it would amount to nothing but "a flivver imitation of departed glory."

The capital of Virginia since 1699, Williamsburg began to fade to a neglected memory when the new state's government retreated up the James River to Richmond in 1780. The Tidewater town slipped into decades of genteel tatters and poverty to become a backwater of historic homes, proud family names, and colonial landmarks. Its surviving 18th-century treasures were fast falling prey to rot and progress in 1924, but preacher Goodwin determined to save them.

It took a discerning eye to see just what was worth saving. Many of the old places sagged beneath the weight of their years; the charm of others had been blemished by 19th-century renovations and additions. The new concrete highway to Newport News ran straight down the main street, tossing off gasoline stations and tin-roofed garages as it went. But after a false start or two, and with patience, charm, and a bit of dissembling, the Doctor had shown John D. Rockefeller, Jr., the need of giving Goodwin the money to buy properties in the village and to invest as much again to transform Williamsburg into the showcase capital of early American history.

When the work began, neither Goodwin nor Rockefeller were sure what the result would be or what the job would take. They hadn't much more to guide them than Goodwin's guesswork, his enthusiasm, and their delight in sharing the dream of Williamsburg restored. To skeptics it was a pipe dream, as amorphous as the smoke that curled from the Doctor's ubiquitous Dunhill briar. But Rockefeller, the Standard Oil heir, had at his disposal the means to give substance to castles in the air.

At first Rockefeller figured on spending $2 million or $3 million, at the outside $5 million. Goodwin would be his resident agent, in charge of on-the-ground research and planning and acquiring likely properties. Rockefeller insisted on anonymity. The financier forbade the mention of his name during Goodwin's studies of the town's buildings, or during his midnight measurements of its greens and streets, or during the Doctor's shuffles through the yellowed leaves in the thickets of the historical record. The deeds and titles would be taken in Goodwin's name, or in blank, as if the parson had suddenly taken up the hobby of city-scale real estate speculation. Nobody was really fooled; Goodwin's restoration scheme was as open as the front page of the newspaper. But for 18 crucial months, no one knew for sure who was backing the suddenly acquisitive priest.

It is impossible to say that one man's contribution was worth more than the other's. Both committed more to the enterprise than they imagined it would require when they began. About $20 million into the restoration—before he was done he would spend more than $65 million—Rockefeller summed up what he thought should be credited to his collaborator's account. He drafted a telegram to be read at a testimonial retirement dinner Williamsburg was putting on for Goodwin. A sometimes Sunday-school teacher, Rockefeller strung together a couple of biblical allusions and wired: "As a dreamer of dreams King Pharaoh was not his equal, while as an interpreter of dreams, Joseph was but an amateur in comparison. Without Dr. Goodwin there would have been no restoration of Williamsburg. To him is due unbound credit. I am happy to join with his many friends in placing at his feet my tribute of appreciation, admiration, and affection."

That was in 1935. By then the postman delivered dozens of accolades—less pious, but as sincere—to Goodwin's office every week. The Doctor believed it behooved him to be modest, and he invariably replied—Goodwin answered all his mail—that the accomplishment was Rockefeller's. Goodwin liked to deflect praise by telling newspaper reporters and other impressionable people a little story on himself.

According to the Doctor, a fellow had stopped him on the street one morning, and said: "I should think you'd have a swelled head from all the wonderful things you have done here in Williamsburg."

The Doctor regarded the man a moment, smiled, pulled the pipe from his mouth, poked the stem at him, and said, "Well, you see, it was God who gave me the idea, and Mr. Rockefeller who gave the money, so I shall probably go on wearing the same size hat."

Merely by retailing the yarn, of course, Goodwin affirmed that he was a principal in the Williamsburg partnership. Already scribes were calling him "The Father of the Restoration." That appellation alone, perhaps more apt than his admirers realized, would justify a narrative of Goodwin's achievement. But it wouldn't be the whole story.

Colonial Williamsburg is the accomplishment for which Goodwin is remembered, and he was proud of his creation. But he had a life before and a life after the Restoration, and the sum of his 70 years is too rich and too ample to be confined by a few square blocks of rescued dwellings, reconstructed halls, and geometric gardens.

Moreover, every father's offspring matures, chooses a future, and slips from his control. So it was with the Restoration and Goodwin. Pushed to the periphery of the endeavor as it developed, its father was, in the end, orphaned. Nevertheless, as a parent does, he closely followed his child's progress and measured the Restoration against the hopes he had at the outset. "It has always been clear to me," he said, "that the supreme worth of this Restoration, and all material memorials, lies in the fact that they are the seen symbols of unseen and spiritual realities. The great problem of the Williamsburg Restoration will be the problem of interpretation of what has been preserved and recreated here, and will be a dead thing unless there can be given to it a silent and voiceful power of speaking for itself of the men and events memorable in history." Dropped the next year from Colonial Williamsburg management's organizational chart, he resigned what had dwindled into an honorary advisory post and quit the board of trustees in 1937. He and Rockefeller, however, maintained a mutually admiring relationship down to the Doctor's death in 1939.

Goodwin's life began in the ruins of Richmond after the War Between the States, the year the Golden Spike was driven at Promontory, Utah, to mark the completion of the first transcontinental railroad in America. It ended a few days after Nazi Germany invaded Poland and started World War II, the same year Albert Einstein told President Franklin D. Roosevelt about the possibility of building atomic bombs.

As a toddler, Goodwin was carried first by canal boat into the obscurity of rural Reconstruction Virginia—to Norwood, a farm market hamlet at the foot of the Blue Ridge where the Tye spills into the James. His father, a disabled Confederate officer, benefited from the kindness of his well-to-do father-in-law but still had trouble supporting his family. Eventually the Goodwins moved deeper into the mountains to Wytheville.

By then young Will Goodwin had been trained up to a Virginian's pride in his past, and he had much of which to be proud. At least one ancestor had fought for Virginia in the Revolution. His father was with Lee at Appomattox. His mother's home had been a hospital for the wounded of Manassas and the Peninsula Campaign. His uncle Thomas, a wealthy merchant, moved in Richmond's most influential circles.

Narrow circumstances have a way of nourishing pride. Though the Goodwins seem never to have been indigent, there was no money to stake Goodwin, the only son and eldest child, to a start in business. When he set out to make his way in the world, he looked down the two paths traditionally taken by young Virginians of means more modest than their ambitions. He would become an attorney or a minister. With an uncle's assistance, he entered Roanoke College in Salem in 1885, supplementing his resources with money he made on his own.

Goodwin tried on the idea of practicing law while he fought with the impulse to preach. In the contest, his view of religion matured and developed a secular cast. Like others of the era, he conceived of a ministry devoted to the community as well as to the Bible. In the beginning, his horizons were as limited as the lectures of missionaries on fundraising tours, the earnest activities of the Young Men's Christian Association, and volunteer preaching in a jailhouse. They expanded to a sort of ecclesiastical humanism.

Goodwin took one more look at lawyering, spent a few months in Richmond considering his options, and chose the church. A private scholarship put him through the Virginia Theological Seminary, and an activist Christian charity became the theme of his life. By the time he took his first parish in Petersburg and was ordained a priest, Goodwin's idea of God's work embraced taking temperance pledges from workmen, promoting laws restricting child labor, visiting among the poor, and teaching in an African-American divinity school. He opened a men's reading room to give factorymen an alternative to slum saloons and raised money to build a church.

He was an earnest and energetic young parson, in the class of men H. L. Mencken derided as uplifters, the kind of guy Goodwin's brother uplifters would call a go-getter and regular fellow. In those days, he took himself as seriously as all young men do when they begin a life's work—not that he ever took his work less than seriously. His diaries of those years are sprinkled with self-exhortation and fervent thanks for opportunities to serve mankind.

Goodwin pursued a belief that bettering families, inspiring hope, lifting spirits, and encouraging morality was as rightfully a part of his calling as the saving of souls. He thought religion should be a part of—as opposed to apart from—everyday life. Which, of course, to a minister it was. He preached the gospel of the abundant life, a life that wove the values of religion into the fabric of the community. He also found time to meet, court, and marry a local girl, and begin the first of his two families.

In those years, Goodwin developed the talent of asking for money in behalf of worthy causes and getting it. The donations, among other things, provided tuitions for black ministerial students, helped support missions in Japan and China, and relieved impoverished parishioners. Fundraising became so much a part of his life that he was at it even on his deathbed.

When in 1903 Goodwin began his first ministry in Williamsburg's Bruton Parish, he turned that talent to the restoration of its church, a cruciform building of brick that dated to 1712. The project, clearly, was not his idea; his predecessor had made a start on the job.

Certainly no one was more conscious of Williamsburg's heritage, talked about it more, or did as much to maintain the scores of colonial buildings that survived as the townspeople who lived in their ancestors' 18th-century homes. In fact, in 1884 the young women of the church formed a preservationist group, which, by the time Goodwin arrived, had been succeeded by the Association for the Preservation of Virginia Antiquities. The women had repaired the old gravestones in the churchyard, acquired the Powder Magazine, and taken custody of the foundations of the colonial Capitol.

Goodwin said more than 30 years later that Bruton's restoration "represented the beginning of the thought of the restoration" of the entire town. What he meant by "represented" isn't plain; and in other recollections, he contradicted this one. But the restoration idea wouldn't have required a flash of inspiration; it should have been a next-to-natural step in the progression of preservationist interest long afoot in the city. Perhaps that's why Goodwin could never put his finger on the moment the idea struck him. It was as much a part of life in Williamsburg as was the past.

The important part of his inspiration, however, was not its moment but his conception of the uses to be made of inspiration itself. In Bruton Church had worshiped the likes of George Washington, Thomas Jefferson, and Patrick Henry. Goodwin felt their presence and the presence of other patriots in the history of his parish, of his state, and of his nation. He communed, as he said, with their ghosts in the evenings as he walked Williamsburg's unpaved streets. He wanted his parishioners, indeed all Americans, to find inspiration not only in the faiths of their fathers but in the whole legacy of the people he called the nation-builders. He was a true believer in the democratic society he was sure they had established under God—as much the body of the abundant life as religion was its soul.

To promote Bruton's restoration, its history, and their

inspirational values, the Doctor researched and wrote a pamphlet and two books that are still the starting points for Bruton Parish historians. The first he used as a promotional tract as he traveled the East Coast soliciting contributions and help.

The parish dedicated the church in a ceremony attended by such luminaries as the Bishop of London and financier J. Pierpont Morgan. The crowd packed the building and overflowed into the churchyard. People elsewhere took notice. Success brought Goodwin promotion.

Wealthy St. Paul's Parish in Rochester, New York, called the Doctor to its pastorate in 1909. Among his communicants were men of means; if not captains, at least lieutenants of the city's burgeoning heavy industries, as well as bankers, lawyers, stock brokers, and real estate executives. The congregation was large, active, and committed to its church.

Goodwin's zeal for the ministry was no longer restrained, as it had been in Virginia, by a dearth of resources. Always energetic, he had come to a parish in which he could invest all his vigor in the pursuit of his ideas. For the next 13 $\frac{1}{2}$ years, he was, in effect, chief executive officer of a small but diverse and well-financed corporation complete with a staff, a board, plant, and investments— as well as politics, infighting, and second guessing.

At work he spent himself on the affairs of church schools, service clubs, vestry committees, and building projects. He wrote more books, raised more money, studied and reformed parish organization, and refined the methods of collecting offerings and pledges. He rose in the hierarchy of the diocese and was sent on a national speaking tour. He was a delegate to national church conventions, participated in Rochester's civic affairs, organized city religious observances, and volunteered to minister to soldiers and sailors in the camps of the First World War. He seldom turned down an invitation to deliver a speech or a chance to share his opinions on the questions of the day.

At home, in St. Paul's rectory, he raised three children and nursed his first wife through a lingering illness that led to her death in 1915. He read. He started another book and composed a never-published epic-length poem, *Emmanuel.* He liked verse and taught its composition to his children. His favorite lines were from Alfred Lord

Tennyson's *In Memoriam*: "A link among the days to knit, the generations each to each." Tennyson was speaking of the church in the figure of a mother, but Goodwin made reflexive use of the passage in historical contexts—much as it has been in the title of this book. A parishioner gave him a set of volumes titled *Modern Painters* and from it Goodwin memorized a John Ruskin epigram: "It is our duty to preserve what the past has had to say for itself, and to say for ourselves those things that shall be true for the future." It nearly became Colonial Williamsburg's motto.

Goodwin sent his children to boarding schools but maintained an attentive, instructive, and often admonitory correspondence with them as they coped with life on their own. He encouraged them to keep daily diaries, just as he had in college, and to mind their expenditures as closely as he did his. In 1918, he courted another Virginia belle, remarried, and began a second family.

The Doctor took on so many jobs and responsibilities that he drove himself to nervous exhaustion. By 1922 he was, he said, "inexpressibly mentally tired." He confided in his bishop his intention to leave St. Paul's, and asked for a less demanding position in the city. As his St. Paul's work wound down, the opportunity came to return to Williamsburg.

It was a chance to take up the quiet life of a College of William and Mary professor and to head up the dilapidated school's endowment campaign. Goodwin quit Rochester in February 1923 and shipped his household south on a train.

J. A. C. Chandler was president of William and Mary. He had come aboard in 1919 to keep the college, the second oldest in the United States, from oblivion and improve upon the start made by Lyon G. Tyler. Thanks in part to a decision in 1918 to make the school Virginia's first co-educational college, William and Mary's enrollments were rising. Chandler could count on state appropriations to support the college's operations and its teacher training program, and some temporary buildings were thrown up to accommodate an expanding curriculum. Still, funds were tight, and the school badly needed more and better facilities if it were to survive.

The president had ideas of building classrooms, laboratories, athletic facilities, and dormitories. Goodwin was eager to teach, but he and Chandler understood the primary importance of Goodwin's money-raising skills. In addition to his professor's salary, Goodwin would draw a commission of five cents on every fundraising dollar.

He brought with him to the job his St. Paul's secretary, Elizabeth Hayes, and their partnership lasted the rest of the Doctor's life. After Goodwin and Rockefeller, she had the most important, and least celebrated, part in the adventure that followed.

Before his first William and Mary year was out, the Doctor landed a $175,000 gift for construction of a gymnasium, and he was railroading up and down the seaboard calling on the well-to-do for more such benefactions. The chief talking point of his appeal was William and Mary's history. Jefferson and James Monroe were among its alumni; Washington was its first chancellor. The main building—the Wren—dated to 1695. On the Wren's left stood the President's House, begun in 1732. On its right was the Brafferton, built for an Indian school in 1733. Only the Brafferton stood now in its original form and fabric, but each was an example of the best in colonial Virginia architecture.

Goodwin wanted the appearance of his gym to harmonize with these 18th-century buildings. But Chandler thought the construction money would go farther with a more modern and functional design. The dispute, which reached the board of visitors, as the trustees panel is called, turned out to be pivotal in perfecting the idea of the town's restoration.

The Doctor enlisted for an ally his old associate, J. Stewart Barney. A prominent New York church architect with Virginia roots, Barney had helped him with the Bruton Church restoration 16 years earlier. Now Goodwin asked him to return to Williamsburg, and argue for a gym with a colonial façade. After a meeting with President Chandler proved fruitless, Barney and Goodwin walked to the apex of the triangular College Yard at the top of Duke of Gloucester Street. They stood talking about the surviving colonial buildings in Williamsburg, and what could be done to preserve them.

Barney advised Goodwin to find a rich man to buy the buildings, renovate them for student and faculty housing, endow them, and deed them to the college. It was precisely the proposal Goodwin would make to Rockefeller and exactly what Rockefeller started out to do.

Before he was done, Rockefeller thought better of the idea and found other ways to help William and Mary. But once he started

on the town's restoration—despite misgivings about the costs and the
complications and regardless of the disasters of the Great
Depression—he pursued the essence of Goodwin's plan, the revival
of 18th-century Williamsburg. New houses were demolished or
moved, old houses repaired and restored. Archaeologists dug out
foundations, and plans were developed for reconstruction of the
Governor's Palace, the Raleigh Tavern, and the Capitol with its
House of Burgesses.

As the work went forward, and the Depression deepened,
the thing that came most to count was the idea of creating in the
now-uppercase Restoration a shrine to the life and the values—as
Goodwin, Rockefeller, and their associates perceived that life and
those values—of America on the threshold of nationhood and
greatness. If their perceptions would later be faulted, at the time they
reflected the faith and aspirations of a country pre-occupied with
itself and sometimes doubting the fundamentals of democratic
capitalism. America wanted reassurance; it was a nation in need of
ideas, and of touchstones.

After even Rockefeller had lost half his money in the
financial collapse, Goodwin's son-in-law Barclay Farr wrote to the
Doctor and asked about the beginnings of the Restoration. He
wanted something he could tell his friends. He wanted to know how
Goodwin had come by the idea, to know the source of the dream.
Goodwin composed his reply with care, and told in three pages the
essentials of his life's grand achievement. He wrote:

> The George Wythe House
> Williamsburg, Virginia
> March 15, 1931

My dear Barclay:

It is very good of you to ask how the thought of the
Williamsburg Restoration began. It is difficult to trace a dream to its
beginning.

Somehow I have always felt that the older people of
Williamsburg, many of whom lived in the Colonial houses, were
largely responsible for the dream of the city restored. They loved the
stories which had been handed down to them from the past. They
were constantly peopling the houses with fascinating ghosts who,

you know, beckoned dreamers to wander with them down the dim lit paths which lead into the past. The dream of the Restoration was nourished and enriched by these human contacts.

The tradition is current in Williamsburg that, while the people here have ever been ready and willing to wage civil war over differences of opinion, they have been held together by a love of the past which they have cherished as a common heritage. They might divide into contending hosts over the location of a School on the Palace Green, or upon such questions as permitting cows to rove at random through the streets, but they would rally with united front to contend against any claim that was made that Fredericksburg, Boston, or Charleston, could possibly be as deserving of historic fame as was Williamsburg.

Memories lingered here of the things which had been said by those of the olden times. The ghosts of the past haunted the houses and walked the streets at night. They were glad and gallant ghosts, companions of the silent hours of reverie. They helped to weave the stories of the past which have found their way into fiction, into current traditions, and into history. While these stories may not have always been entirely true to fact, they were true to life. They grew as they were told on moonlit verandahs or on winter nights by those gathered around a blazing fire whose flickering light illuminated the faces of ancestral portraits which still graced the Colonial walls. These ancient personages had been too long silent. Words were put into their mouths, and these words wove themselves into the charming stories of the vanished days of the long ago.

Letters were found which had lain long hidden in secret drawers or in hide-covered trunks. Through them Washington entered Williamsburg with Rochambeau to join here the gallant LaFayette or the romantic love of a young French officer was rapturously revealed as it sought to awaken responses of the heart of a Virginia belle.

Amid such familiar scenes the Palace ballroom was again peopled by "the lovely and the beautiful, the light of other days." The music of the minuet and the fragrance of the mint again filled the "Hall of Apollo" in the Raleigh Tavern as Jefferson returned to dance with his fair "Belinda," or to listen to the eloquence of Patrick Henry in the House of Burgesses.

These scenes lingered in the thought and fancy of the older

people here, but the public buildings with which they were associated were no more, and many of the ancient homes of spirits recalled had vanished from the scene.

As one listened to these stories and traditions of the past, one felt that they may have been embellished, but that after all they were not more embellished than were the days and the scenes which they recalled. They were the result of the desire to recapture the glory of the past, which was finding its resurrection through the glamour of memories. These stories were akin to the effort of the poet to people again the halls of King Arthur with the Knights of the Round Table, or like the desire of an artist to catch and hold the lingering twilight of a departing day.

But alas, the canvas was coming to be little more than a thin worn fabric of dreams. The frame which held it was fast falling to pieces. It was evident that unless something was done there would soon be left in Williamsburg nothing but memories of what was no longer here, and regrets for the loss of the tokens and symbols of a glorious past.

Then, too, there were the nightmares that disturbed the dream, as nightmares will. They blurred the picture. Corrugated iron buildings on the Duke of Gloucester Street mixed in with highly colored filling stations. Unsightly shacks and stores and cheap modern restaurants were like blots on the painting of a master artist. They held no lure for ghosts, and broke the harmony of dreams as the noise of sledgehammer blows would mar the music of a Beethoven symphony.

It gave a real hurt to the soul to see a beautiful Colonial building bought to be torn down to make place for a garage or to see ancient garden spaces covered over with tin shops and tin cans.

The hope had long been indulged that some one might be found to respond to the appeal of Williamsburg for restoration and preservation. We knew that America would respond with gratitude and appreciation when the significance of a restoration of the city was understood.

In my mind was always the hope that Mr. John D. Rockefeller, Jr., might visit Williamsburg. The knowledge of what he had done and was doing to "preserve what the past had to say for itself" gave encouragement to the hope that he would vision the great education value of the restoration of the Colonial city and become interested in making this additional contribution to the enrichment of culture and the promotion of human fellowship.

It would, we felt, be evident to him that Williamsburg stood unique among the cities of America associated with the past. The bonds of an ancient fellowship existing here between Old England and Virginia, and between France and America, would, I believed, make appeal to his expressed interest in promoting international accord.

With these thoughts and hopes in mind we sought first to interest him in the College. This endeavor was destined to failure because the appeal was ignorantly made in the wrong way. His interest in College and University education was, we found, being amply expressed through other channels.

It is terribly hard when one makes a wrong approach to a very busy man, to undo the error. It is not because of a diminished faith in the man approached, but because of a diminished faith in oneself. Consequently, I turned to others with no results except an unexpected publicity given through the papers to the restoration idea.

Fortunately Mr. Rockefeller's interest in the proposed memorial hall of the Phi Beta Kappa Society brought him twice to Williamsburg.

These visits in the end proved to be very expensive to him! This was not because he was asked for money. This appeal was not made to him. The soul of Williamsburg appealed to the soul of a rare and cultured man. He gave himself in response to hopes and dreams otherwise incapable of fulfillment.

The Restoration of Colonial Williamsburg, now in process of a beautiful completion, is the result of his sympathetic understanding and his generous and glad willingness to enshrine a glorious history in the simple beauty of the capital of Colonial Virginia as it is now being restored.

This, in brief, because it is a long story, is the answer to the request which you have made.

No one can ever know how happy I am to have been instrumental in some measure in helping in what Mr. Rockefeller is doing through the Restoration to save a city that will now speak to the future of things both noble and beautiful in our Nation's past.

Faithfully yours,
Wm. A. R. Goodwin

Foreword

No book-length biography of the Reverend Doctor W. A. R. Goodwin has before been published. Often cursory and sometimes jumbled accounts of his role in the restoration of Williamsburg began to appear in 1927, just after the project started, but no writer paid much heed to the rest of his long life. And no treatment of his Williamsburg days has been as forthright as that in this volume. Much of the material within is printed for the first time.

That material comes mainly from records Doctor Goodwin compiled for institutions he served, or kept of himself and his family. His business files are rich with correspondence, journals, pictures, and other documents. But his personal and still-private archive is a biographical treasure trove. It contains letters, diaries, family photographs, telegrams, manuscripts, tax returns, jottings, canceled checks, sermons, wills, speeches, pamphlets, deeds, poems, bills, newspaper clippings, even an informal autobiography of his first 53 years.

This book, like earlier accounts, focuses on Doctor Goodwin's signal accomplishment—the creation of Colonial Williamsburg. It is, however, a biography, not an institutional history. Nevertheless, the Williamsburg chapters trace Goodwin's passage through the restoration's first 15 years, and readers will find here facts available nowhere else in the public prints or that elsewhere have been glossed over.

Folklore, and wishful thinking have mantled the memory of Goodwin. In his last year, he wrote, "Research takes much joy out of life by curbing the cherished traditions long recited as if they were the proved facts of history." Charming fictions about Goodwin do not stand up to comparison with the record. But a candid relation of his life is just as interesting—and more instructive—without embellishment or invention.

In every respect this is a journalistic, not an academic, work. It endeavors to capture the vitality, energy and humor that characterized Goodwin's life, a life not without blemish.

In one of Goodwin's puckish moments he offered some wisdom on this score to a Baltimore historian sketching the lives of Virginia's great men. Goodwin said: "It is exceedingly hard to clothe dry bones with flesh, with vigor, and with beauty. The man who assembles these bones and who correctly articulates them and then breathes into them the breath of life, answers, as he alone can answer, the question of Ezekiel—'Can these bones be made to live again?'"

Resurrection work was, of course, the Reverend Goodwin's day job. But he was a writer, too, and he often raised with himself the Ezekiel question. Goodwin published six books and was at work on another when he died. In his correspondence are scores of essays masquerading as letters. Selective but generous use is made in these pages of Goodwin's literary bones, because his words as he articulated them capture the breath of life as he exhaled it. Such verisimilitude also serves the interests of accuracy.

In 1923 Goodwin sent to a friend a just-printed copy of the first volume of his *History of the Theological Seminary in Virginia*. In a letter dispatched with it, he said: "A work of an historical nature requires such painstaking accuracy in every respect. In history, facts are facts and dates are fixed, and one cannot guess at such things. There will, of course, be discovered minor errors, but I think there are very few. I suppose no book was ever printed that did not contain some."

A biography is, of course, a history of a life, and Goodwin's penchant for preserving records simplifies the work of telling his story faithfully. But no man commits all that he does or says to paper. Moreover, Goodwin saved very little material that touched on his family life, and his most personal letters have been destroyed. The temptation to fill the gaps with informed conjecture—to guess, as Goodwin put it—has been resisted. Readers will find facts enough from which to draw conclusions.

If, as Goodwin supposed, no book has ever been written that didn't contain errors, this volume cannot claim to be the exception—though it is to be hoped the flaws are few and minor. They are, in any case, the author's. Credit for what is right with the work is due the colleagues, associates, archivists, family, and friends without whose help and encouragement this book would not have been attempted.

Chief among them are Howard and Alice Goodwin of Charlottesville, Virginia, who generously permitted me unrestricted access to Doctor Goodwin's personal files, and who over the years received me with gracious hospitality during my visits to their home. I introduced myself to Howard, Doctor Goodwin's son, by telephone while writing a script for a video biography of his father in 1994. Howard's cooperation, and that of his wife Alice, has been extraordinary, patient, and unfailing from that day to this, and I am deeply appreciative. Among the chief rewards of the endeavor has been the chance to make the acquaintances of two people who define the word Virginian.

The affection of three other people for Doctor Goodwin and his memory—three people I never met—was of fundamental help as well. Between them, the late Rutherfoord Goodwin, who was Doctor Goodwin's oldest son, and Rutherfoord's late wife Mary preserved, protected, sorted, and supplemented Doctor Goodwin's personal papers until shortly before Mary's death in 1990. Their work and research illuminated subjects that might otherwise have remained obscure and smoothed my way over some stumbling blocks. So, too, did the unflagging efforts of the late Elizabeth Hayes Goddard, Doctor Goodwin's secretary and assistant from 1922 to 1939. She was the original clerk, custodian, and compiler of the records during Goodwin's years with St. Paul's Church in Rochester, New York; Grace Church in Yorktown, Virginia; the College of William and Mary; Bruton Parish Church; Colonial Williamsburg; and the Yorktown Sesquicentennial Association. From them she wrote invaluable narratives of his activities before, during, and after Williamsburg's restoration and helped Goodwin draft, edit, and revise his own accounts of his endeavors. Her daughter Diane Bergh of Los Altos, California, kindly and unselfishly permitted me the use of her mother's Williamsburg papers and became a delightful correspondent.

The attentive, courteous, and friendly cooperation of the Colonial Williamsburg Foundation's archivists opened all but confidential files to me and cheerfully gave every assistance for which I asked. Manager Steve Haller and his staff Donna Cooke, Betty Stewart, Patty McIntyre, Pat Hickey, Alexandra Curran, as well as former manager Bland Blackford, provided valuable documents and assistance.

No less valuable was the tolerant and willing help of Colonial Williamsburg's John D. Rockefeller Jr. Library staff. Susan Berg, Liz Ackert, George Yetter, Del Moore, Laura Arnette, Cathy Grosfils, Marianne Carden, Gail Greve, and Mary Keeling each contributed their professionalism to the research.

I first sought their help in 1993, when Kenneth Wolfe of Colonial Williamsburg's development department asked if I could create a slide show for the foundation's W. A. R. Goodwin Society. Barry Dress, Colonial Williamsburg's director of development, commissioned the writing and research, and later asked for the video. These endeavors, collaborations with Colonial Williamsburg Productions, are the genesis of this biography.

It would not have succeeded without John Hamant, the shows' narrator and advisor; Priscilla Waltner; photographer David Doody and his staff, Tom Green, Mary Norment, Tom Austin, Kathy Dunn, Lael White, and Kelly Mihalcoe; producer Mike Durling and his staff, Pete Roberts and Chuck Smith; and Nancy Gulden.

Dress's support and advice as the projects passed through their phases were fundamental to their completion. Also essential was the encouragement of Wayne Barrett, editor of *Colonial Williamsburg*, and production assistant Brenda DePaula; Richard McCluney, director of Colonial Williamsburg Productions; and designer Helen Mageras of Colonial Williamsburg's publications division. Barrett edited the manuscript and designed these pages.

Finally, my thanks are due my wife Joyce and my daughters Charity, Harmony, Honor, Carla, and Grace for tolerating my absences, real and figurative, and answering my calls for help during the research and writing.

Claremont, Virginia
1998

Chapter One: **1934**

At precisely 11 a.m. on April 19, 1934, a Thursday, the
Reverend Doctor W. A. R. Goodwin was cued. A quarter inch shorter
than 5-foot-10, he drew himself up behind the microphone and
commenced to speak. "It is an honor deeply appreciated," he began,
"to be privileged to address this distinguished gathering on the
Restoration of Colonial Williamsburg, capital of Colonial Virginia,
which restoration is now being consummated through the cultured
interest and munificent generosity of Mr. John D. Rockefeller, Jr."

It was the kind of opportunity preachers prayed for in the
1930s. The National Broadcasting Company had set aside half an
hour to carry live and coast-to-coast a homily from the rector of
Williamsburg's Bruton Parish Church. Radio then was still novel—
NBC itself was barely seven years old—but already glamorous, and
powerful, especially in its appeal to the imagination. Eleven months
earlier, Franklin Delano Roosevelt had adroitly used that power,
inviting America into the White House for the first of his fireside
chats. People listened as respectfully as if they were in the
President's living room—which vicariously they were—as he
described what he was doing about the nation's economic crisis.

Goodwin also spoke from Washington, though his forum
was several blocks away at Constitution Hall, where had assembled
the 43rd Continental Congress of the Daughters of the American
Revolution.

The microphone, a big metal affair emblazoned with the
network's initials, made it harder for the conventioneers to see
Goodwin's face. But they could hear him, standing there at the
zenith of his fame. His voice was mellifluous, smooth and sweet,
somewhat nasal but low-timbered and honeyed with the long-
voweled accents of Virginia's Tidewater. "About" was "ah-bauwght,"

and "house" was "hauwze."

To Elizabeth Hayes, his secretary, he was a "born orator," eloquent "whether in conversation or when speaking from the pulpit, platform or public rostrum." She said that "he not infrequently became so enthusiastic when delivering a sermon or making an address that one feared he might lose his balance and come hurtling down, as he leaned far out . . . in hammering home an idea." He piled his words up backwards in phrases that rolled his sentences over little hills of expression. His rhythms were leisurely, almost halting. His start-and-stop cadence underscored his thoughts and made an audience listen to hear if his clauses would sort themselves before he fetched up on a period.

The Daughters were attentive. "It is," he said, "a subject which naturally is of vital interest to you and your associates and friends throughout the world. What Mr. Rockefeller is doing in Williamsburg is in reality the creation of a visible and monumental symbol of the high sentiment and unselfish devotion of the patriot fathers, which you and other patriotic societies of America are seeking to preserve and perpetuate."

It was the sort of high-flown sentiment that had made him a darling of the sons and daughters of every flag-waving cause, the poster boy of the preservationists, a friend to the rich, and a confidant of the powerful. For Williamsburg was as much a monument to the lives his listeners led as to the lives of their patriot fathers. It represented a way of life they were trying to recapture, preserve, and perpetuate. That a session of a D. A. R. convention would be broadcast nationally is an insight on the state of the national psyche. Williamsburg was a concrete answer to the question of what, in those distracted days, the country really stood for.

Williamsburg was a 3-dimensional lesson in the values of 100-percent Americanism, a fasthold against the uncertainty of the times, the dread of creeping socialism, the threat of another war, the fear of immigrant influences, and the spectacles of underclass lawlessness. In the Southwest, bank robbers Bonnie Parker and Clyde Barrow were on the loose. "Pretty Boy" Floyd had gone to ground in Ohio. Back East, G-men were closing in on a German stowaway, Bruno Hauptmann, for the 1932 kidnap-murder of the Lindbergh baby. Gangbuster J. Edgar Hoover had made himself a legend, and Alcatraz was in everybody's vocabulary.

But here at the podium stood Goodwin, scion of

respectable British-American stock, reassuring, the upright son of a poor man, the self-effacing member of a Mayflower family, a courtly Virginian, an affirmation of the rightness of traditional conservatism and the Anglo-Saxon Protestant creed. Or so he seemed.

The Doctor's patriotism was as sincere as the D. A. R.'s—maybe more—and he believed what he said. But he had no use for xenophobia or intolerance. Though proud of his heritage, Goodwin spent no time digging among the roots of his family tree. His admirers and patrons tended toward staunch Republicanism, but Goodwin's politics were New Deal Democrat.

On race, he was more flexible than most Virginians. Like almost everyone, he didn't capitalize the word negro. He counseled blacks to remember their place and blamed racial discord on outside agitators. But he was a trustee and fund raiser for an African-American seminary, insisted on admittance of blacks to historic Jamestown Island, pestered two governors for the parole of a repentant African-American convict serving life for murder, and preached to black chain gangs.

Within his state he participated, enthusiastically, in the endeavors of patriotic societies, but he never spent a dime to join one; all his memberships were honorary. From start to finish, he was at heart an everyday Anglican minister to ordinary men and women, though better spoken.

Goodwin turned his page and spoke again into the microphone: "The past and the present are the parents of the future. Therefore, so Ruskin says, 'It is our duty to preserve what the noble past has had to say for itself, and to say for ourselves what shall be true for the future.' To this ennobling task your organization is dedicated. To this end, also, is dedicated the restoration of Colonial Williamsburg."

He took a small liberty with Ruskin by adding the word "noble"—Goodwin said he liked to "improve" on a quote. He had a weakness for displays of erudition; a big gold Phi Beta Kappa key depended from his vest. That vest had grown a little tight, though the Doctor carried not much more than 160 pounds on a rather large-boned frame.

He had stowed in a suitcoat pocket his briarwood pipe, its bowl still warm from the last load of Prince Albert tobacco. These days he clinched it between false teeth. Baldness long ago had established a beachhead above his bushy eyebrows and begun an inward march. He was 64. But he was still handsome, a man with whom women liked to pose for photographs.

"It is impossible to restore a vanished past," he said to his radio audience and the convention delegates. "It is possible, however, to preserve the memorials of the past and to re-create the architectural and artistic setting of vanished days. Through historic buildings restored or reconstructed, and through revived colonial gardens of boxwood, crepe myrtle, and roses, the imagination is stimulated to recall the scenes and associations of bygone centuries, and to link the life of the past with the thought of the present, and thus enrich the life of the future.

"In the re-created environment which the Williamsburg Restoration seeks to recall, one may hear echoing voices which come to us out of the past and catch visions of men who are written down as dead, but who still live as an inspiration in the memory of mankind. These memories are awakened by the vision of the homes where they lived and the places where they nobly wrought."

What Goodwin and Rockefeller had wrought since the first property had been purchased in 1926, the Doctor said, was 63 buildings restored, 72 reconstructed, 345 removed or destroyed. They had opened 28 shops with colonial façades in the two blocks at the west end of the city's central thoroughfare, mile-long Duke of Gloucester Street. The Governor's Palace, to be dedicated four days hence, was the latest step in the quickening march to wrap up the Restoration's first phase.

He took up the subject of the Colonial National Monument, a national park Goodwin was instrumental in creating. It linked Jamestown, site of the nation's first permanent English settlement; Yorktown, the field of Washington's triumph over the British; and Williamsburg, the city restored, with a wide, tree-shaded parkway.

"In Williamsburg," he said, "the Colonial College buildings of William and Mary, including the Christopher Wren building, have been restored. The Governor's Palace, the Capitol, and the Raleigh Tavern, have been rebuilt. Most of the Colonial houses on the Duke of Gloucester Street and the spacious city greens have been restored. Within a year the telephone and power lines, which in Williamsburg as in China hinder the return of ancestral spirits, will go underground; concrete streets and pavements will have vanished.

"Along the graveled street the hitching posts, mounting blocks, and wayside wells and watering troughs of other days, will reappear, and, with them, the ghosts of the past will return to say things in the twilight hours to spirits attuned to hear their voices speaking in boxwood and rose gardens revived, and from quaint artistic ancient houses, and from spacious and ornate public buildings restored."

Goodwin believed in ghosts. Not the sort that hid in closets or under beds but the kind that lived in the mind as the memories of the people of the past. The spirit embodied by the Restoration, by the writing of a Jefferson, by the colonial cabinetmaker's chests of drawers, whispered in Goodwin's imagination.

"To those who will have had the wisdom to come and linger here, and it is necessary that one should linger here, these voices will speak," he said. "The Colonial National Monument road will beckon them into silent forests. . . . Children, with their God-given fancy, unblinded by unrealities, will sense the presence of fascinating ghosts in shadowed haunts and glimpse the Indians of other days through the beckoning greenery of the forest glades, or seek to trace the footsteps of Pocahontas through the wood lands where she dwelt, or follow the warpath of King Powhatan, her father.

"Children of the larger growth of time, who have been spoiled and blinded by the 'light of common day,' as they have passed in their journey away from the dawn, will come, and if wisdom lingers, will linger here through restful and restoring days. To them will come, amid these ancient habitations of the city restored, visions of reality, and they will return home inspired and enriched by those things which live because God has thus linked them through deathless memories with the immortalities of human life."

It was the end of the beginning for the Restoration and, conversely, the beginning of the end of its need for the individuals Rockefeller had hired to shape and build it. The first phase of the project was nearly done. The reconstructed Capitol had opened in February. The first exhibition building, the reconstructed Raleigh Tavern, had been in business for 17 months.

The Restoration was terminating its contracts with, but retaining as consultants, Perry, Shaw and Hepburn, the Boston architectural firm that had redesigned the city, and contractor Todd & Brown, the New York construction outfit that had carried out the plans. Goodwin had resigned as a director of Williamsburg

Restoration, Inc., and as assistant treasurer of that organization and
its sister company, Colonial Williamsburg, Inc. He had gone on half
pay in February. Hayes had taken an almost two-thirds cut in her
Restoration salary.

They were rushing to put on the finishing touches. About a
month after the D. A. R. speech, Goodwin wrote to a friend:
"Williamsburg at present looks as if it had been struck by about ten
earthquakes all at once. The streets are in a condition of upheaval
incident to undergrounding telephone and power lines, laying new
sewers, and preparing for putting down of a gravel roadway and
appropriate sidewalks. The unprecedented winter weather which we
have had is delaying this work about six weeks, but we hope, by
June, certainly by October, that things will be straightened out."

Roosevelt was coming in October for a 21-gun grand
opening of Duke of Gloucester Street. It would be the second great
Williamsburg ceremony of the year.

In February the Virginia General Assembly returned to
Williamsburg for the first time since 1780, conducted a
commemorative session in the colonial Capitol, and made
Rockefeller an honorary Virginian—an honor before bestowed only
on the Marquis de Lafayette.

Rockefeller's acceptance speech was broadcast live from the
House of Burgesses, and the newsreels were there. He praised
Goodwin for the restoration dream, thanked the governor and
legislators, wished his father could have been on hand, and concluded:

"What a temptation to sit in silence and let the past speak to
us of those great patriots whose voices once resounded in these
halls and whose far-seeing wisdom, high courage, and unselfish
devotion to the common good will ever be an inspiration to noble
living. To their memory the rebirth of this building is forever
dedicated. Well may we say to ourselves in the words which the
Captain of the Lord's host spoke to Joshua: 'Loose thy shoe from off
thy foot, for the place whereon thou standest *is* holy.'"

The scripture appears twice in the Old Testament, first as
Exodus 3:5, and again as Joshua 5:15. In Exodus it reads: "And he
said, Draw not nigh hither: put off thy shoes from off thy feet, for the
place whereon thou standest *is* holy ground." Then the words are
delivered to Moses by the Angel of the Lord speaking out of the

burning bush.

　　Moses and Joshua aside, Rockefeller had compounded some historic facts into the sort of overstatement great men are prone to make. No patriot's voice, or anyone else's, had resounded in the Capitol earlier than the year before, when construction of the brand-new H-shaped building neared completion. It was a reconstruction, not a restoration; a from-the-ground-up re-creation, not the salvation of an 18th-century original.

　　Certainly the new Capitol rose above original foundations, but, at that, it was an anachronism, and perhaps an inaccuracy. The first building on the site, finished in 1705, featured semicircular apses on the south ends of its two mirror-image wings. That Capitol burned in 1747, and construction of its replacement, the building that

Goodwin, fifth from left against the wall, John D. Rockefeller III, sixth, Kenneth Chorley, seventh, and Governor George C. Peery, eighth, watch John D. Rockefeller, Jr., enter the reconstructed House of Burgesses to deliver his 1934 dedicatory address.

stood at the Revolution, began in 1751. Its wings were rectangular.
Though Colonial Williamsburg was intended to represent the city on
the eve of independence, that consideration was put aside, and the
first Capitol was reconstructed for the greater architectural interest
of its semicircular elements. "The rebuilders of the reconstructed
Capitol have now been accused of redesigning it," architecture critic
Ada Louise Huxtable wrote in 1997. "More recent scholarship has
suggested that the original documents and foundation remains were
misread in the 1930s. Taught to think in terms of the formal classical
symmetry of their Beaux Arts training, the reconstruction architects
could not believe, or accept, that the building's axis could have been
off center. The entrance contradicts the evidence of the foundation
and is probably in the wrong place. Other spatial relationships are
also questionable."

But by its nature, Colonial Williamsburg was intended to be
more a representation of the ideal than the reality. The enterprise
and its buildings were abstractions of artistic, philosophical, and
polemical constructs. "I have felt from the outset," Rockefeller said,
"that the restoration of Williamsburg, that ancient center from which
there went forth those intellectual, spiritual and patriotic influences
so largely responsible for the making of our country, would perhaps
some day have much to do with the recreation in our people of the
qualities of their forebearers."

Rockefeller and his wife, the former Abby Aldrich of
Providence, Rhode Island, relaxed in town awhile afterward. The
next day they attended Sunday services at Bruton. They heard
Goodwin read, as the Anglican calendar called for, the lesson about
it being easier to thread a camel through the eye of a needle than to
navigate a rich man through the gates of heaven. Some parishioners
thought it tactless, and Goodwin apologized, but Rockefeller took it
in stride. The rector assured Rockefeller he thought the
philanthropist had already secured the keys to the kingdom.

On Monday, Rockefeller called at Goodwin's office on the
second floor of the Wythe House for a conference. They discussed
the construction of a hotel, theatrical effects in the historic district,
the educational ends of the Restoration, who should be its
custodian, and Goodwin's future.

The custodianship question was touchy. At the inception of
the project, Goodwin represented the College of William and Mary.
President J. A. C. Chandler had brought him back to Williamsburg

from Rochester in 1923 to be director of the school's endowment
campaign. Goodwin's proposal to Rockefeller in 1926 was to take on
the restoration in behalf of the college and deed the town's buildings
to the school for classrooms and student and faculty housing.

As Goodwin was swept up in the project, he agreed with
Chandler "that it would not be expedient, in view of the Restoration
endeavor, that I should actively prosecute the Endowment
Campaign work, but rather to take advantage of such opportunities
as might offer, to call the needs of the College to the attention of
persons whom I met from time to time whose interest might be
enlisted." For the meantime he would remain on William and Mary's
faculty, but his most active interests would henceforth be the
restoration and Bruton Parish Church.

There was no question what Goodwin had in mind when he
approached Rockefeller, but in 1928 the Rockefeller organization
backed away. Rockefeller spent $514,000 to restore the school's main
building and more on its two other colonial structures—for which
Goodwin declined his fund-raising commission—but balked at
conveying Colonial Williamsburg properties to a creature of the
state. As Goodwin understood it, Rockefeller worried what
politicians might do with the project.

In a memorandum of the February 1934 meeting, Goodwin
wrote: "The suggestion was made that, if the College of William and
Mary could be taken from political control and made a cultural
institution of very high grade, it might be well to consider the
advisability of having the guardianship of the city committed to the
Board of Visitors of such a college, if and when created; the thought
being that either the Board, through some committee of the Board,
might have supervision, or else that the Board might appoint some
carefully selected committee to which this responsibility might be
delegated."

In other words, Goodwin wanted to take the school away
from the state and make it a private college, its future secured by a
private philanthropic endowment. Rockefeller didn't contemplate
contributing to that endowment, but he was willing to cooperate.
Goodwin saw the plan as a way to demolish the wall of separation
between church and state at the taxpayer-supported school and
infuse its curricula with religious instruction, just as it had been at
the school's founding in 1693. That was another of the Doctor's
dreams. He believed that "all education should be related to Spiritual

development and the spiritual expression of human personality" and "learning without a Christ-like purpose is knowledge without either power or wisdom."

Chandler died after a lingering illness on May 31. Goodwin did as much as he could to make good on his original commitment and to meet Rockefeller's objections, before the transition was made to a new administration with its own plans and goals. On June 8 he drafted a seven-page proposal to the board of visitors. "Dr. Chandler committed himself unreservedly to the suggestion that an effort be made to establish the College upon an independent Endowment and authorized the solicitation of funds for this purpose," Goodwin told the visitors. "It was, of course, evident that such an Endowment fund would be conditioned upon a changed objective and the ultimate separation for the College from political control."

On the 26th he presented a two-page version to the president-designate, newspaper publisher John Stewart Bryan and on the 30th, Bryan's *Richmond Times-Dispatch* printed it as an article. Goodwin told the newspaper's readers that the chief obstacle to raising money for the school was that it was a state college and emphasized the narrow specialty of teacher training. He envisioned its transformation into a "cultural college," an institution of higher moral purpose. "The great need of today," he said, "is for that type of education which will create a new sense of values." He would also end coeducation.

In a passage that could not have endeared him to Chandler's waiting replacement, Goodwin said: "I have ventured to make this appeal for a review and consideration of the high future Mission of William and Mary, and of the conditions precedent to her largest possible usefulness as a means for creating culture and enrichment of life, prior to the election of a long term permanent President.

"It is evident that the opportunity of establishing the College upon an independent foundation would, of necessity, involve a complete freedom, on the part of the reconstituted College, to make choice of its personnel for leadership, untrammeled by any previous commitments."

In any case, Goodwin's formal associations with the college were all but at an end. He had been on unpaid leave of absence from the faculty since 1931, when the national financial crisis forced the General Assembly to slash state education appropriations. Because of the Depression, Goodwin had given up even his passive fund raising in 1933. He had collected $1,089,375.76 from private sources, though no large gifts had come in since 1928. Among other things, the money, combined with state funds, had helped build 11 major buildings. During Chandler's presidency, according to the college, the value of William and Mary's buildings and grounds rose from $450,000 to $4,772,311, annual expenditures from $84,000 to $763,940, and enrollment from 333 to 1,269. Goodwin's contribution to the success of those years spoke for itself.

With Bryan's selection and Goodwin's restoration responsibilities winding down, the Doctor attempted to revive his academic and fund-raising connections to the school. In August he wrote to the president-designate: "The consciousness of growing old has of late been vividly present in my mind. . . . I no longer feel equal to carrying the full burden of teaching work at the College in connection with my other duties. And yet I do not want to entirely withdraw from the College just as my cherished hope is being fulfilled in your acceptance of the presidency." Goodwin proposed that he and an unemployed professor friend divide the duties and salary of teaching a course called "The Life of the Spirit and the Life of Today." A physician had warned Goodwin to curtail his activities, even to the point of giving up his practice of showing tourists around the city. In effect, Goodwin was asking to return part time to active teaching duty. Perhaps because he spoke so late in the summer, the class was not listed in the fall quarter catalog. One student heard about it anyway and enrolled, but Bryan couldn't justify offering a course for a single pupil.

"This being so, it is obvious to me that it will be impossible to get your salary approved under present conditions," Bryan wrote to Goodwin. "I hope very much that we can find some other way to work out a method by which the College may avail itself of your valuable services, and in case we do I will be glad to confer with you about that. If we are not able to employ you we will continue you on the leave of absence."

Goodwin promptly submitted his resignation but offered to stay as Bryan's fund raiser. If he remained, Goodwin said, he wanted a contract, and he would prefer to collect money only for professors' raises, selected student aid, "or to pursue the purpose of setting the College free from political control." Goodwin had in mind a full-time post. Bryan put him off, but the Doctor insisted on an answer. With the backing of the board of visitors, Bryan finally offered no more than to consult the Doctor on special fund-raising projects. Thus ended the work that had summoned Goodwin to Williamsburg, the work that had resulted in the Restoration.

With Hayes' help, Goodwin closed his fund-raising books and began to prepare a final report. It noted that he and Rockefeller had discussed deeding the Restoration to the school, but "It was felt that Colonial Williamsburg restored, would, itself be a contribution to the enrichment of the life of the college." The Doctor wrote that he had abandoned his effort to help build "an endowment which would be adequate to establish the College upon a foundation independent of State aid control." So stood matters for now.

While Hayes typed the report, Goodwin prepared to leave for a general convention of the Episcopal Church in Atlantic City. The college and the Restoration turned their attention to the final plans and preparations for Roosevelt's visit. The president would arrive by train the morning of October 20, dedicate Duke of Gloucester Street, and motor to the college to deliver the principal address at Bryan's installation as William and Mary's 19th president. As Goodwin left town, he asked Hayes to send the college a list of his 28 most important donors to consider for the guest list. Five days before Roosevelt's arrival, someone noticed Goodwin had been left out of the college ceremonies.

Bryan wired the Doctor at the beach, asking him to hurry back to deliver the inauguration benediction. Goodwin returned in time to greet Roosevelt at the Capitol. "For nearly a year Williamsburg had no Duke of Gloucester Street," he later wrote, "for in December 1933 ground had been broken to place all telephone and electric power lines underground and to pave the street to resemble the dirt road of the eighteenth century."

A 21-gun salute from the National Guard boomed out over the city with the arrival of Roosevelt's train. The chief executive boarded an open limousine and motored to the Capitol. He remained in the car while Mayor Channing M. Hall presented a scroll of welcome. At 11 o'clock, the driver pulled away for the college. "Large flags near the Capitol were parted and the President's journey up the shady old street signalized the formal opening of the street restored, with its grassy curbs, flagstone and brick walks and old type street lamps." Goodwin said. "The street was lined with citizens who cheered lustily as the presidential car passed by." They also cheered for Eleanor Roosevelt, Mrs.

Woodrow Wilson, Admiral and Mrs. Cary T. Grayson, and Senators
Carter Glass and Harry Flood Byrd.

At the College of William and Mary, President Roosevelt
said: "What a thrill it has been . . . to have the honor of formally
opening the reconstructed Duke of Gloucester Street, which rightly
can be called the most historic avenue in all America. What a joy to
. . . see 61 colonial buildings restored, 94 colonial buildings rebuilt,
the magnificent gardens of colonial days reconstructed—in short to
see how through the renaissance of these physical landmarks, the
atmosphere of a whole glorious chapter in our history has been

Goodwin (left) and Kenneth Chorley greeted Franklin Roosevelt when the President
visited Williamsburg in 1934 to dedicate Duke of Gloucester Street.

recaptured.'"

The next day Goodwin wrote to Rockefeller to describe the festivities, noting: "A congressman had his pocket picked—he now knows how it feels."

Rockefeller returned to Williamsburg in November and called on Goodwin at the Wythe House the morning of the 3rd. The only topic this time was Goodwin's separation from the Restoration.

The Doctor never asked Rockefeller for money, but Rockefeller always insisted on rewarding Goodwin and Hayes for their labors. Neither otherwise could have afforded to devote so many working hours to the Restoration. Nevertheless, the arrangement, which Goodwin recapitulated for Rockefeller in a memorandum of this meeting, was private.

Colonel Arthur Woods, Colonial Williamsburg's first president, "very wisely took the position that I could best serve your interests, by not being connected, on a salary-relationship, with any Restoration organization," Goodwin wrote. "He felt that, with no such connection, there would be given me larger freedom in forming my judgments and in the expression of opinion. Consequently my salary was paid direct from your office."

Goodwin had volunteered for salary reductions as his duties diminished, but Woods and Rockefeller demurred. About a year earlier, however, the new president, Kenneth Chorley, "discussed with me the question of a new salary basis for myself and for Miss Hayes." They were moved to a payroll Chorley controlled; their salaries were slashed, and were to be cut to nothing at the end of January. Carefully spelling out the details of his personal finances, the Doctor noted he still had his Bruton Parish Church salary, a housing allowance, and a little annual income from stocks and bonds. Then he offered his resignation and Hayes'. He said:

> In handing you my resignation you will know that it is done with unqualified and unreserved appreciation of your unfailing kindness and consideration.
>
> If, as you further formulate your plans in connection with the Restoration, there should appear to be any service which I can render, which will be of real help to you and this endeavor, it would give me supreme pleasure to render such service.

If on the other hand our official and financial relations should be terminated, I will always cherish with supreme gratitude the memory of my relationship with you and to the work of the Restoration.

You will also be assured that it will be my constant desire and pleasure to render at any and all times loyal and willing help and cooperation with you and your representatives here to the end that harmony and good will and mutually desired results may attend the further developments of the Restoration plans and purposes.

In closing, the Doctor offered to sell the Restoration his home, a three-story house on Francis Street, for what Goodwin paid for it in 1923. The next day, Chorley wrote to Goodwin asking him to close out his Restoration expense and office accounts, but within a week Chorley, too, called at the Wythe House for a conference. Goodwin and Hayes would stay on the payroll until the Restoration closed the deal for Goodwin's home. Thereafter, the Doctor would remain a Colonial Williamsburg trustee and play an informal role in the day-to-day work.

Rockefeller wrote on the 14th: "Your personal letter of November 5th is received. I appreciate deeply the spirit which has prompted you to write as you have. The association we have had together in the restoration project has been one of the notable experiences of my life. As I told you the other day in your study at the Wythe House, I could not bring myself to contemplate a severance of this happy relationship. You will, therefore, realize how pleased I am to hear from Mr. Chorley today of the new arrangement with you which he has consummated in line with the talk I had with you."

If Goodwin regretted the acceptance of his resignation, he kept faith with his dream and with Rockefeller. The Restoration hostesses, costumed women employed part-time to lead tourists through Colonial Williamsburg's buildings, invited Goodwin to address them at the Capitol. He prepared another speech, "The Background and Beginning of the Williamsburg Restoration." The title was very close to a document Hayes had presented to Goodwin in April for his signature, a history of the Restoration compiled from their letter files. She seems to have hit upon the idea while copying for Colonial Williamsburg the Doctor's Restoration correspondence. Long stamped "Confidential," it remains the single most important document of the project's beginnings.

The Doctor began his remarks with a rhetorical question: Why was Williamsburg restored? He spoke for a minute about the ghosts and talked about what now picture-perfect Williamsburg had looked like when he began. He was measuring his accomplishment, saying what he had done, remembering what he had imagined in his evening walks:

When the dreams and visions of the night vanished and the stars were gone, one could see the desecrated Williamsburg, from which the ancient glory and beauty had so largely departed.

In the background of the Restoration there were not alone dreams of vanished loveliness but there were nightmares also. There was the nightmare of Palace Green with its modern and inartistic public school building standing obtrusively where the Governor's Palace had stood. There was the hideous nightmare of Market Square green with its motley array of eighteen modern buildings. Near where the Travis House now stands was the corrugated iron Palace Theatre and east of it a line of buildings vying with each other in ugliness, including the bank building which the owners managed to tie together until they could sell it to the Restoration. Did any city ever have such a firehouse and city hall as the ones that faced South England Street, on which stood, next to the Powder Magazine, a corrugated iron garage with its flaming red invitation painted on the door 'Toot-an-Kum-In?' Next to this were two dilapidated negro houses. A three-story brick building towered from the corner of the Duke of Gloucester Street near which stood the Greek temple pillared Baptist Church, flanked by an A. & P. Store true to color and form, and next to it a hideous building which encased what was once a part of the ancient Market Square Tavern.

Up nearer the College was a row of tumbled-down modern stores and disreputable houses of some very reputable negroes. They had inherited the houses, as negroes often do, when no white man was left who would live in them.

And who can forget Casey's Store? It was exhibit A, with its gables and its annexes, each part painted or white-washed in the color of its pristine construction. This building stood across the side street from the present site of the Peninsula Bank and Trust Company, while where the Raleigh Tavern now stands there was a brick store, with false front, flanked by other stores of hideous mien.

Colonial buildings were, in many places, crowded upon by fire-trap structures. In other places old homes of colonial days hung over caved-in foundations being held up by their rotten framing timbers. In one instance the negroes who slept in one of these colonial buildings slept in rainy weather with umbrellas over them. They slept there without paying rent. Some sense of humanity was left, for who would seek to collect rent from dwellers in a colonial house whose only protection from the rain was an antique umbrella which leaked also. This house is now restored on Francis Street and is known as the Orrell House. It was not entirely unique among some of the dilapidated colonial buildings in pre-restoration Williamsburg.

This is not either a complete or in any sense an adequate description of Williamsburg as it was. Some few colonial houses retained a fair measure of their ancient grace and beauty, but no one of them was protected from fire and very few from the fire menace of neighboring fire-traps. The extent to which this was true may be realized when it is recalled that 442 buildings of modern construction have been demolished.

So much, and much more could be said, of the Background of the Restoration. Only one who paused to recall the unique glory of the vanished past, or who looked upon the conglomerate mixture of the then thought-provoking and fear-challenging decaying city can understand how compelling the thought of and desire of a Restoration would be.

Gasoline station advertising disguises the 18th-century origins of the Prentis Store in the dog-eared days of 20th-century Williamsburg.

Williamsburg's Bruton Parish Church in 1886.

Chapter Two: **1869-1889**

Some of Richmond was still burning when the Union Army marched in. The heart of the city lay in ashes. As they evacuated the Confederate capital the night before, the rebel troops who guarded the city put the torch to the stockpiles left behind. The blazes spread on a wind that drove flames through the business district and showered sparks on the brick rowhouses and wooden homes beyond. As the Yankee columns turned into the streets that April 3rd in 1865, officers ordered men to pitch in to stop the fires from spreading further. Strands of smoke still drifted from the ruins when Abraham Lincoln, thronged by just-free blacks, strolled up from Rocketts Landing the next day.

Cold rubble choked Main Street when Lieutenant John Francis Goodwin, C. S. A., of Richmond's home guard made his way into the shattered city more than a week later. The Stars and Stripes flew from the peak of the Capitol on Shockoe Hill. A blue-coated sentry stood at Robert E. Lee's gate on Franklin, protecting the family's peace.

Frank, as John Francis was called, entered the army— probably as a conscript—in 1863. He answered his first muster as a sergeant, reporting October 13 to Company B of the 6th Battalion of the Virginia Infantry, Local Defense. Commanded by Captain John McDonald, the battalion styled itself Tredegar's 6th Light Dragoons.

At the end of April 1864 Goodwin won election as a junior second lieutenant, the rank he held in September when the 2nd and 6th battalions were consolidated to form the 2nd Regiment of the Virginia Infantry, Local Defense. That November he was detached from Company E to serve at Chaffin's Farm along Richmond's collapsing eastern defenses.

As the months passed, the city's position grew desperate,

and the Confederate Congress authorized enlistment of African-Americans to shore up the lines. Goodwin wrote March 18, 1865, to Major J. W. Pegram: "Being anxious of raising a company of colored men for field service, I respectfully request that you will have me ordered by the Hon. Secy. of War to you for duty." McDonald endorsed the request, saying "I consider Lt. Goodwin well qualified for the duty upon which he desires to be ordered. He is an efficient faithful officer & I would not be willing to give him up except for his own promotion."

What progress Goodwin made in recruiting, the records that survive don't show. Perhaps none; he soon reported to Petersburg to join Lee's defense of the town and the railway lines Richmond depended upon for communication and supply. When Grant drove the rebels out of their trenches April 2, Goodwin joined the Army of Northern Virginia's retreat toward Danville as an additional aide de camp in Battle's Brigade.

Like Lee and the Army of Northern Virginia, Goodwin made an enforced return to civilian life at Appomattox on April 9. He carried back to Richmond with him a parole filled in with his name and rank, which identified him as a member of the headquarters staff. He was not in good health, having suffered from exposure in the field or, by other accounts, a wound.

Frank was the son of a New England man, Episcopal missionary minister Frederick Deane Goodwin. His father had come south more than 30 years before to attend the Theological Seminary of Virginia near Alexandria. After graduation in 1836, he wed Mary Frances Archer, the daughter of an Army surgeon at Fort Monroe, opposite Norfolk. They settled in Nelson County, about 80 miles up the James from Richmond, and raised four sons. Frank was born in 1843. Frederick moved to Wytheville in southwest Virginia, where he was rector at St. John's when the church was built in 1858. By then Frank and his uncle William M. Archer had become partners in Richmond's Vulcan Iron Works. During the war, Frank divided his time between the army and answering the East Byrd Street factory's bell. Partner or not, he worked at such tasks as cutting tacks.

After the war the disabled veteran found a wife in Richmond, Letitia Moore Rutherfoord. Born in 1848, she was one of seven daughters of Samuel J. Rutherfoord, a man of property and means, and the former Frances Watson. Samuel, the son of a wealthy immigrant Scottish merchant, had opened their Richmond house for a hospital. The girls nursed wounded and dying Confederate troops returning from the battlefields after First Manassas. When fighting slackened, the daughters entertained soldiers around the piano in the parlor. One married a doctor who went into practice after the war with the surgeon who treated Stonewall Jackson for his fatal Wilderness wounds.

Frank and Letitia were wed July 14, 1868, at St. Paul's, just across the street from the Capitol and Richmond's most fashionable church, by the Reverend Doctor Charles F. E. Minnigerode. A German refugee and once a Williamsburg college professor, the rector had baptized President Jefferson Davis. Davis was now imprisoned at Fort Monroe, but President Andrew Johnson, who had survived impeachment in May, granted Christmas Day pardons to the rebel rank and file.

Eleven months after their union, the Goodwins produced a son. He was born June 18, 1869, perhaps on Franklin Street, where

Letitia Rutherfoord Goodwin in 1896, the year her son entered Roanoke College.

Frank and Letitia lived in 1870. His parents carried him to Amelia County, a Rutherfoord family outpost, where at Grub Hill Church he was baptized William Archer Goodwin. Years later, out of affection for his uncle Thomas, he took Rutherfoord for another middle name. For the most part his family called him Will, or Willie.

The South was in economic tatters, but the Vulcan works look to have gone on well enough. In 1870 it was producing bolts, nuts, washers, grating, fencing, and iron railing; did smiths' work, and made machines. The Northern economy was robust. At the outset of the year, John D. Rockefeller, Sr., of Cleveland incorporated his limited partnership into Standard Oil of Ohio with $1 million capitalization. In September there was a financial panic, but an outbreak of smallpox in Richmond was likely of more concern to Frank than any threat to his business. That year he quit the city, though the move was not prompted by the contagion. "My father's health having been undermined during the War," Will said in a narrative of his early years, "he was ordered to remove to the country. He knew nothing about the country and had neither the health nor experience which were essential to successful farming." Letitia was no better prepared; she once asked her husband which of their cows gave buttermilk. She did, however, sew all her oldest son's clothes from country-store cloth until he was grown.

Will recalled the events of these and later years in an *Autobiography* prepared in 1924 as a Christmas gift for his children. Before he was two, he wrote, his parents bundled him aboard a packet boat that floated them up the James River and Kanawha Canal to Nelson County's New Market. Oxen and mules walked beside on a towpath, pulling the low wooden craft against the current and through the locks. Will broke out in measles on the way. Suspecting the pox, cautious fellow passengers kept their distance.

New Market, a hamlet clinging to a rise at the confluence of the James and the Tye, stood with its back against the Blue Ridge and looked eastward into the Piedmont. At the turn of the century, it was renamed Norwood. Will's uncle Edward Lewis Goodwin had been rector of its Christ Church. William H. Ribble was the town doctor and the husband of Fanny Goodwin, Frank's sister. "It was in order that my father might be near him and have the benefit of his professional skill that Nelson was chosen as the place where we 'pitched our tent,'" Goodwin wrote. At first they lived with the Ribbles—Will's cousin Frank became a life-long buddy—then they took a house next door. "My first memory is of the winter afternoon when the snow was falling, when I was wrapped in a blanket and carried from Doctor Ribble's home through a gate in the fence to a home into which we then moved." It was just above the church, on the east side of the village.

In September 1876 Letitia's father gave her $5,060 to acquire a 563-acre farm on the river bottoms a mile east of the house. Frank took title as trustee for his wife. He seems never actually to have grasped the plow. Will said his father "farmed from a distance;" tenants worked the place on shares. "We always believed that the tenants made a very good living from the farm," Will wrote. "We were never quite certain that we did." Frank remained an absentee partner in the iron works at least until 1878.

He and Letitia had one other son, Frank, Junior, who died in infancy, and four daughters, three of whom lived to adulthood. "We also became the possessor of a horse, several cows, of a garden, and of a spring down at the foot of the hill, a quarter mile from the house," Will remembered, "which . . . together with an axe and hoe and a water bucket constituted the chief implements and tasks of my early education. Later on I acquired a dog and some white rabbits, which still later on were eaten by the dog, which was the first tragedy of my youth. A little later still the dog had his eye pecked out by a rooster."

The boy rose at dawn to kindle a half dozen household fires, then he helped his father with the milking. When Will was a teenager, his father hired a man called Uncle Sam to help with the farming, but Uncle Sam "went crazy, made him a bed of jimson weed under the oak tree in the backyard, and died." Will's most onerous duty always was lugging buckets of water up the hill from the spring.

Molly Roberts, his first teacher, conducted school across the road in a room with one window, one door, and many children. "It was a bare room in a log building, the other end of which was presided over by Mr. Matthews, the shoemaker. . . . Miss Molly was noted for her ability in handwriting, and I can well remember the ambition which came to me in my boyhood days to copy the well rounded and beautifully slanted letters which she wrote on the top of a sheet of paper for us to copy." Nothing would ever be more distinctive about Will than his penmanship, which he began in these years to perfect. At age 11 or 12, he entered a private school taught by Miss Kemp Kinckle at Montezuma, a plantation house a quarter of a mile below town. In 1881 or 1882 he won a prize for spelling, and somewhere in between he fell in love for the first time. Her name was Lila Hubbard. When Norwood opened a public school, Will left Montezuma for a seat on its benches.

After class was another round of chores, and at about sunset, with the mail train's approach on the Virginia Midland Railway, he was sent to Norwood's combination post office, store, and barroom for letters and groceries. Captain Stratton, who weighed 380 pounds, presided over the place. Although Will disliked the drunkenness of Stratton's patrons, he "first learned from him how much real goodness could be in a barkeeper." At Christmas, the captain dispensed firecrackers for the day's celebration. "In fact it was the only celebration which we had, because, in those days, the Fourth of July was not a day that was marked in the calendar of Virginia." The War for Southern Independence had become the Lost Cause, and memories and resentments lingered.

The family was active in the little red-brick church just below the house, and at 14 Will was confirmed. "Very clear in my memory are the religious influences brought to bear upon my life while at Norwood," he said. "Chief among these was the influence of my mother. She was a living epistle and the letters were written so large that even a little boy could read the divine revelation as it was written in her daily life. She was superintendent of the little Sunday School which was held down at Christ Episcopal Church at the foot of the hill. My father was the senior warden and I was the sexton." Five of the boys in the sexton's Sunday school class, taught by a Mrs. Peters, became ministers, one advancing to bishop.

Will remembered his aging grandfather Goodwin as a man of austere piety. Will said the patriarch developed a Southern temperament to compliment his New England conscience, "which is about as bad as a combination of rheumatism and St. Vitus dance." The ministry seemed to run in the Goodwin family. Along with uncle Edward, uncle Robert Archer Goodwin followed the cross and served, among other places, in Salem and Petersburg, Virginia. Both ministers influenced their nephew's choice of a career and its development. In Petersburg—where Will would eventually succeed his uncle—Robert had charge of two African-American institutions, St. Stephen's Church and St. Stephen's Normal School, which later became the Bishop Payne Divinity School. In 1893 he was appointed rector of St. John's in Richmond, the church where Patrick Henry had given his "Give me liberty, or give me death" speech 118 years earlier. Uncle Frederick Goodwin, Jr., became an Arizona territorial judge.

Will's summers passed in hoeing the garden, swimming in a branch of the canal or a dirt-dammed pond below the spring, playing baseball, and shooting marbles. "The only other real fun I remember was the actual skinning of a cat which Frank Ribble had managed to kill and with which we made a mask which made the boy who was privileged to put it over his face, the wild Indian or the barbarian man of the afternoon." Some summers the family took the packet down to Richmond and rode on for Amelia County to visit Grandfather Rutherfoord's estate at Castles.

There were other boyhood excursions. "My grandfather Goodwin, having grown old and feeble, it was thought by the family that it might help him, and it might help me, to spend a winter in Wytheville," Goodwin said. He took a bed in the house his Aunt Ella shared with her husband Clarence Repass, his grandparents, and one or two more members of the clan. It was an especially religious household, and Will carried some of its piety home when he returned the next year to Norwood. Frederick Goodwin died soon after, in 1881. Will's other grandfather, Samuel Rutherfoord, had died the Christmas before.

In his 15th summer, Will made his first trip alone, an excursion by train for a long-term visit with friends in Culpeper County. He had to get his trunk over the mountain to Montreal Station seven miles away. He ran a rope around Uncle Sam's waist, tied the other end to a wheelbarrow, put his baggage in, took the handles, and away they went.

The next year Will enrolled in Roanoke College in Salem, just outside of the city of Roanoke. He took lodgings with his uncle Robert, rector of St. Paul's. "I could not have afforded to go to College had it not been for his kindness," Goodwin said. "My father's health was bad and the farm provided little more than a very limited living. . . . My uncle invited my parents to let me come and live with him, which I did without any charge to them." Frank Ribble, his cousin of cat-skinning fame, went along, too.

Freshman Goodwin studied history, philosophy, and divinity. He remembered little of his first year at the Lutheran institution, but that summer's vacation stuck in his mind. He was studying French at home, and his tutor brought along a 17-year-old cousin from the

Rockfish Valley. Goodwin fell hard for her, a young woman whose "hair was deeply golden, and her eyes were of liquid blue." One summer night he traced in the dark, using matches for a pen, *"Je vous aime de tout mon coeur."* "I love you with all my heart." Goodwin never forgot her.

That September he came by another treasure: For the first time he bought himself a book. Will had worked four sweaty 50-cent days pulling down fodder in a cornfield. With the $2 he purchased a tome with a dark blue cover embossed with gold pictures of the Promised Land. Inside, he inscribed the flyleaf with his lacework signature. Goodwin kept the volume all his life, three times embellishing his inscriptions. The title page said:

Buried Cities Recovered
or
Explorations in Bible Lands,
Giving the Results of recent Researches in the Orient and Recovery
of Many Places in Sacred and Profane History
Long Considered Lost

By Frank S. DeHass, D.D.
Published by B.F. Johnson and Co.
Richmond, Va.
1884

Williamsburg, the city Goodwin and John D. Rockefeller, Jr., would recover, wasn't buried, but the sands of time were obscuring its 18th-century treasures. Will, who liked to read the newspapers, may have noticed a headline that June reporting the destruction of the Eastern Lunatic Asylum in the old colonial capital. Superintendent James D. Moncure blamed the disaster on its new-fangled electrical wiring. Originally called the Public Hospital, the 112-year-old-institution was the first facility in British America devoted to treatment of the mentally ill. Dating to 1773, it had been among the surviving originals of old Williamsburg's public buildings, among them Bruton Parish Church, the college buildings, the Public Records Office, the Courthouse of 1770, and the Powder Horn.

Bruton had been modernized and remodeled in 1839, the work completed in 1840 with the installation of the town clock in its steeple. The interior was divided to provide Sunday school space,

the altar moved, and new pews put up. Much of its 18th-century
simplicity had been lost.

In 1862, after Williamsburg's occupation by Union General
George McClellan's soldiers, members of the 5th Pennsylvania
Cavalry set ablaze the College of William and Mary's main hall to
deny cover to rebel snipers. Now called the Wren Building, it was
the college's primary classroom and dormitory facility. Its walls and
foundations withstood the fire, the third in its history, but little of the
interior survived.

In the spring of 1865 the garrison blocked and loopholed the
Wren's west windows and doors and installed a cannon to guard
against Confederate raiders. After Appomattox, William and Mary
classes resumed despite the condition of the building. It was rebuilt
in 1869.

The Governor's Palace burned in 1781 while serving
Revolutionary War soldiers for a hospital after the Battle of

The College of William and Mary's Wren Building and members of its student body
much as they appeared when Goodwin first visited Williamsburg.

Yorktown. Union troops pulled down its two advance buildings in
1863, so that officers at Fort Magruder, east of the city, might have
bricks to build chimneys in their huts.

By 1880 the octagonal Powder Horn—later called the Public
Magazine—had become a livery stable. It had served previously as a
market house, a Baptist meeting hall, and a dancing school. There
was more use for it now, in any case, than for the Wren, which
closed again in 1881 for lack of students and funds.

That was the year of the Yorktown Centennial celebration,
when the railroad reached Williamsburg at last. The remaining
above-ground vestiges of the Capitol of 1751 were removed, so that
Chesapeake & Ohio magnate Collis P. Huntington could run
temporary tracks down Duke of Gloucester Street and through
Capitol Square. The cars carried people out to the battlefield a
dozen miles away and to the new Yorktown Victory Monument.
Despite its promoters' ambitions, the centennial turned out to be not
quite so historic as an affair in Tombstone, Arizona, reported in the
penny press that month—the gunfight at the O.K. Corral.

But a woman who assisted with the Yorktown celebration,
Cynthia Beverley Tucker Coleman, would make a lasting mark on
Williamsburg's future. Former principal of the Female Seminary of
Williamsburg, she organized the first preservation organization that
appears in the Williamsburg records. Formed in 1884, it was a girls,
club, the Catherine Memorial Society, named for a 12-year-old
daughter who died the year before. The society was a Bruton Parish
Church auxillary and raised money for church projects through bake
sales and such.

When Bruton's congregation undertook extensive repairs,
remodeling, and alterations of the church two years later, the
Catherine Memorial Society contributed $300 for interior work and
furnishings. As the job progressed into 1887, the girls requested
permission of the vestry "to repair the old monuments in the Church
Yard and to otherwise put in order the yard as their means may justify."
Many of the colonial gravestones, which lay flat on the ground in 18th-
century fashion, were cracked and crumbling. Coleman set the girls to
mending the tablets and underpinning them with bricks.

Though the church looked less than ever as it had appeared
originally, it was called by the vestry a restoration. At least the
building had been brought into a better state of repair than the
Powder Horn, one of whose walls fell in 1888 under the weight of 173

years and the cold breath of a February night. Part of a second wall crumbled the next day. Coleman secured funds to purchase the building and repair the damage. Her contacts with other preservation-minded women put Coleman among the founders of the Association for the Preservation of Virginia Antiquities. Her home, the Tayloe House, was the site of its organizational meeting in 1889. The APVA acquired the Magazine for $400. Fire destroyed the roof later that year, but the walls stood. The college's affairs began looking up: William and Mary acquired state aid to reopen.

Goodwin returned to Roanoke College in the fall of 1885. His uncle Robert had moved, so Will and his cousin Frank took a second-floor room in the main college building. To save money they made a tin coal stove small enough to hide beneath a bed and, against the rules, cooked in their quarters. When the faculty discovered the infraction, it warned the roommates to desist. Too poor to eat out, the boys began to look for other lodgings and found them in the recently vacated offices of the college treasurer. They depended on a fire hydrant for water, tapping it at night.

In class Goodwin pursued such subjects as science, political economy, mathematics, and ancient languages. Out of class he joined Phi Gamma Delta fraternity, and the YMCA, and volunteered to preach Sunday afternoons to the inmates of the Roanoke jail. The jailer once forgot Will was there and left the young proselytizer locked in the common room with his congregation for four hours.

"As the spring came on my money completely gave out," Goodwin wrote, "and I returned to Norwood. . . . I hired myself to Julian Brown, who kept the store at the foot of the hill. . . . The contract called for the payment of one hundred and fifty dollars a year, with room and board. I do not recall why it was that I was expected to sleep at the store unless it was to help guard the old place from burglars who might think of entering it, not knowing what it contained."

Goodwin contracted a chills-and-fever malady but was well enough to take instruction in the art of the Virginia reel. "About every other day I would have a chill, and about every other night I would go to a dance." In the winter he attended night classes with a Mr. Talbott, an Ohio schoolteacher who had taken over the now-disbanded high school, and "made a failure of running it."

"Mr. Talbott was a learned school master," Goodwin said,

"but an ignorant Yankee in the South. He made himself somewhat unpopular by his views freely expressed with reference to social intercourse with negroes. He began by acting in accord with the honesty of his convictions and even went so far as to ask several negroes in the neighborhood to dine at his house. This, however, did not last very long, as one of them stole all of his silver spoons, and another one took some of the few clothes that he had in the house, which resulted in his conversion to the southern point of view."

Will earned enough money to enroll that summer in the University of Virginia's law school. He intended to return to Roanoke College in the autumn to finish work on his degree, then come back to resume the law course. He was advised not to interrupt his legal studies but to begin again in Charlottesville the following summer, and take the course straight through. That year in Salem, just before Christmas, Goodwin changed his mind. He decided to become a minister.

"It was the one thing I didn't want to do," Goodwin said, "and yet it seemed always to be pressing in upon me as a subject which had to be considered. I did my best to suppress any voice which seemed to sound as though it might be the voice of a clear call to the ministry of the Church. I stopped going to the YMCA. For a time I entirely stopped going to Church. I danced furiously. I tried to be mildly wild (although I was never led at any time to resort to strong drink of any kind)." But after he put to paper his arguments for and against becoming a preacher, he went home for the holidays and announced his decision to enter the seminary.

He graduated from Roanoke in June 1889, a week before his 20th birthday, with a bachelor of arts, a master of arts, and "quite a number of bills, with no money with which to pay them."

He had been offered the headmastership of a boy's school, but he had no interest in teaching, and, anyway, he hadn't finished educating himself. To get out of debt, he took a summer job as a book agent. Four years earlier, Mark Twain published *The Adventures of Huckleberry Finn*, and now he was out with *Wit and Humor of the Age*. Goodwin carried a sample of that and a teacher's reference Bible door-to-door in Roanoke, asking for orders. "My chief obstructions with which I met in pursuit of my chosen vocation were dogs and typhoid fever, both of which were raging in Roanoke at that time." He was mildly surprised that Twain sold better than the Bible—though he confessed he himself read modern Mark more than ancient Paul—and perturbed that people pretended they weren't home when he knocked. In his diary, Goodwin sketched a picture of a woman hiding in her house while the dread book salesman approached. Nevertheless, he made money enough—$51.82 in the first month—to pay his debts and, with some commissions still due, gave the business to a friend.

Thomas Rutherfoord, Goodwin's maternal uncle, was a prominent Richmond businessman and a member of its Westmoreland Club, a retreat of the male elite. He believed Goodwin should forget the ministry, enter business, or take up farming to support Letitia, who had moved with Frank to Wytheville. Rutherfoord asked his nephew to stay away from the country for a year and attend Richmond College at his expense. He hoped the attractions of city life would tempt Goodwin away from the cloistered existence of a rectory. For his part, Goodwin wanted to study Greek, and Richmond College's Greek teacher was the best in the state. To supplement his studies, he took up literary society work, but he also went to the theater, sampled metropolitan social amusements, polished his rustic manners, and dated. He didn't always pay the strictest attention to the young women he escorted. His mind wandered. He said that "when making love to several Richmond girls, I often looked down from Gamble's Hill at night, into the seething and molding masses of iron which continued to flow through the furnaces many years after my father and uncle had retired from the Vulcan Iron Works."

At school Will won a literary society debater's medal—he preserved a transcript of his address as well as the elaborate star-shaped gold badge for the rest of his life—and founded a chapter of Phi Gamma Delta fraternity. "We lived the simple life except on certain rare occasions when banquets were served," he said. "I well remember one of these banquets when jelly was made for the special purpose on the part of others of finding what effect it would have upon the founder of the chapter who was known not to be addicted to the drinking of spirituous liquors. The jelly, as a matter of fact, was only used as a binder and tradition has it that before the banquet was ended the effect of that which the jelly bound together had produced a very hilarious effect upon your present correspondent."

He remained, however, too sober to give up the seminary.

On an outing from Virginia Theological Seminary to Washington, Goodwin (left) and the Ribble brothers.

Chapter Three: **1890-1893**

Perhaps 80,000 people marched down Richmond's Franklin Street that May in a column led by 50 former Confederate generals and 15,000 Confederate veterans representing every state in Dixie. As many as could laid hold of a rope and helped pull a six-story-high statue of Robert E. Lee past his old brick home at 707, and out to Monument Avenue in the city's new western suburb. Two of Lee's sons and two of his daughters were there. So was Will Goodwin, whose father also had lived on Franklin Street. Will marched with his school chum Thomas Nelson Page.

"The confederate flag was everywhere conspicuously displayed," reported the correspondent of *Harper's Weekly*. "The military companies affectionately bore it in the line of march, but with it they bore the Stars and Stripes and bore them loyally. The paradox is explainable only by the fact that the former no longer meant disunion. It stood, rather, for past trials and heroism in adversity looked back upon from the standpoint of changed views and unforeseen prosperity." Be that as it may, the men and women who took their places on the dedication platform stood at the high-water mark of the Lost Cause in its capital.

Jubal Early, James Longstreet, and Joseph E. Johnston were among them. Early followed the new governor, Philip Watkins McKinney, to the podium. Then the Reverend Doctor Charles Minnigerode, the priest who married Goodwin's parents, said a prayer. Colonel Archer Anderson gave the keynote address, and Johnston, who surrendered command to Lee during the Confederate retreat up the Peninsula 28 years before, pulled the cord that unveiled the big bronze-and-stone monument.

French sculptor Jean Antoine Mericie had posed Lee on Traveler, a horse almost as beloved as its rider, and put them on a

39-foot-high pedestal. The general and his mount rose another
22 feet 2 inches. Richmond's blacks had objected to the cost,
$83,000. But it was an era of monument building, marching veterans,
and patriotism. The Washington Monument had been dedicated only
five years before, the Statue of Liberty a year after that.

Will, who idolized Lee, noted this day in his diary: May 29. If
Goodwin saw the *Harper's* account, he should have remarked how
close it came to describing his own view of the day and the war.
"General Lee personified what was best in a bad cause. His
individual virtues gave the Southern people, who craved a
demonstration commemorative of an indelible epoch in their lives,
something substantial and unquestionably creditable to rally
around. The honor to the hero of their vain struggle has been paid. . . .
It may therefore be surmised that in the great outpouring of the ex-
Confederates at Richmond the final obsequies of the war of
secession have taken place, and the circumstances attending it show
how completely the wounds of the conflict have been healed, and a
most important chapter of American history closed." But the
bittersweet tides of Southern sentiment would wash Virginia for the
rest of Will's life and carry him as well to the rostrum at similar rites.

As the college semester drew to a close, he packed up his kit
and carried the memories of the crowd and the old soldiers and the
speeches and the ceremonies home to his mother and father. Home
was now Wytheville, a southwest Virginia community in the lee of
Lick Mountain among the folds of the Alleghenies. He spent the
summer in suspense.

Come autumn, Will intended to enroll in the Virginia
Theological Seminary, at the other end of the state, entering as a
junior. But tuition was a problem. Someone, perhaps one of his
father's minister brothers, tried to interest people who might help
the promising young parson-to-be. That August a Richmond woman
offered him $900 for a scholarship. He wrote in his diary, "How
blessed I am." His benefactor was one of the Misses Stewart, "four
patrician ladies" who lived at Brook Hill, in Henrico County. Will
didn't mention which one, and characteristically misspelled her last
name. In any case, the four contributed generously to the Episcopal
Church, and they financed the final years of Goodwin's education.

In September he set out from the mountains by train, bound
for Alexandria, which he reached on the 22nd late in the afternoon.
Walking or riding from the station for the seminary, he got turned

around, and the short journey took him until sunrise. "In some unaccountable way the road had twisted around so that the west seemed to be east," he wrote. "Having once gotten wrongly oriented, I was never able during my whole three years at the Seminary, nor have I been ever able since, to twist the sun around so that it would rise and set in the proper place.

"On the first night at the Seminary I climbed the cupola and looked down on the forest in which the Seminary is embosomed, and out to the lights of Washington gleaming in the distance. I can well recall the thoughts and feelings which came to me in those silent moments lit with the light of spirit-enkindled emotions."

Goodwin moved into Room 15 in Aspinwall Hall, bunking with at least one other student. Will took his studies seriously, probably with more gravity than his roommate. He wanted his classmates, and perhaps his professors, to be aware of it. On his door he posted a sign:

> Study Hours
> 8 a.m. to 2 p.m.
> 3 p.m. to 5 p.m.
> 7 p.m. to 11 p.m.
> Very Busy.

He studied, among other things, systematic divinity, Greek, and Hebrew. When he wasn't writing his lessons, he was filling his diary in a handsome hand and sparing no religious sentiment.

Nevertheless, there was time for diversion. Frank Ribble was at the seminary, along with his brother Fred. The trio went to Washington just before Thanksgiving to have their pictures taken and to see "the place in Union Depot where Garfield was shot." Charles J. Guiteau had fatally wounded the president there eight years before.

On November 18, Will wrote in his diary: "I moved this p.m. I am glad to have a room alone for although I was charmingly situated still one wants much time for silent thought and communion with his Maker. . . . I long to become more nearly drawn to his blessed will. I long to decrease while he in me increases. I long to have every passion overcome by the influence and perpetual presence of the Holy Spirit."

The thoughts of the 21-year-old acolyte were full of prayer and self-exhortation. A typical diary entry: "God grant that I may not be led to accept any opinion which will hinder me from preaching to men any doctrine taught in the blessed word." In December he

received a letter from Bishop Francis M. Whittle, which read: "Dear
Sir, You are received as a candidate for priests' orders in the
Protestant Episcopal Church."

Goodwin was assigned to practice preach each Sunday at
Langley Mission in Fairfax County, 12 miles away, which he reached
by hired horse. When he returned, he often gave an afternoon
service at Colonial Falls Church. The echo at Colonial Falls was so
bad that it repeated Will's words to him. The acoustics were better at
Langely Mission, but the congregation could be distracting.
Northern Virginia was rural, and services were not so straitlaced as
to exclude a parishioner with his dog. One Sunday a mastiff went
after a pup just outside the chancel rail. "They rushed around

The Williamsburg Courthouse crowd lounges on the porch while a more vigorous
group plays ball on the green around the turn of the century.

underneath the pews on the right hand side of the Church,"
Goodwin said, "the big dog after the little one, and everybody on
that side of the Church standing up on the seat of the pews until the
big dog chased the little dog out." Another Sunday, as Goodwin
began a sermon, a deaf gentleman planted a chair a few feet from
him and held his ear trumpet in the budding minister's face.

But when Will went home for Christmas, it was as a man
entitled to wear clerical garb. He soon found need of his
professional services. "My father was exceedingly ill," he wrote. "We
prayed and God spared him."

Before the next semester was out, Goodwin added a pair of
eyeglasses to his wardrobe. He blamed a case of the grippe–
influenza–for making his eyes weak. That year, 1891, he got his first
look at Williamsburg. The seminary sent him on a recruiting trip to
Virginia's oldest college, which itself had been founded to train men
for the pulpit. He noted in his diary: "On the 26th of March was sent
down to William and Mary College to speak about the ministry. God
blessed the meeting."

He later remembered his intense interest in that first visit to
historic Williamsburg, although he did not record at the time what he
saw of the former haunts of Washington, Jefferson, Henry, and other
"gladsome ghosts" of the city. But we know how in the 1890s
Williamsburg appeared in the eyes of a young man who would be
one of Will's friends and restoration collaborators–as well as
Williamsburg's mayor–Cynthia Coleman's son George.

"Williamsburg on a summer day!" Coleman wrote years later.
"The straggling street, ankle deep in dust, grateful only to the
chickens, ruffling their feathers in perfect safety from any traffic
danger. The cows taking refuge from the heat of the sun, under the
elms along the sidewalk. Our city fathers, assembled in friendly
leisure, following the shade of the old Court House around the
clock, sipping cool drinks, and discussing the glories of the past.
Almost always our past! The past alone held for them the brightness
which tempted their thought to linger happily."

They liked a good story, especially ones that poked fun at
themselves. Among Williamsburg's favorites–it would be one of
Goodwin's, too–was the yarn about Billy Gilliam's funeral. Just after
the War Between the States, Captain Richard A. Wise organized

Wise's Light Infantry Blues, a group part militia and part fraternal. Captain Dick, as he was called, recruited his men mostly among the town's veterans and from the government offices of James City County and Williamsburg. They kept their rifles and uniforms at an armory at Duke of Gloucester Street's west end. Money was scarce, and the Blues carefully husbanded their martial trappings and accoutrements.

Several years later—no one remembers how many, exactly— one of the Blues, Billy Gilliam, died. A bachelor, he had lived with his mother on Waller Street, at the city's east end. Captain Dick called his comrades together at the armory to furnish Gilliam with a military funeral, the company's first. A mule-drawn wagon was pressed into service for a hearse, and the captain led his men down Duke of Gloucester Street in the mile-long march to the Gilliam house.

When they came to the first bar, just outside the armory, Captain Dick ordered his troops to stack arms; and he furnished them with drinks. Thirsts quenched, he ordered them to fall in, and they marched east to the bar on Market Square. There the company repeated the libation maneuver—as it did again at the Colonial Hotel bar, where Chowning's now stands, and once more at Dickerson's Bar, apparently today's Wetherburn's. At length, it reached the Gilliam house.

Captain Dick ordered a detail inside to bring out the remains. Poor Gilliam's coffin, made by a local carpenter, was a box of bull-pine boards nailed together quickly; and it was very heavy. In it the detail found Gilliam wearing his militia uniform—an extravagant waste of the company's slender resources. His comrades took him out, closed the lid, and carried him upstairs to remove the outfit and save it from the grave. As they worked, a second detail came in and carried the coffin to the hearse.

Captain Dick asked his musicians for a dirge. The drummer was young Archie Brooks, the fifer a patient from the Eastern State mental asylum. Between the two, they knew one tune: "Hop, Light Ladies, the Cake's All Dough," a lively melody of the day. Captain Dick commanded them to play it very slow.

The Blues about-faced and headed back west on Duke of Gloucester Street. It had almost reached Dickerson's Bar, and Captain Wise was about to give the order to fall out for more refreshments, when a boy came yelling down the road. He was saying that Billy's mother had noticed her boy's corpse in the house, and that the coffin consequently might be empty.

Raising the lid and finding that was so, Captain Dick about-faced his men, and they slow-stepped back for the house at the pace of the improvised "Hop Light" dirge. Impatient of the progress he was making toward mending his mistake, Captain Dick said to his band, "That's too damn slow; can't you play it a little faster?" and the musicians resumed the melody's step-lively cadence. Billy, less splendidly dressed, was carried out and laid in his coffin, and the company retraced the route to Dickerson's. Refreshed again, Captain Dick led them away for the Colonial.

After a final round on the commander, the company made its way to a graveyard adjoining the Public Hospital compound. As the bull-board casket was lowered into the grave, Captain Dick ordered the squad to fire a salute across the grave. In their eagerness to do military honors, the men had not thought about blank cartridges, so their rifles were loaded with standard ammunition.

Some of the patients had come to see the ceremony and were sitting on a brick wall that separated the hospital grounds from the graveyard. Just behind the onlookers grazed some of the hospital's cattle. The Blues leveled their rifles and fired. The patients fell backward off the wall, and a cow dropped, too. In one version of the story, the patients had been wounded and the cattle killed. In another, the patients were merely brushed from the wall by a branch blasted from an overhanging tree. In either case, that was the story of Billy Gilliam's funeral.

The story of Miss Nancy's reticule was often told, too. Williamsburg ceased to be the first resort of Virginia's polite society when Thomas Jefferson moved the state's government to Richmond in 1780 and set the old colonial capital in decline. Nevertheless, the leading families of the proud little village maintained as many of the trappings of gentility as their increasingly shabby circumstances would support.

Cynthia Coleman moved in Williamsburg's best circles. In 1890 she preserved a few memories of *her* Williamsburg in a private monograph.

In 19th-century Williamsburg, social standing was as much a function of descent as wealth, and the better sort, no matter how beggared, made a weekly round of afternoon teas conducted in one another's parlors. It was an age when the gentlemen suffered the discomforts of celluloid collars, and the gentlewomen made their ways through the dust and mud and heat in full-skirted frocks. A proper lady often carried a reticule—a handbag made of network— and in it a vinaigrette, a small ornamental box or bottle full of aromatics like smelling salts.

Though not all could well afford it, each member of the Williamsburg circle put out plates of sweets and baked tidbits like biscuits, as cookies were called, for the satisfaction of their callers. Among the most noteworthy in the matter of refreshments was Miss Nancy Craig, a nearly insolvent descendant of a family so distinguished that a county had been named for one of her progenitors.

She had, Coleman said, "an ungovernable passion for other people's biscuits. She was in all other respects a most exemplary character, so people winked at this amiable weakness. Whenever Miss Nancy came to drink with her neighbors there always depended from her arm a long and very lank black silk reticule, which somehow had grown into surprising plumpness when the hour for departure arrived. No matter how lean it might be at coming, it invariably went away fat. That black bag's appetite and capacity never failed so long as the tea tray passed around and there were biscuits on it. Still nobody actually saw the skillful process of feeding.

"On one occasion at a tea party . . . a local wag determined to probe the mystery. Accordingly after supper he gave out that a small article of value had been lost, and that every lady in the room must submit to a searching of her reticule, or else bestow upon him a kiss.

"The company saw into the joke and immediately acquiesced. The wag constituted himself searcher and went the rounds, without finding anything more than handkerchiefs and an occasional vinaigrette. Finally he stood before Miss Nancy, whose bag lay abnormally distended on her lap.

"'Well Miss Nancy,' he said, 'it is painful to subject ladies to such an indignity, but the penalty is heavy, so it must be done.' There was a moment's hesitation. A sweet confusion passed across the spinster's face. Then the plump bag fell to the floor as she rose to her feet.

"'Law', Aleck,' she cried, a soft color suffusing her withered cheek, 'I'd just as soon kiss you as not.' Her arms were about his neck, and she had paid the penalty."

Miss Estelle Smith, another member of the party, said the

last thing Aleck wanted was a kiss from Miss Nancy. "She taught him."

Whatever Goodwin thought of the tumbledown town and its keeping-up-appearances people, his mind was focused on his classes, his books, and perfecting the delivery of his sermons. He styled himself "the fearful Demosthenes;" a classmate called him "Weeping Jeremiah." A newspaper notice described him as "an able and forcible speaker."

Goodwin took charge of Zion Church at Fairfax Courthouse in his senior year. Confining himself closely to his duties, nevertheless he found time to fall in love once more—with a local coquette named Annie Hoston—and to watch a president sworn in. The March 4, 1893, entry in his diary says: "Went to Washington to see Cleveland inaugurated—cold wind and snow—immense crowd—heard part of speech and left—caught cold." Goodwin was ill for the next 16 days.

As he had at Roanoke College, he got away for YMCA conventions, church meetings, and missionary lectures. He visited Nashville, Tennessee, in 1891 and Auburn, New York, in 1892. He'd been to Norfolk and later traveled to Baltimore. But it was his preaching excursions that he noted most faithfully. They were carrying him so far into the countryside that in his final year he had to take the train and stay overnight.

The most private matters he confided to his diary in code, but he wasn't afraid to poke fun of himself in plain English, and one of these outings gave him the chance. Coming home from an April service, Goodwin called on a parishioner who "gave me a letter to mail addressed:

THE CHIEF OF THE WEATHER DEPART.
WASHINGTON, D.C.

"On train, stuck it in the band of my hat, leaving the top line above the band, and then walked through Alexandria wondering what people were looking at me for, and it never occurred to me until a young lady asked me if that was my hat with the envelope in it."

With graduation nearing, he began to get job offers that would have taken him farther afield. The bishops of Texas and Missouri invited him to take positions in their dioceses, but Goodwin had already decided to remain, at least for now, in

As new to the ministry as his surplice, young Parson Goodwin about the time he graduated from the seminary.

Virginia. His decision may have been influenced by events in Wytheville. His father was fast failing and, as the eldest child, he owed a son's duty to his mother. Before the year was out, she was a widow. Frank died at age 50.

In June, Will graduated and was ordained a deacon, the rank below priest, and prepared to step into the world on his own. He took up his profession at a time when America was moving from a wagon-wheeled past to a self-propelled future. The frontier, opened at Jamestown in 1607, was closing with the Oklahoma land rushes of 1889. Candles and woodstoves had long since given way to lamps and ovens fueled by Rockefeller's kerosene, and they were being replaced with appliances that used natural gas and alternating current. In the course of his three seminary years, the last great Indian battle of the West, the Wounded Knee Massacre, was fought in South Dakota, and Frank and Charles Duryea test drove what is believed to be the first gasoline-powered automobile in the United States. Basketball was invented, and the bank-robbing Dalton Gang was all but wiped out at Coffeyville, Kansas.

Smaller, less noteworthy events slipped by in the stream of change that was shaping Goodwin's life. William and Mary won a reparation from the federal government for the damages done by Union soldiers. Phi Beta Kappa, founded by 50 of its students at the Raleigh Tavern in 1776, revived its William and Mary chapter in 1893. That year in Providence, Rhode Island, John D. Rockefeller, Jr., entered Brown University, from which he would graduate with a Phi Beta Kappa key and the nickname Johnny Rock. Brown's president, Elisha Benjamin Andrews, became Rockefeller's mentor. A veteran of the 1st Connecticut Heavy Artillery, Andrews had lost an eye at the Battle of the Crater in Petersburg, fought at the Wilderness, and participated in the Peninsula Campaign—during which, Williamsburg fell to the Union. If Rockefeller indulged a young man's curiosity about the war, he may have heard his first descriptions of Virginia and its colonial relics from Andrews.

From such disparate threads would be woven the fabric of Williamsburg's restoration. But that was for the future. Goodwin's immediate prospects were more apparent and pragmatic. "I had always said that I would never teach," he wrote, but "the assignment of the Bishop of Southern Virginia led me almost immediately into the professorship in the Bishop Payne Divinity School for colored students located in Petersburg, near St. John's Church where Bishop Randolph sent me to serve my diaconate."

Deacon Goodwin (top right) and his associates on the faculty of Bishop Payne
Divinity School soon after his arrival in Petersburg, 1894.

Chapter Four: **1894-1902**

Deacon Goodwin arrived in a Petersburg of cotton mills, luggage works, tobacco factories, and railroads, a city built of brick and business, crowding down the banks of the Appomattox River. A manufacturing town. Petersburg had its share of well-to-do people living in handsome Victorian homes on quiet avenues. But the grid of cobblestone streets at the city's core rattled with teamsters and pulsed with men, women, girls, and boys going to and from round-the-clock shifts at the plants. Those people were Goodwin's people.

He made his way to the 5th Ward, a district of poverty and saloons, looking for St. John's Church. In addition to teaching at Bishop Payne Divinity School, Will was now to take over St. John's pulpit. His uncle, the Reverend Robert Goodwin, had been rector as well as Bishop Payne's principal. But Uncle Robert had just been called to St. John's in Richmond, and Will was on his own.

A photography studio made a portrait of Bishop Payne's five-man faculty soon after Will's addition. Arranged in front on two chairs and a stool are three men, two sporting mustaches and one a pointed beard. None of them knows what to do with his hands. The one in the middle seems to be braced against the photographer's powder flash.

Behind them stands their only African-American colleague in the African-American school, a rumpled fellow of about 30 who looks fed up. Next to him is Will, smooth shaven, well brushed, erect. His suitcoat is buttoned up all the way, and there is a small round pin in his lapel. Wide-eyed, he seems a little too aware of himself. All five men are in clerical collars. Will augments his with a dark tie carefully tied with a lopsided half-Windsor, a young man's knot. He is the picture of someone eager to make a good impression—a junior associate anxious to fit in and wondering, perhaps, what he's gotten himself into.

The teaching wasn't going as well as he'd hoped. The students arrived with little Latin, less Greek, and were often deficient in English as well. Deacon Goodwin prided himself on knowing all three, essential in his mind to interpreting and teaching the Gospel. He hadn't trained to be a pedagogue. He worked hard at teaching but not always well, and he sometimes blamed his frustrations on his pupils.

"Truth," he said, "had to be made very simple to these students and the thought and study necessary to present the truths of redemption to these earnest but uncultured people demanded clearness of thought and simplicity of language, or else there was a complete failure to secure results."

There was no race malice in him. He shared the attitudes of polite society towards blacks that prevailed North and South. In some respects his thinking was as advanced as Booker T. Washington's and, on both sides of the color line, Washington was the most admired African-American of the time. Goodwin had taken a post many of his fellow seminarians would have regarded as unpromising, and he had committed himself to the work with enthusiasm in the spirit of Christian charity. For the times, he was enlightened on race and social issues generally. He would earn regard as a Southerner worth hearing on the improvement of black-white relations, and he worked in behalf of Bishop Payne Divinity until he was an old man. He was sincerely anxious for its students to follow the path of achievement. But there is no denying his paternalism, and he doubted their capability to get far down that road.

Will found more satisfaction in the work of the parish than of the school. Within a year he cut his classroom duties to an hour a week to pursue his pastoral obligations. St. John's was a plain wooden church at the rear of a lot left otherwise vacant against the hope of one day building something grander. He went about a minister's work methodically, scorecarding visits to the sick and widows, collecting building-fund pledges, and so on. In his diary he drew precise columns in red and blue ink and kept an account of his calls in rows of numbers, measuring himself against his goals.

"The parish was composed almost exclusively of the extreme poor," he said, and life was poorer in the 5th Ward than usual.

Goodwin doubted more than three of the church's families owned their own homes. He thought the biggest part of the problem was that John Barleycorn was claiming too large a share of the parish paychecks.

"There were five bar rooms within one square of the Church," he said. "I soon came to know the men who kept these bars and also the men who kept them running." A particular friend was the saloonkeeper in business diagonally across the street from St. John's. What the teetotaling deacon learned of what he called "the drink evil" at the bartender's elbow became the basis of Goodwin's first big sermon, "Hard Times in the Fifth Ward and the Principal Cause of Them."

"It was a panic year," Goodwin said; there was a depression on, "and the fact that the sermon had been advertised produced a most astonishing congregation which filled the Church and all the windows looking into the Church, and the yard and street around the Church. The point of the sermon was to show that most of the poverty in the parish resulted from the drink evil, which was unquestionably the truth. As I refrained from abusing the bar-keepers and the bar patrons, what I had to say was kindly received and I think ultimately did good, as the man who gave me the facts shortly afterwards gave up his bar business."

For the former patrons and other men of the drinking class, Goodwin opened a reading room and men's clubroom in a vacant house on the next block. Men flocked to the place, Will said, perhaps overstating the case in his enthusiasm. But he was making progress, and he had cause to be proud.

In little more than a year, Will became a full-fledged parson, marking the event in a new diary that day. On the first right hand page, he wrote: "Ordained Priest in St. Paul's Church Petersburg, Va. July 1, 1894 by Rt. Reverend F. M. Whittle DD Bishop Randolph being sick. . . .Sermon preached by Reverend E. L. Goodwin who also presented me." E. L. was uncle Edward Lewis. That night at 8:15 p.m. the new reverend delivered at St. John's his first sermon as a priest. For his text he took Exodus 3:2: "And the angel of the Lord appeared unto him in a flame of fire out of the midst of a bush: and he looked, and, behold, the bush burned with fire, and the bush was not consumed." The "him" of the passage was Moses, who, according to Scripture, was visiting the backside of the desert.

Of course, Goodwin was not all Bible and business. He was as interested in, and attractive to, women as ever he would be. He called on young ladies at their homes and walked out with them in Gay Nineties fashion. "I had not been long in Petersburg," he wrote later, "before seeing one day in the bookstore of Mr. T. D. Beckwith a graceful and beautiful girl who had come to the store with a friend to look over some music from which task she sufficiently diverted herself to look me over. I knew what was going on because I could overhear the whispered conversation of Mr. Beckwith who shortly came over to where I was and took me over and introduced me to these two girls. One of them, Evelyn Tannor, subsequently became Mrs. Goodwin."

She lived immediately behind St. Paul's, of which she was a member, and had been born the daughter of Major Nathaniel Mitchell Tannor, CSA, of Locust Grove in Dinwiddie County on July 17, 1869. She first appears in Goodwin's diary July 17, 1894. "Walked with Miss E. 6:30 a.m., drove with H to Mr. Layne's," the entry says. Four days later he wrote: "Called with Miss Evelyn at Battersea," a former Randolph family plantation that dated to colonial days. On October 1, Will wrote: "E's Birthday. Sent Bible and love." The entry for November 22 is: "Spoke to Uncle Thomas about marriage."

They were wed February 19, 1895, at St. Paul's by Bishop A. M. Randolph, the reverend doctors E. L. Goodwin and Claudius R. Haines, the rector, assisting, along with Goodwin's Norwood chums, the reverends Frank and Fred Ribble. Frank was best man. "It was the only wedding with which I ever had anything to do which took place five minutes before the appointed time," the groom said. "Her brother insisting that the wedding must start on time, started the procession sufficiently ahead of time to make a very large number of people who intended to be present at the wedding arrive at the Church when the ceremony was practically over." Somewhat ambiguously, Goodwin's diary entry for that day is: "was married, hope to be worth twice as much after the honeymoon."

The couple took a bridal tour that carried it west into the state's interior. He stopped in Rutherfoord country to preach at Grove Hill and Amelia Courthouse on February 24. When they returned to Petersburg, they moved into two rooms of St. John's rectory, but took meals with a woman who rented the rest of the house. It would be a year before the Goodwins had the place to themselves.

When or where Evelyn met her mother-in-law, Will didn't record. Surely he introduced Letitia to his betrothed early on, and certainly she was at their wedding. In August the couple visited her in Wytheville, and he wrote: "Evelyn, Mother and I went to Church together. It was the first Communion I had taken with my wife and the first time for many months that I had gone to church with my mother. She grows dearer to me as I grow older, and learn better to

The Reverend Goodwin, wife Evelyn, and children about the time the family moved from Petersburg to Williamsburg.

appreciate true self sacrifice and love."

Nor did the marriage inhibit Goodwin's activist ministry. That December, in the interest of Bishop Payne Divinity, he took his first fund-raising trip, a week-long excursion in the North to solicit individuals for scholarships and operating funds. Though Goodwin's extant records do not say, he must have been successful; he later became the school's financial secretary.

It was a few months before he strayed so far from home again. Evelyn was, as they said, in an interesting condition. On February 2, 1896, at 1:15 a.m. she delivered their first child, a daughter. They named her Evelyn, too—Evelyn Withers Goodwin. The proud parents took her to see the United Confederate Veterans Reunion in Richmond that July 1, and the next day, as he underscored in his diary, they "Saw Confederate Parade." The keynote speaker, former rebel soldier and Richmond College teacher J. L. M. Curry, sounded the note of reconciliation the *Harper's* correspondent had tried so hard to hear at the dedication of Lee's statue. Curry said that "recognition of the glorious deeds of our comrades is perfectly consistent with loyalty to the flag and devotion to the Constitution and the resulting union." That became precisely Will Goodwin's belief, and one in which he would raise all his children.

The next time Goodwin went to a photographer's studio to have his picture made, he went alone. The pose he struck is full of animation and self-assurance. The thumb of his left hand is hooked in his waistband, his forearm pinning open his long black preacher's coat. His head is turned to the right, opening up his shoulders, and his feet are spread at an angle to the lens. His face is decorated with a mustache and a pair of spectacles. His eyes are focused, theatrically, on something in the distance. His clerical collar is complimented by a black tunic with two vestlike pockets from which depends a chain hung with a cross. He has become the picture of a confident young man on his way up.

As the years of his St. John's ministry accumulated, so did the jobs Will gave himself. Sunday school started at 9, services at 11, more Sunday school at 4, and another service at 8. Two Sundays each month he went to Chester, 14 miles away, and conducted a chapel service. He ministered at the Alms House and still called on parishioners. He

Goodwin, his self-confidence showing, as his Petersburg ministry prospered.

collected $7,000 or $8,000 a year for the construction of a brick
church, bringing himself into touch with such people of means as the
future Mrs. Molly McCrea, the fabled owner of Carter's Grove
Plantation just outside Williamsburg. He served as assistant minister at
St. Paul's, so he could preach at outlying Blandford's Chapel. He
taught five hours every day except Saturday at Bishop Payne Divinity,
lecturing in theology, philosophy, and history.

The Goodwin household grew with the addition of
daughter Mary Katherine on November 1, 1898. Son Thomas
Rutherfoord LeBaron arrived before the family doctor did on
January 5, 1901. A nursemaid helped their mother mind the brood,
and sometimes Letitia lent a hand. After a visit in 1896, Goodwin
wrote: "mother came over and spent the week with me. God has
placed before me a noble example in the life of her whose
beautiful Christian life springs from a living and working faith in
Christ." The family usually spent August in Wytheville or in
Bedford County at Lowery.

Will testified before the Virginia Legislature in behalf of a
bill to prohibit children from working all night in the cotton mills.
Labor reform and social welfare were the liberal causes of the era,
and by that measure he was a liberal. At home he fought a more
pressing social problem by collecting temperance pledges and
preserving them in the back of his diary. A typical pledge read:

> Petersburg, Va.
> Nov. 26th, 1898
> I do solemnly and sincerely promise and swear that by
> the help of Almighty God, I will not drink intoxicating liquor of
> any kind, unless under written prescription from a physician for
> a period of five years (Nov. 26, 1903.)
> Signed,
> J. F. McKinney
> Witnessed by
> W. A. R. Goodwin
> 5 Years.

Construction of the new St. John's church began May 25,
1897. A Mr. Egerton "struck the first pick into the earth and Mrs.
Goodwin and I threw the 1st spade of earth into the cart." As the
new church rose, a druggist whose shop was across the street, a Mr.
Partin, interested himself in the work. Goodwin had planned "to

build a tower only up to where it stuck out through the roof. To my joy and astonishment Mr. Partin asked me one day why we were roofing the tower over at that point, and when I told him, he said he did not want to have to look at anything like that all the time and he told me to finish it and send him the bill."

That was the year John D. Rockefeller, Jr., 22, graduated from Brown, went to work in his retired father's office on the 9th floor of 26 Broadway in New York, and began to build a philanthropic empire. Goodwin was learning about charity, too. "I never lend money to people with the hope of getting again," he confided to his notebook. "I[t] breaks friendships. I ask myself how much can I afford to give then if it comes back I am richer than I made allowance for. There was one man who[se] intimacy was oppressive until he asked me to lend him $1.00. I let him have it and have never asked him for it. He has not been around since. Cheap price." He was something of an easy touch, and he found it all but impossible all his life to refuse the requests of needy parishioners, hard-pressed friends, and out-of-work family for gifts or loans of small sums. His home was always open to relatives in need of shelter or the kindness of kin.

He led a fight to keep Bishop Payne open when the church's mission society proposed to close it in favor of a Washington institution. The society wanted to concentrate its resources on King Hall, "which we of the South," Goodwin said, "felt would be a most serious disaster to the negro men preparing for the ministry of the Church." Goodwin won.

Rockefeller was advancing the cause of African-American education in the South, too. In 1901 he and 50 other prominent persons took a train trip through Dixie organized by Robert C. Ogden, a merchant interested in improving educational facilities for blacks. Among the places they visited was Hampton Institute, about 30 miles from Williamsburg. A former Union officer founded the school after the war, using surplus Union Army buildings next door to Fort Monroe. Rockefeller's association with the school endured, providing the occasion 25 years later for his first visit to Williamsburg. On the group's return trip north, St. George Tucker, namesake of a famous Williamsburg judge and president of Washington and Lee University, made an impassioned speech. It helped persuade Rockefeller to found the General Education Board, chartered in

1903. Established to help black schools, it masked the object of its philanthropy by contributing as well to white institutions to avoid offending Southerners.

Life in Petersburg had exciting if less uplifting moments. One evening Goodwin took a visiting minister to see the men's club reading room, now in the charge of a Mr. Hawkins who lived upstairs with his family. Barkeeper and 5th Ward politician Juney Quarles had gotten drunk, picked up his pistol, and gone to the reading room in search of a political and saloon-keeping rival. Failing to find him, Quarles shot out the windows and lights and turned over the tables for exercise, then left to hunt his quarry up the street. But he threatened to return. When Goodwin and his friend arrived, Hawkins was on the porch waiting for Quarles with a shotgun, and a crowd had gathered hoping to see a shoot-out. Goodwin stepped in, persuaded Hawkins to take his gun and go back inside, and got the disappointed crowd to disperse.

Quarles didn't reappear until the next morning, when he knocked on Goodwin's door to apologize and ask forgiveness. The police had arrested him, and he had to be in court at 10 a.m. to answer a disorderly conduct charge. Summoned as a witness, Goodwin declined to file a complaint and add to Quarles's troubles. In gratitude, Quarles repaired the reading room damage, bought materials, hammered together improvements, and became the rector's fast friend.

At the next election, Quarles and his political-bartending antagonist asked Goodwin to be an election judge and see that the voting was on the up and up. Goodwin agreed to it on the condition Quarles would stay sober during the day. Taking up a position in the polling place, Goodwin helped keep an eye on the ballot box. He wrote that Quarles "afterwards told me when he found the election going against him that he would have shot up the place if he hadn't known that I was inside."

Will's reputation as a rector as well as a peacemaker spread from Petersburg on the church grapevine. He was invited to remove to parishes in Brooklyn, Missouri, Ohio, Maryland, Texas, Pennsylvania, and two others in Virginia. The ninth call he answered, and it put him again in the role of a mediator between rival political factions.

The Reverend William Thomas Roberts of Chase City, Virginia, had accepted a call to Williamsburg's Bruton Parish in 1894, the year Goodwin became a priest. He took up the rounds of the parish, joined the rotation of local clergy serving William and Mary as chaplains, took the rector's place among the community's leaders, and began looking around for things to improve. He made the obvious choice: the church.

The building had been renovated in 1886, financed in part by a $300 donation from the Catherine Memorial Society. Nevertheless, more repairs were needed. Two years after his arrival, Roberts secured funds for the purpose from the family of wealthy Eastern State Hospital mental patient Marie Marshall, and Cynthia Coleman's ever-active young women staged a historical exhibit to raise more money.

The rehabilitations Roberts and the vestry now undertook may have sparked—or been the result of—an interest in restoring the church to the dignity of its colonial past. In either case, a sign of the renewed reverence for old Bruton is found in the vestry meeting minutes of 1897. James D. Moncure, superintendent of the mental hospital, and Dr. Van F. Garrett, a William and Mary professor, were appointed "to so fix the gates that cattle may be prevented from trespassing in the churchyard."

Coleman had repaired the Powder Magazine, turned it into a museum, and sold the building for safekeeping to her new Association for the Preservation of Virginia Antiquities. The year before Roberts's arrival, Mr. and Mrs. Edward Barney gave Coleman's APVA the 17th-century church ruin at Jamestown and 22.5 adjoining acres of the island. The same year the College of William and Mary won from Congress a $64,000 appropriation in compensation for damage done the campus during the Civil War. The APVA conducted the first of its annual Jamestown pilgrimages in 1895 and raised a plaque in 1896 commemorating the first settlers' landing in the Chesapeake Bay. Mary Jeffrey Galt of Norfolk—with Coleman the group's co-founder—supervised the first archaeological investigations at Jamestown in 1897. Two years later the association persuaded Collis P. Huntington to turn over the colonial Capitol site at the east end of Williamsburg's Duke of Gloucester Street and got a Richmond architectural firm, Noland and Baskervill, to stabilize the crumbling foundations. The property was conveyed through the Old Dominion Land Company, a wholly owned subsidiary of

Huntington's Chesapeake & Ohio Railroad, which had taken over
the site for the Yorktown Centennial train.

America was of two minds about its past and arrived by
different routes at some of the same conclusions. A certain turning
inward, an isolationist introspection born of weariness with Old
World machinations, was encouraging a patriotic pride in the nation
and its history. Yet the same pride and Americanism was fostering
the jingoism of Manifest Destiny adventures. Both were encouraged
by politicians and the popular periodicals. A magazine, *The Youth's
Companion,* composed the first version of the Pledge of Allegiance
in 1892. Six years later, the yellow press of William Randolph Hearst
and Joseph Pulitzer capitalized on the need of national self-
verification with bloody-shirt reporting that fostered the Spanish-
American War.

In the competition for patriotic distinction at home,
Southerners, particularly Virginians, felt an imperative to defend
their claims to having founded the country. Northern historians
dominated their field, wrote the textbooks, and quite naturally told
the story of America's founding from a Yankee point of view.
Generations of school children grew up under the impression that
the first settlers were the Plymouth Rock Pilgrims of 1620, not the
Jamestown colonists of 1607. Virginia historians like Alexander
Brown, Edward D. Neill, and, later, William and Mary President Lyon
G. Tyler set out to correct the record. The APVA itself served as a
counterbalance to the formation of a New England preservationist
society.

In 1901, the year Vice President Theodore Roosevelt told a
Minnesota State Fair crowd that America should "speak softly and
carry a big stick," Rector Roberts took up the cause of Bruton's
restoration. The community believed the building was the oldest
American church in continuous use, and Roberts proposed to return
it to its colonial appearance. He got the vestry's permission to raise
funds to remodel the interior, remove the partition erected in 1839,
and rid the building of Victorian embellishments. By April he had
collected about $1,000, and he thought he could raise $5,000 more.
But without consulting the vestry, he had already spent the first
$1,000 to buy from R. J. Armistead a rectory for himself across the
street from the church. When the vestrymen asked him to justify his
unilateral decision to use the restoration funds on a purpose for
which they weren't donated, Roberts said he knew they agreed on

the need for a rectory, and there hadn't been time to call a meeting before Armistead's offer expired.

Whatever misgivings the vestry may have had, it allowed Roberts to embark on a two-month fund-raising tour of Norfolk, Richmond, Washington, Philadelphia, New York, and Boston. He gathered money and pledges totaling $4,365, on an outlay of $130 for expenses. He also found time to pick a poisonous fight with Tyler, president of the college.

Roberts had sought and been denied a seat on William and Mary's board of visitors. Now he publicly spurned the institution as a "once honorable but now dishonored seat of learning." It was one of the choicer phrases he employed in a six-page screed that he dispatched to the Virginia Constitutional Convention meeting that winter in Richmond.

Roberts quite reasonably objected to a proposal before the convention to subsidize William and Mary with state funds; it was not yet a state school. Less convincingly, he opposed a move to make Tyler, the president of a private school, a member of the state board of education—and he attacked Tyler personally.

Tyler, 48, was almost as much a Williamsburg institution as the College of William and Mary. He was the son of the most recent Virginian to serve as president of the United States, John Tyler of Williamsburg. William Henry Harrison's vice president until Harrison's death in 1841, John Tyler was at his Francis Street home when a courier arrived April 5 to notify him he was needed in Washington.

Roberts contrived to drag the nation's newest president, Teddy Roosevelt, into a tortuously reasoned diatribe against William and Mary's chief executive. It went like this: Roosevelt, who had become president in September with William McKinley's assassination, angered much of America by inviting Booker T. Washington to dine at the White House. Tyler's daughter was attending Wellesley College in Massachusetts, where Washington's daughter was also enrolled. Roberts said: "Was it a crime against society for the President of the United States to sit down at the dinner table with Booker T. Washington? Then it must be equally a crime for the daughter of the President of William and Mary College to sit down in the classroom and at the dinner table with the daughter of Booker T. Washington." Roberts hoped the convention would not "endorse such monstrous things" as "Mixed Schools, Social Equality and Miscegenation."

It may have been in connection with this harangue that some young men of the college painted Roberts' horse green.

Tyler spread his reaction across an eight-page letter to the Bruton Parish vestry. "It is simply inconceivable to me that such poisonous thoughts could find lodging in the brain or the heart of any human being!! . . .It is wonderful how well the College has done with such an enemy as W. T. Roberts in our midst, who it can be proved has advised students not to come to this institution." Tyler said he regarded Roberts "as a fire-brand, as a marplot, as a headstrong, passionate, vindictive man, as a fanatic who would throw everything into confusion."

Throwing things into confusion had become Roberts's strong suit. In some quarters he was suspected of having less against the drink evil than some of his colleagues. He could be as belligerent as any boozer. One day at the train station he said something disagreeable—just what isn't recorded—to Coleman's niece Annie, a member of Bruton's congregation. She slapped him. He banned her from the church. The word "excommunication" was bandied about. Coleman, who taught Sunday school and Bible study classes, decided that if Annie wasn't welcome, she wasn't either. She quit attending services and, in the bargain, moved her Sunday school class to her house. Roberts was incensed; she antagonized him more.

The church's roof leaked, and the Catherine Memorial Society had collected funds for its repair. Coleman told Roberts she would turn the money over on condition it was spent for a new roof. Roberts objected. He told Coleman she had no right to the money, that it had been collected in the name of the church, and he would decide how to spend it. Coleman who had seen what he had done with other moneys collected for the church, appealed to the vestry. Its leader, Bruton's senior warden, was her neighbor Dr. Garrett, a Roberts critic. He referred the question to Bishop Alfred Magill Randolph of Virginia's Southern Diocese. Randolph ruled for Coleman and gave Garrett the pleasure of making the official notifications.

The vestry now directed Roberts to withdraw his letter to the Richmond convention. In addition, five vestrymen called for disciplinary action. Three thought the reprimand sufficient. Roberts claimed the right to vote as rector if the question of his punishment was put to a ballot. The debate over the propriety of Roberts sitting in judgment of himself resulted in another appeal to the bishop and forestalled immediate action. But the anti-Roberts faction, led by Garrett and treasurer Henry Dennison Cole, demanded Roberts giving an accounting of the Bruton restoration money. If Roberts bridled under the implication of further fund-raising chicanery, he rendered a detailed report. But bad feelings finally led to blows. Professor Garrett and the Reverend Roberts had a fistfight on the Palace Green.

Late in March the congregation conducted a regular election of vestrymen. As bitterly divided as its leadership, the members broke into two factions, and each elected its own slate. Williamsburg's newspaper, the *Virginia Gazette*, ran a headline April 5 that read, "Two Sets of Vestrymen: Bruton Parish Now In That Condition." Bishop Randolph was drawn into this dispute, too, as were an ecclesiastical tribunal and a state court judge. The settlement of all the affrays was reported in the May 10 edition of the newspaper under the headline: "Roberts To Leave." Garrett was reelected senior warden, and the hunt was on for a new rector.

Bruton's rectorship could not have sounded like a very attractive opportunity. Whatever Goodwin heard in Petersburg of all its troubles, or whatever Williamsburg interest may have lingered in him from his visit as a seminary student, he was busy finishing construction of St. John's and getting the building dedicated. When at length Bruton's search focused on him, Bishop Randolph urged Goodwin to accept, but Roberts urged him not to. Goodwin said that Roberts wrote him "a letter of twenty pages or more giving me the reasons why I should not go to Williamsburg, and stating in detail the condition which would confront me." Goodwin said he wrote back that the situation "seemed so deplorably bad . . . that if I had had any doubt in the world about coming, his letter had convinced me that there was no place which seemed to require the service of a Christian minister in a larger degree, and that I had decided to come."

Goodwin was ready to take over Bruton's pulpit but anxious not to assume Roberts's place in the church war. He conditioned his acceptance of the call on the vestry's agreement to make no more reference to the disputes. Before packing up, he dedicated Petersburg's new St. John's Church, his first building project.

Goodwin formally became Bruton's rector February 15, 1903.

The young new rector of Williamsburg's Bruton Parish Church packed his small
gas-lit Main Street rectory with family, furniture, books, and pictures. Wife Evelyn is
at left in this circa 1905 photo. At the desk is son Rutherfoord.

Chapter Five: **1903-1908**

The morning after Goodwin arrived in Williamsburg, an elderly man with a cane made his way up dusty Duke of Gloucester Street toward the Bruton Parish rectory. He reached the big mimosa opposite the minister's quarters, arranged himself on the bench beneath the tree, and waited for Goodwin to come out. It was 7 a.m.

Two hours later, Goodwin opened his door. The old-timer rose on his walking stick and hurried into the road, beckoning for Goodwin to cross. "He wanted," the new rector said, "to tell me the truth about the situation in the Church before the damn liars on the other side got hold of me."

Goodwin wanted no part of either side in the Bruton Parish wars and, anxious to discourage the retelling of past engagements, declined the old man's offer. By way of changing the subject, he asked whether the fellow had fought in the Battle of Williamsburg in 1862. "Some strange intuition told me that he was a fighting man," Goodwin said, "and so it happened that from nine o'clock until lunch-time he fought over the whole Civil War, and took out on the Yankees the wrath and indignation which he had kept stored up to pour upon the rival factions in the Church row." And so the new rector hit on the tack he would take whenever he wanted to avoid being drawn into a dispute among the natives: Ask about the Battle of Williamsburg. The veteran became one of the first friends Goodwin made among the townspeople, and the attachment lasted until the old man's death.

Thirty-six years later, a few months before Goodwin himself died, the preacher wrote out his impression of the rest of what he found in Williamsburg when he arrived in 1903:

Gardens, devastated by war, were remembered and regretted. Ancestral homes were however preserved in spacious yards until necessities growing out of poverty often compelled yard and garden curtailments. The ancient houses looked askance at the new houses built on the sold-off lots and seemed unconscious of unseemly crowding.

As poverty increased, the city lost in a measure its civic pride and yielded to the temptation to secure revenue without imposing additional taxes by disposing more and more of its public domain.

Lots were leased for building west of the Public Magazine on the Market Square. There a Baptist church of Greek Revival architecture arose, and other buildings including a galvanized iron garage, a fire house, a shack converted into the City Hall and a plumber's shop—all tied together by iron rods. The Methodist church building, two stores, a bank and two houses of the 1890 period, with the galvanized iron Palace Theatre ranged along the Duke of Gloucester Street across from the Court House Green . . . Behind these buildings was a tumbled-down house which was occupied by negroes.

The Court [House] Green was spared, save for the presence of a modern hotel which tried to look old, but couldn't. Next to it stood a revamped building concealing the remnants of an ancient stairway.

The approaches to the college along Duke of Gloucester Street constantly called forth the apologies of this venerable institution.

Next to the college entrance was a shanty occupied by a respectable negro family. Pigs grunted in the pen, and a cow and a horse and chickens were at home under the apple trees.

In a motley array of houses on this square most of the city's business was conducted, the stores being kept open at such hours of the day as suited the convenience of the merchants.

It was evident to those who saw the city as it was then that it cried aloud for a restoration and its relics for preservation.

Not all of what he recalled then actually dated to 1903, and his memory of the city's cry for restoration that year wasn't any more precise. He was by then, of course, familiar with Roberts's plans for Bruton's preservation—one of the other things that had divided the congregation. Many of Bruton's communicants favored leaving things just as they were, just as things had been all their lives. Others wanted things as they had been in their grandparents' lives. On May 8, 1903, the vestry authorized the Reverend Goodwin to canvas his flock and put the question to a vote, with the understanding that work would not begin until funds were in hand. Two days later, Goodwin secured without dissent his parishioners' approval for a restoration, and on the 23rd he collected the vestry's endorsement.

Williamsburg began as a settlement called Middle Plantation about 1632. It became Virginia's capital when the government quit Jamestown 67 years later. The present church is the third erected to serve the town's Anglican community. The first was built of wood in 1660 on a different site. The parish, formed in the consolidation of Marston and Middletown parishes, was named Bruton 14 years later. Bruton, Somerset, England, had been home of the governor, Sir William Berkeley, and Thomas Ludwell, secretary of the Virginia colony. The first rector was Rowland Jones of Burford in Oxfordshire, who served until 1688 and was an ancestor of Martha Washington.

Planter John Page donated a farmed-out field and £200 to put a brick church on it in 1677. Finished in 1683, it rose a few yards northwest of the present structure. This second church stood near the center of the city plat when Middle Plantation was christened Williamsburg in 1699. Perhaps the primary impetus for the incorporation of the city was the establishment of another ecclesiastical institution, the College of William and Mary, in 1693. The Reverend James Blair, Virginia deputy of the bishop of London, had traveled to England to obtain a charter and funds for the school. The Virginia General Assembly directed it be built "as neare the church now standing in the Middle Plantation old fields as convenience will permit."

By 1710, the second church had fallen into a ruinous condition, and the vestry proposed construction of the third. Governor Alexander Spotswood presented architectural drawings for a cruciform design early in 1711. Also of brick, the new building would be 75 feet long and 28 feet wide with two wings 22 feet wide and 19 feet long. The east end chancel was 25 feet shorter than the west-end pew area. There was no tower. Construction began the next year and was essentially finished late in 1715.

A short flight of stairs wound up to the pulpit, which hung from the southeast wall and was crowned by a sounding board that reflected the preacher's voice into the congregation. Spotswood took a canopied wooden chair opposite the pulpit, inside the rail. Less distinguished worshipers sat in boxes—the men north of the aisle, women south of it. As the years passed, overhead galleries were added to accommodate college boys, slaves, and servants. In 1744 the building was enlarged, and eight years later the vestry voted to extend the east end to make it as long as the west. The parish installed an organ in 1768—it lasted until 1835—and a tower was added to the west end in 1769, in part to accommodate a bell donated by merchant James Tarpley.

The Episcopal faith was colonial Virginia's official religion, and Bruton, the principal church in the colony's capital, was the resort of its chief executives, leading politicians, local merchants, and nearby planters for 81 years. The earliest graves in Bruton's churchyard date to the 17th century. Prominent Virginians were sometimes interred beneath the floor of the church itself.

During the Battle of Yorktown in October 1781, Bruton served for a hospital or storehouse, perhaps both. At the end of the century it was dilapidated, but no major renovations were undertaken until 1839. Within a year, carpenters partitioned the interior to create Sunday school space. They put the classrooms behind the partition on the west and moved the chancel to the middle of the hall. The pews faced west toward the tower, and a new main entry was opened in the east wall. The old entry, the lower tower, became a coal bin, and the town clock was installed in the upper tower. During this renovation—or perhaps when some work was done in 1886—the marble slabs and gravestones underfoot were replaced with wooden flooring.

Goodwin proposed, in essence, to get rid of the 1839-1840 partition and remodel the church on the form it had in 1769. But it was not a restoration as the term is understood in Williamsburg today. Eventually he would see the job as "partial and incomplete." But it "resulted in saving the Church from collapse threatened by structural disintegration . . . and restored the interior to its Colonial appearance in so far as information then available made possible."

Before Goodwin got started, he nearly re-ignited the William and Mary war by accident. He had started off well enough, taking his turn among the clergy of Williamsburg's four churches to serve as college chaplain. But in a conversation with a member of the board of visitors, Judge Robert M. Hughes, he faulted the institution's efficiency and said he doubted he could recommend it to young scholars. Shades of Rector Roberts. Word of this circulated, reaching L. B. Wharton of the faculty, who took up his pen and wrote a letter to Goodwin three blocks away. It began with all good wishes from Wharton and his colleagues. Then it got to the point:

> We think at the same time, that your attack upon the efficiency of the College as shown in the training of young men neither kind, nor just, and also an attack that came at a very bad time, when we all wanted peace to pursue unhindered our several vocations, we in our secular employments, you in your higher spiritual work as a minister of Jesus Christ, who is not a master but a servant of men, refusing to become a judge, or a divider among men in their worldly and secular occupations. And all this came at a time when you had been a sojourner among us for only about three months and might be supposed not as yet to have gotten the full bearings of things among us, not to be yet fully competent to pass authoritatively upon the workings of our public institutions as to their efficiency or non-efficiency.

Goodwin unearthed 28 graves when he undertook to repair the Bruton Church floor during the building renovations begun in 1905. Daughter Evelyn, who helped identify coffins, long remembered the "musty smell of earth, the strange odor of sanctity."

Goodwin scrambled out an explanation by way of apology. He had shared his opinions only when Mr. Hughes had asked for them, he wrote, and had said he could not conscientiously recommend "young men preparing for the ministry and deficient in literary attainments" to attend William and Mary because a student instructor was employed in teaching entry-level Greek. Peace was thus preserved, and Goodwin busied himself in matters closer to home. He began laying the groundwork for his restoration fund-raising campaign.

The first step was to prepare a promotional pamphlet he called *A Sketch of Bruton Parish Church,* based largely on entries in the old parish registers and vestry books. Goodwin conveyed the tract's central message in a single epigram: "What time has spared so long and hallowed must not suffer from man's neglect." He paid for the printing out of his own pocket, but the vestry reimbursed him 50 cents for each copy used. Included in the booklet was an advertisement for the restoration fund.

In the creation of the pamphlet, perhaps, is found the germ of Goodwin's enthusiasm for the restoration of the city. It led him to undertake his first book and his second, both devoted to Bruton and its historical setting. "This research and writing," he said, "developed

In his first attempt to return Bruton to its colonial appearance, Goodwin removed the 19th-century pews, altar, and other furnishings.

and intensified my sense of appreciation of the historic background and environment of the church and helped to develop the thought of the value and need of a more extensive restoration of colonial Williamsburg."

In October, pamphlets ready, Goodwin began a 22-day fund-raising trip that took him as far north as Providence, Rhode Island. He offered contributors the chance to pay for memorial plaques, pew nameplates, furnishings, silver, and prayer books, and he returned with $3,717.50 in cash and pledges. Included was $1,125 from Andrew Carnegie toward a new $3,000 organ. The rector expected more pledges to follow, more gifts to go with the approaching celebration of his first Williamsburg Christmas.

During the city's first century, Christmas observances were reverently modest. In its second, they grew more elaborate. In 1842 a young professor of Latin and Greek at William and Mary introduced the town to the first Christmas tree noted in local lore. A political refugee from the principality of Hesse-Darmstadt, he was a Yuletide guest in the St. George Tucker House, across Palace Green from Bruton Church. In the tradition of his German homeland, he erected a small evergreen on a table in the parlor for the Tucker children. Among its young admirers was the woman Goodwin knew

In 1839, Bruton's congregation divided the church with an altar partition, moved the entry to the east, and turned the pews to face west. The baptismal font is from the church at Jamestown.

The St. George Tucker House, one of Williamsburg's finest 18th-century homes, as it appeared about 1904. The lad in the foreground is Rutherfoord Goodwin, son of Bruton Parish's rector.

as Cynthia Coleman. The professor was Charles F. E. Minnigerode, the minister who baptized Jeff Davis and wed Goodwin's parents.

By the start of the city's third century, Christmas had become a day of candle-lit evergreens, gift-giving, firecrackers, feasting, and visiting. Bruton's service was always a centerpiece, an anchor in a sea of change all around. This year, seven days before Christmas Eve, two inventors from Dayton, Ohio, flew their first airplane at Kittyhawk, just 120 miles away.

Goodwin spent the following year collecting money, ministering, and perfecting plans. In the course of his fund-raising calls, he earned the friendship of the Reverend Dr. William S. Huntington of Grace Church in New York. Huntington agreed to chair a restoration advisory committee, steered Goodwin to new prospects, and recommended J. Stewart Barney as an architect.

Trained at Columbia University and the Ecole des Beaux-Arts in Paris, Barney became partner in a New York office about 1894 that specialized in ecclesiastical architecture. Later he practiced on his own. Among his New York projects was Grace Church Chapel and the Church of the Holy Trinity. His family had lived in Richmond, where Barney designed another Church of the

Holy Trinity and All Saints Episcopal. When Goodwin met him, he
was doing Richmond's Church of the Covenant. Barney agreed to
help with Bruton on two conditions: The architect would accept no
compensation, and the goal would be a colonial restoration. Those
conditions suited the rector fine.

As Barney drafted the plans, Goodwin collected all the
Bruton records he could find and edited them for publication in the
volume *Bruton Parish-Historical Notes*. The book, Goodwin's first,
came off the press in 1905, the year he was ready to start the
renovations.

They began May 15 with a 4 p.m. ceremonial service and
sermon by the Reverend Dr. Beverley Tucker of St. Paul's in Norfolk.
Tucker's topic was "to be true to a trust." The service, Goodwin said,
was "held not so much to inaugurate the beginning of the
Restoration of Bruton Parish Church as to mark the passing out of
existence of the innovations made in 1839." It was "arranged in order
to conciliate certain conservative members of the congregation who
objected to any change whatsoever, insisting that the Church should
be kept as they had always known it."

It was not an auspicious start. After that morning's regular
services, a man from the Hutchings-Vetey Organ Company of
Boston had opened the old pump organ to see what its restoration
would require. In use for 70 years, it was held together by wires,
shoestrings, and prayer; and the man may have undone some of
them. That afternoon, when sexton William Galt began to push the
instrument's pedals, and the organist struck the keys for the opening
hymn, the organ "gave a long and horrible moan, and passed into
eternal silence."

"This was the beginning of the horrors," Goodwin said. "A
thunderstorm came up. A cat and dog took refuge under the Church,
and began to dispute with each other sole possession of this refuge
from the storm. The air became black with darkness, so that it was
impossible to read the service." Galt, dressed all in white, descended
from the organ loft, looking rather ghostly in the gloom. He carried
a stepladder and a box of matches to light the chandelier candles.
"After this, amid terrific claps of thunder, the service proceeded to
its end," Goodwin said. "Some of the conservatives hinted that it was
all an omen of disaster and of divine disapproval." The next
morning, however, everyone returned to help remove the furniture,
cushions, and books, so the work could begin. The discarded pulpit

and pews Goodwin sent back to Petersburg.

After the partition was taken down, the floor was torn up and the plaster ripped from the brick walls. The red tin roof was inspected and the walls plumbed for straightness. Goodwin found in the ground large bundles of bullets secreted during the Civil War and 28 graves. He identified nine burials by comparing to parish register-entries the letters and dates shaped with brass tacks in the coffin lids. Daughter Evelyn helped with the excavations, or at least he let her think she had. As an adult she wrote a brief memoir of him that mentioned the mysteries beneath the floor. "There is a picture of Father standing among those ancient tombs," she said, "but as I write I need no picture to bring back the musty smell of the earth, the strange odor of sanctity, and the feeling of awe that it stirred in me as a little girl." Goodwin discovered that the foundations had disintegrated and that the roof timbers had spread, pushing the transept walls outward. The workmen repaired the foundations, installed new timbers, tiled the roof, put the chancel back at the church's east end, and laid a marble floor over a base of concrete and iron. The work went on for about 18 months. Worship services were conducted in the parish house, just northwest of the churchyard.

Goodwin became secretary of the Diocese of Southern Virginia. He still served as financial secretary of Bishop Payne Divinity and was soon to become a trustee. He made trips to Richmond, back to Petersburg, and struck out on fund-raising forays up the coast for the school as well as for Bruton. In August of 1906 he was invited to teach at a conference in Richfield Springs. He decided to take the children with him, while Evelyn went to Canada with her sister Lizzie.

Goodwin found rooms in a private home, where young Molly Seaton looked after the little ones while he taught. One day Molly took Rutherfoord, now five, to a drugstore for ice cream. He came home with a pocketful of change. His father learned "he had been put up on a counter and had preached a sermon on 'Noah and the animals going into the Ark.' Someone had suggested he take up a collection and had loaned him a hat, and he had passed it around with lucrative results."

Goodwin himself was asked to make a presentation at the conference, to deliver a paper titled "The Education of the Negro. The Greatest Need." It was a lengthy document, the product of first-hand experience, and it may have taken an hour to deliver. The gist of it was that Goodwin believed blacks should be educated for the work they were most likely to secure. He counseled against creating more black high schools and colleges until society provided more outlets for the skills those institutions would teach them. Otherwise, he said, the result would be unrest born of disappointed expectations.

Of the African-American, he said, "To tell him that all men are equal is to simply tell him what is not true. But to deny him an equal chance and equal justice is a social and political crime. To tell him that the line of division, which has been run between the races,

A trio of workmen takes time out from their renovation labors to strike a lighthearted pose before Bruton's south gate.

which is designed to prevent their mixture and social mingling, is subversive of his rights, is simply to encourage in him a spirit of resentment and rebellion which will result in race clash and social discord." Goodwin saw no promise in desegregation. On the contrary. He thought more thorough segregation was the solution. He envisioned a separate black society in which African-Americans would build independent communities, establish their own businesses to serve one another, create the need for and train their own professionals, and accumulate their own capital.

Removed from the context of 1906, the paper may be unpalatable. But what it proposed is hardly novel, then or now. Thomas Jefferson sketched a similar separation of the races in the 1780s, and the founding of Liberia by American blacks in the early 1800s was an attempt at creating a separate nation for blacks. African-American leaders like Marcus Garvey espoused black independence in the 1920s, and African-American separatists still offer variations on the theme.

Goodwin shared Jefferson's gloomy views about the capacities of African-Americans for equality. Several months later he wrote: "Now when we come to examine the negro mind we find that it is weakest in its power to reason, to reflect, and to deal with practical issues in a common-sense way. He has a good memory and is very quick of perception. He is disposed to want the training which his race has not mastered, not, I am convinced, for the purpose of equipping him for service, but because it is unusual."

In Williamsburg, Goodwin's mind was occupied with problems more mundane, like the community's agitation over the question of paving Duke of Gloucester Street, "someone having presumed to suggest this should be done." Some said the mud in which Washington and Jefferson had walked was good enough for them. Others favored more solid footing.

Next door to Goodwin's home stood H. Dennison Cole 's shop, and in front of that shop grew an old mulberry tree. Beneath it met the Pulaski Club, a sidewalk society founded in 1779, a still-functioning loose-knit group of 31 men who like to see things go their way. Certificates of membership are written longhand on the back of an Octagon Soap wrapper, and the initiation fee is a quart of Virginia bourbon. Nailed to the club's mulberry was the community bulletin board, a clearing house for town notices and important newspaper clippings. It announced great outside events like the San Francisco Earthquake in 1906. To the board Goodwin tacked his contribution to the paving debate, a mathematics problem: "The Duke of Gloucester Street is one mile long from the college to the Capitol. How deep is it, allowing six inches that you go down in the mud for every eighteen inches that you step forward?"

The school superintendent happened along, read the question, looked around, took down the paper, and put it in his pocket. Goodwin, watching from a rectory window, said nothing, "as I did not want my connections with the matter known." At day's end, all Williamsburg was engaged in the calculation.* "The superintendent had taken the problem as one of the arithmetic problems of the school and through the children it went all over town. It may have been one of the forces' contributory to the getting of the greatly needed sidewalks."

One of Goodwin's fellow college chaplains, "a Baptist minister of a sensational disposition of mind," also looked to the bulletin board for items of interest and news. Still current was the story of the morning in 1889 when he stopped on his way to deliver the school's morning prayers and read a clipping about the Johnstown Flood. In the chapel he thanked God, without mentioning any of the particulars, for sparing the city from the most disastrous flood since Noah's. It sounded as if Williamsburg was the new Mount Ararat. Immediately after chapel, there was "a wild rush of students downtown to the bulletin board to find out the ground and reason for the parson's prayer of thanksgiving."

The college's fortunes were improving under Tyler's administration. In March 1906 the General Assembly voted to accept it as a state institution, solving the objection Roberts and others had raised to the outlay of state funds for a private school. The Carnegie Corporation gave the college $50,000 to build its first library.

John D. Rockefeller, Jr., was doing better, too. He had recovered from a nervous collapse the year before and partly for therapy built his parents a $1.1 million house in New York State's Pocantico Hills. Almost half the sum went for landscaping. A Broadway wag described the grounds as an example of what God would have done if he had only had the money. As it happened, the senior Rockefellers disliked the place and had it rebuilt.

---

* The street would be 1,760 feet deep when it reached the Capitol.

Rutherfoord, Evelyn, and Mary—The Reverend Dr. W. A. R. and Evelyn Goodwin's three eldest children, about 1906.

Letitia was living with the family now, helping Evelyn manage the household. On June 23rd the Goodwin's had a second son, William Archer. "His birth," Goodwin said, "marked the beginning of the physical illness which some years later resulted in the death of his mother." The boy lived a year, dying July 14 during a visit to Carter's Grove plantation. He was temporarily interred at Cedar Grove Cemetery in Williamsburg and removed to Bruton Parish Churchyard in September, when it was clear of restoration work.

The church had been ready for services that May; it was consecrated on the 12th by Bishop Randolph. The dedication was put off to give the ceremony a bigger role in events surrounding the Jamestown tercentennial celebrations of 1907. They were the grandest historical observances in Virginia's Tidewater since the Yorktown festivities 16 years earlier. The centerpiece was the international Jamestown Exposition that opened in April at Norfolk. But there were elaborate memorial activities at Jamestown Island, eight miles from Williamsburg, and Goodwin took a prominent role.

The federal government erected a 103-foot-tall, $50,000 obelisk on the island to mark the spot of the first permanent English settlement in America. To make it easier for people to reach the monument, Goodwin engineered the improvement of the boulevard that led out of town toward the site. He persuaded a quarry operator to donate gravel, a railroad man to donate hauling, and the governor to provide convict labor. Some in town objected to this modernization, too.

The day before Bruton's consecration, the Society of Colonial Dames unveiled the memorial church at Jamestown, a chapel built over 17th-century foundations. Goodwin gave the sermon for the dedication of a monument and tableau honoring the Reverend Robert Hunt, the settlement's first Anglican clergyman. Hunt had delivered his first sermon beneath a canvas strung up in the trees; so did Goodwin, in whose parish the memorial church stood.

Goodwin finished writing his second book, *Bruton Parish Restored and Its Historical Environment,* and worked on arrangements for the dedication ceremonies. The city council passed an ordinance "prohibiting the running at large of cows and horses."

The dedication was to coincide with a national meeting of the Episcopal Church, a general convention conducted this year in Richmond because Virginia was the state in which the Episcopal Church had taken American root 300 years earlier. On October 5, a Saturday, the participants adjourned to Williamsburg for 11 a.m. ceremonies at Bruton. Among them was steel tycoon J. Pierpont

Steel magnate J. Pierpont Morgan was the center of attention when delegates of the Episcopal General Convention traveled from Richmond to Williamsburg to join in Bruton's 1907 dedication. Goodwin is at left in the derby.

Morgan, lay representative from New York. "Special trains were run
down from Richmond," Goodwin said. "The attending crowd
overflowed both the Church and the churchyard." He said he thought
2,000 people came.

Two representatives of all the dioceses in the 13 original
states attended, as did the Reverend Dr. William Huntington and
Bishop William Lawrence of Massachusetts. Another bishop
preached in the churchyard to the people who could not get inside.

Though in colonial days the lord bishops of London had
charge of the church in Virginia, none had before been to America.
Dr. Arthur Foley Winnington-Ingram became the first, steaming
across the Atlantic to present a gift to Bruton Parish from King
Edward VII. It was a specially bound Bible tooled in gold and made
up to commemorate the establishment of the English Church in the
Old Dominion. J. Young, a British Embassy attaché, had the honor
of delivering it by hand. The lord bishop put it on a bronze lectern
presented by Bishop Saterlee of Washington in behalf of President
Theodore Roosevelt.

The lectern was designed on Barney's drafting table, and
Goodwin had a tactful hand in the Bible's design. The Archbishop of
Canterbury proposed the reverse binding of the Bible be embossed
with the Virginia state seal. Perhaps he had not seen the emblem.
Designed in 1776 by George Wythe, master of the house next door
to Bruton, the seal shows Virtue, dressed as an Amazon and holding
a spear, with her foot on the prostrate form of Tyranny, a man whose
crown lays nearby on the ground. Its motto is *"Sic Semper Tyrannis,"*
Latin for "Thus Always to Tyrants." Doubting the propriety of that
sentiment being conveyed by the King of England, Goodwin
suggested the substitution of a colonial emblem. It portrayed Virginia
as the fifth jewel in Great Britain's crown, after England, Scotland,
Ireland, and France, all claimed by the crown at the time. His
recommendation was adopted, and royal face was saved. But not so
for the American bishop who introduced Winnington-Ingram at the
presentation of the Bible. He told the congregation it was the gift of
King Henry VIII.

When the train had reached the Williamsburg station that
morning, there had been a rush for conveyances to the church.
Morgan, Huntington, Winnington-Ingram, and Lawrence had seized

a wagon, but British attaché Young and his wife had to settle for a closed "carry-all with horse, harness and vehicle evidently dating from ante-bellum days." Morgan helped them into the broken-down coach, put the Bible on the driver's seat, "and had," Goodwin said, "the utmost amusement in watching the representative of the successor of King James and George III drive to the ancient church."

After the service, the joke was on Morgan. There was a luncheon at the rectory for special guests. When it was done, Morgan wanted to drive around town. "It was before the days of automobiles in Williamsburg," Goodwin said. Henry Ford would not introduce his Model T, priced at $825, for another year and a month. "The one vehicle which could be requisitioned was a spring wagon owned by Professor Hugh Bird of the College, which was standing in front of the house, having arrived with the ice-cream for the luncheon." It was a creaking rig that wobbled on its wheels behind a rickety horse held by dilapidated harness. Because Bird was Bruton's junior warden, Goodwin asked if Morgan would assume the risk of the wagon's use. He would. "Mr. Morgan, the Lord Bishop of London and Bishop Lawrence climbed up and seated themselves on the front board seat," Goodwin said. "Dr. Huntington and I climbed into the rear end and sat on the floor of the wagon with our feet dangling out." Word of their approach proceeded them to the college; classes adjourned, and students and faculty assembled on the lawn. When the wagon arrived, the bishop of London got down, looked at the spring wagon, and said, "Young gentlemen, if you haven't got a sense of humor, pray for it." Then he told them he had come to see what they had done with the money he had sent by Blair in 1693.

When the guests left, Williamsburg took a breather. The year to come would be remembered chiefly for the death of Cynthia Coleman and the raising of a Confederate monument on Palace Green by the local chapter of the United Daughters of the Confederacy. It was inscribed: "Lord God of Hosts, Be with us yet / Lest we forget, Lest we forget." Goodwin regretted Coleman's passing immediately; the monument would cause him grief 24 years later. For now, his endeavors with Bruton's rehabilitation brought him new prospects.

He was dispatched in June to London as a representative to the Pan-Anglican Conference. With him went Tyler and J. B. C.

Spencer. They traveled as the guests of Mrs. Sarah Bowman Van Ness of Lexington, Massachusetts. Tyler, of course, was president of the college. Spencer was owner of the Colonial Inn on Courthouse Square and a bit of an eccentric. He is best remembered for his hospitality, the satisfying quality of the traditional Virginia meals served in his dining room, the pleasantness of the toddies served at his bar, and for his disposition to sit on his house porch with a loaded gun in his lap.

The Duchess of Marlborough invited the trio to a garden party at 4 p.m. on the 25th. On the spur of the moment, the Archbishop of Canterbury presented Goodwin to the King and Queen of England and the Prince and Princess of Wales to thank the King for the Bible. "The King was very gracious and very democratic," Goodwin said, "and asked me how the people liked the Bible, to which I replied that the people seemed to listen with more

Goodwin, matured by his first Williamsburg ministry, looked the very picture of success for churches in the market for a new rector.

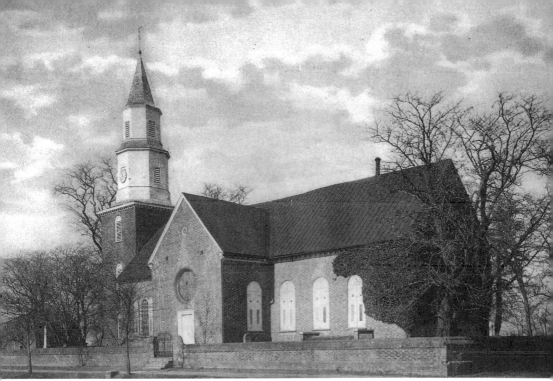

Tin-roofed and ivy-covered, Williamsburg's Bruton Parish Church as it stood when Goodwin came to town in 1904.

marked reverence when the Lessons were being read from the book given by his Majesty." Goodwin walked away in a fog; he could never remember whether he had turned his back on the King as he took his leave. It bothered him.

Three days later, Goodwin preached at Bruton, Somerset. The church gave a banquet for Goodwin and Tyler at the Guild Hall, and later Goodwin went with Vicar Douglas L. Hayward to stand beneath the Ludwell Oak. Thomas Ludwell of Hayward's parish was one of the Englishmen who carried the name Bruton to Virginia. Ludwell died there in 1678 and is buried at the north transept door of Bruton, Virginia.

After a jaunt on the Continent, Goodwin returned to Williamsburg and his family. In December the William and Mary chapter of Phi Beta Kappa made him an honorary member in recognition of the books Goodwin had published on Bruton. Dr. Garrett of fist-fight fame presented him with a fraternity key of colonial design.

Before the year was out, a church in Blacksburg asked Goodwin to take its pulpit, and the American Church Missionary Society in New York offered to hire him as its secretary. Goodwin stayed put until he got a better offer. Besides, he wasn't quite through in Williamsburg.

The interior of Goodwin's new church, St. Paul's in Rochester, New York, looked big enough to contain all of his old one, Bruton Church in Williamsburg.

Chapter Six: **1909-1918**

Bruton Parish Church restored stood as a memorial to the spiritual government of the men and women of 18th-century Williamsburg. Perhaps that's what suggested the resurrection of a monument to the regulation of their civil life, the big brick Capitol at the end of Duke of Gloucester Street.

It has the earmarks of a Goodwin idea, but the notion as easily could have come from the APVA, the organization that owned the Capitol's site and foundations. It could have occurred to anyone who wandered, as Goodwin had, among the capped footings of the vanished building, thinking of its history, stepping off the General Courtroom, the offices, and the Hall of the House of Burgesses. In middle age, Goodwin made a point of starting a new project the day he wrapped up an old one. The record doesn't show whether, at 38, he began to consider the Capitol's reconstruction as quickly as he got J. P. Morgan back aboard the Richmond train. But he was turning the project over in his mind and writing to people about it at least as early as March of 1909. "I wish to thank you for your kind favor of the 11th," a correspondent said, "and am very glad to know that the house of 'Burgesses' is likely to be restored. I think the country can thank you for a good deal of this restoration that is going on."

No doubt the building stood already revived in Goodwin's head, rising course by course on the base of the original. But he would have to raise real money before he could raise real bricks, and that was the first thing on the minds of the members of the APVA. The association had already organized a Capitol reconstruction committee; but the panel was having trouble getting started, not finding a chairman until April 15, when it asked Goodwin to accept the job. "The only duty of this committee," he was told, "is to ascertain and report to the Association the probable cost of the work and the feasibility of raising the money. The Association will then take the necessary action and probably enlarge the powers of the committee and enlarge its membership." That was pretty much how he had begun the Bruton project. If he thought the Capitol's reconstruction was probable, it was perhaps because of how well things had come together for Bruton's restoration. As he said, the responsibility for the raising of funds for the job had given him "wide and interesting contacts." After his labor at Bruton, St. John's, and Bishop Payne Divinity, he had learned, as he put it, "to think big."

He was, in fact, thinking of bigger things than Williamsburg and the Capitol. He was thinking of building a road linking Jamestown, Williamsburg, and Yorktown, and he asked his congressman for legislation to construct a federal highway across the storied Peninsula. Nothing practical could be done about it at the time, his representative said. It took 22 years to gain federal funding for the Colonial Parkway, which was not finished until 1957. But Goodwin's aspirations the last year of his first Williamsburg tour of duty foreshadow what he would accomplish when he returned.

There was in 1909 another portent of things to come—though Goodwin had nothing to do with it. John D. Crimmins of New York had found in a Norfolk bookshop a faded drawing labeled *Plandela Ville et environs de Williams burg envirginia.* Dated May 11, 1781, it was a curious rendering, probably a preparatory sketch for a formal plan of colonial Williamsburg's streets. An unknown French army officer had made it, perhaps for use in billeting Rochambeau's troops the winter after Yorktown. Crimmins sent it to Betty Custis Ambler to present to the College of William and Mary. It is still the most precise representation yet discovered of the locations of the buildings and the geography of the 18th-century city. It is called by two other names: "The Frenchman's Map" and "The Bible of the Restoration."

Goodwin, however, was closing his book on Williamsburg to accept the call to another church.

St. Paul's in Rochester, New York, needed a replacement for the Reverend Doctor Murray Bartlett. It sent down vestrymen Hiram Sibley, Granger Hollister, and Benjamin B. Chase, with their wives, to evaluate Goodwin in March. St. Paul's was one of Rochester's wealthiest parishes, and this party of well-to-do men and women could not have been much impressed with down-at-the-heels Williamsburg. Moreover, they "ran into a blizzard and nearly froze to death at the Colonial Inn," the ramshackle hotel J. B. C. Spencer ran on Courthouse Square.

Christ Church in Norfolk was shopping for a new minister, too, and it dispatched a delegation on another winter Sunday. "I was afterwards told," Goodwin said, "that I was not called because I read my sermon . . . one of perhaps a half-dozen occasions during my whole ministry on which I ever read my sermon from a manuscript."

Sermons, of course, are supposed to be delivered as if they were extemporaneous, not read. Usually, Goodwin spoke from notes. His chagrin over this lapse was still palpable 15 years later. No doubt in 1909 he still would have preferred advancement within Virginia. But four days after the APVA asked him to chair the Capitol committee, St. Paul's offered Goodwin the Rochester job. The vestrymen had warmed to his more spontaneous sermon that blizzardy Sunday in March.

Before giving his answer, Goodwin traveled north incognito to get the lay of the land. He arrived late the evening of April 24, a Saturday, and took a room at the Osborn House. Eager to see the church, he asked the clerk for directions. The instructions led him instead to The Happy Hour Motion Picture Theatre on St. Paul's Street in a building that had been the church 15 years earlier. Goodwin concluded it had been that long since the clerk, a Mr. Snake, attended services. The next morning, dressed in what he called "citizens clothes," Goodwin went to the corner of East Avenue and Vick Park B and got his first look at St. Paul's.

Compared with Bruton, the church was a cathedral, a large stone Gothic-style building with soaring spires and stained-glass windows made by Tiffany Studios. Framed by stately elms on a parklike lawn, the church looked big enough for Bruton to fit inside.

Goodwin entered and took a seat halfway up the left aisle as the service began. About the same time, he said, "a little minister, with a long-tailed coat reaching down below his knees, entered the Church accompanied by his low, but by no means little, wife, as I am sure that she measured almost as much across as she did lengthways. They were ushered up the main aisle of the Church to the seat just in front of the pulpit. As the minister who had been called was expected that day, this parson . . . was supposed to be

myself. I had the pleasure of hearing the whispered comments of my
nearby neighbors on the appearance of their prospective rector and
his wife."

He returned to Williamsburg, and wrote to the vestry May 3:
"After mature consideration I have decided to accept the call
extended me." He resigned as Bruton's rector the same day,
effective June 20, and said he would take up his duties in Rochester
July 1 or soon thereafter. When he delivered his final Bruton
sermon, the church was packed with Methodists and Baptists as
well as Episcopalians. But rather than talk about his
accomplishments or departure, he made it an opportunity to
promote church mission work.

Letitia returned to Wytheville; and the rector, his wife, and
their children left Williamsburg June 24, stopping in Charlottesville
for a week. The day of his departure the *Virginia Gazette* said:
"When Rev. W. A. R. Goodwin came here seven years ago he found
a parish actually torn to pieces by unfortunate differences in
the congregation. The dissensions had not been confined to that
congregation alone, but had spread over the town. The parish was
wracked with turmoil and an unhappy state of affairs existed. It was
a herculean task this young man of God faced, but how well he met
and conquered the difficulties; how by his tact and wonderful
personality he united the factions in the common cause of Christ all
know, and he leaves behind a record of which any minister should
feel proud. The work of restoring the church was merely incidental
with him, but it stands as a beautiful monument to his energy."

The Goodwin children had their first automobile ride when
vestryman Granger Hollister in his Packard chauffeured the family
from the station to the rectory at 65 Barrington Street. For the first
few days the youngsters played with the novel push-button light
switches "and showed their appreciation of their new home," their
father said, "by announcing to the people that they had three
bathtubs in the house."

Goodwin had adjustments to make, as well. "In
Williamsburg, he said, "if the Lord hadn't put something inside of
you to make you wake up you would have slept forever. In Rochester
it was exceedingly hard amid the many and varied duties and noises
to find chance and opportunity to sleep at all.

"In Williamsburg one was waked up in the morning by a man blowing a seashell and then calling up to your window to know how many oysters you wanted. You told him that you wanted a pint or a quart, and threw out either fifteen cents or twenty-five cents to pay the bill. In Rochester one was waked by the siren calls of many factories."

His congregation numbered close to 1,200—more than half the number of people who lived in the whole of Williamsburg. He preached his first sermon to them July 4, and he was acutely aware that his reading of the epistle that Sunday made the first two words out of his mouth a cornbread Southern expression: "I reckon that the sufferings of this present time are not worthy to be compared to the glory which shall be revealed."

Goodwin's new parishioners called him "the Parson," and among them he developed close friends. The family spent its first Rochester Christmas with the Hollisters, whose tree was lit with electric bulbs instead of old-fashioned candles. Young Rutherfoord, accustomed to the gift of a Christmas-morning penny, got instead a slightly smaller $5 gold piece.

There was an embarrassment of riches, and that for Goodwin posed a problem. In the course of his Virginia fund-raising trips, the Parson had become comfortable in the occasional company of the wealthy. But his workaday parishioners and vestry had always been of modest means. Now he had to deal with an affluent congregation led by a wealthy vestry, and he was conscious of the difference.

"This constituted a barrier which I realized had to be broken down," Goodwin said. "For any such barrier is artificial in its nature and is distinctly obstructive if allowed to separate mind from mind and heart from heart in cooperative endeavor." He went to each vestryman—among them such men of means as James Goold Cutler, Benjamin B. Chase, Edward C. Minor, George F. Johnston, Hiram Sibley, Watkin W. Kneath, and Kingman Nott Robins—to say he was not willing that money should stand between them or hinder free and open relationships. He said he had higher regard for them than their money, needed ready benefit of the wisdom that underwrote their prosperity, and wanted to feel free to ask for counsel on church projects and policies without being suspected of asking indirectly for financial contributions. Goodwin said he hoped their decisions in such matters would be made in mind of what they would cost the

rank and file instead of themselves. Then he moved to "free the
congregation from the paralysis of inefficiency and
irresponsiveness, which had resulted from their having grown
almost entirely dependent upon the rich to carry the full burden of
the Church's responsibility."

The Parson also busied himself in life beyond St. Paul's
Parish. He became a member of the Chamber of Commerce, the
Genesee Valley Club, transferred his Williamsburg membership to
the local chapter of the Masons, and joined the city's Ministerial
Association. He helped start the local Boy Scouts council and
served on the boards of the Rescue Mission and the Federated
Churches of Rochester. He joined the South Park Golf Club, the
Rotary, the Alpha Chi Society, the Humdrum Club, and the
Country Parsons.

The Alpha Chi Society was an organization of ministers that
included professors from the University of Rochester and Rochester
Theological Seminary. The Humdrum Club, composed of lawyers,
doctors, academics, and other professional men, dined monthly to
read formal papers on topics of the day. Goodwin, the only minister,
was chaplain. The Country Parsons, his favorite group, was a let-your-
hair-down collection of 12 Episcopal ministers who five times a year
spent a day in fellowship and shoptalk. The membership invitation he
got in February 1911 said the priests gathered with the "object of
freeing our own minds, hearing the others free their minds, and of
having a good time together. Our bonds are supposed to be, common
work and intellectual and spiritual interests and congeniality."

Some members of St. Paul's thought Goodwin spent too
much time in the congeniality of outside affairs to the detriment of
the parish's. He said the genius of Christianity was its outgoing
spirit, and to him it seemed natural the parish should relate to every
movement in Rochester "which was designed to make the city a
cleaner and more beautiful home for the Father's children." But his
extra-parish pursuits got him into dutch with his bishop, as well.

The flash point was Goodwin's organization of the
Rochester Church Extension Society, an interdenominational lay
missionary group. Bishop William D. Walker of the Diocese of
Western New York was a formalist—a "High Church" man—certain of
the supremacy of the Anglican faith. He was wary of endeavors in
which every denomination necessarily stood on an equal footing.
Goodwin solved the problem by making Walker the chairman of

every committee except ways and means, but using that panel to conduct all the society's business. He conceded that the bishop's opposition and resentment were conscientious and principled. But Walker, according to Goodwin, regarded the rector of St. Paul's "as being disloyal to the Church," which he felt sworn to protect. Goodwin said his superior "felt it his duty to denounce me as a traitor to the Church and her orders." The last straw was Goodwin's sponsorship of a resolution at a national Episcopal General Convention in New York that authorized the church's Board of Missions "to cooperate with other Christian people in the extension of the Kingdom of God through conferences" and other means. It passed almost unanimously. Election as a delegate to a general convention was a mark of distinction. Before the diocese made its selections for the next national meeting, the bishop censured Goodwin in an address to the church council, and made certain the defeat of his candidacy.

There was, as well, more trouble at home. In a congregation so large, there was always room for dissatisfaction and despite his reputation as an orator, a few criticized the subjects on which Goodwin preached. Some resented his frequent remarks on his pet subject—missionary work. Others wanted to hear about Babylon and Nineveh and biblical archaeology. Goodwin went on delivering the sermons he thought St. Paul's needed to hear. He was "glad to be able to say that I am not conscious of having in one single instance brought the level of my preaching down to any of these demands." He did not scruple to declaim what he believed to be the truth merely because wealthy or prominent people were in the pews who objected to the message. Goodwin thought that was his duty, essential to maintaining his self respect. "I know now, and I knew then," he later wrote, "that this level of teaching was antagonizing to some of those whose relation to the Church was evidently not primarily and principally of a deeply spiritual character."

But no one ever accused him of being a slacker. When he wasn't in the pulpit, or at one of his outside functions, the Parson, among other things, officiated at weddings, funerals, and baptisms. He taught confirmation classes and special study groups. He organized and attended meetings of the Woman's Auxiliary, the Altar Guild, the Young People's Fellowship, Sunday School, the Brotherhood of St. Andrews, the Men's Club, and the Mother's Club. He engineered the introduction of a more sophisticated system for

taking up collections—the dual-envelope method—led an annual
fund-raising drive called the every-member canvass, and called on
the sick and the well. He found time in between to edit the church
newspaper, write another book—*The Church Enchained*—and
compose, publish, and distribute a booklet called *The Family Prayer*.
In 1914, he delivered to the alumni association of the Virginia
Theological Seminary an address on the institution's founding,
agreed to compile a history of the school, and returned to Roanoke
College to accept the degree of doctor of divinity.

He was obliged to attend to private business as well. After
the death of his father, Goodwin became trustee for his mother. She
turned over to him the management of the Norwood farm, and
some lots on Richmond's Church Hill inherited from her father. He
and Evelyn from time to time returned to Virginia to visit
Williamsburg and to call on Nelson County and Wytheville kin. But
Goodwin had to try to oversee the farm tenants by mail, relying on
the postman and his brother-in-law S. H. Coleman of Roanoke to be
his local agents. An inexhaustible source of aggravation, the place
produced cash crops no better now than it had when Goodwin's
father was in charge.

For relaxation, Goodwin played golf—though that became
another source of annoyance. He agreed with his parishioners that
Sunday was set aside for worship, meditation, mental and spiritual
rest, and communion with the Creator; but it never seemed to him
"that these purposes were in the least transgressed" by a Sunday
afternoon game of golf. He did not object to his parishioners taking
to the links after church, and he resented being forbidden the same
indulgence merely because he was a minister. "The time will come,"
he wrote, "when the fanatics who insist upon making rules for others
which they do not keep themselves, who go riding in motor cars run
by chauffeurs whom they insist on taking away from their families
and their churches on Sunday, and spy out for possible clergymen
playing golf out in the open sunshine, will be ruled out of court."
Nevertheless, Goodwin refrained rather than lose influence among
the respectable.

Daughters Evelyn and Katherine had gone off to attend the
National Cathedral School in Washington, D.C., and Rutherfoord,
after stints in Rochester public and private schools, became a

student at Episcopal High in Alexandria, Virginia. While they were away, Goodwin said, "their mother, who had not been well for a number of years, grew continuously worse, passing at last through a most painful and distressing illness, which had its origin in kidney trouble."

Before Thanksgiving of 1914, it must have been apparent to him that the disease was terminal. In mid-November he composed a poem, "To My Wife." It read:

> *Let not thy spirit brood over by gone years;*
> *They stand before God's judgement Throne.*
> *And poison not Thy soul with spectral fears,*
> *The present hour is thine alone.*
> *Then fill this hour with love and light,*
> *And banish from Thy heart the night;*
> *Eternal day is thine, Oh child of God.*

Her illness and his distress deepened with the winter. Just after Christmas, Goodwin took a moment away from his fears to write to a Washington, D. C., minister. He began: "Please excuse the confused form of expression in which my letter is written, but I am stealing a moment from the bedside of my wife who is desperately ill to answer your letter as well as I can."

Evelyn Tannor Goodwin died January 15, 1915. She was 46. "The people of the parish were exceedingly kind," Goodwin said. With two vestrymen friends, he took her body to Williamsburg to be buried beside their son William in the Bruton Parish Churchyard. "Every expense incident to these last rites, including the trip down to Virginia, was paid through the kindness of friends in St. Paul's and in addition several hundred dollars were given to me with which to go South for rest and recuperation." He took two weeks in Savannah, he said, "Where I spent a good deal of time playing golf with the Jewish rabbi."

Williamsburg had resumed its long slow slide into somnambulance. At least for the present. In the six years since Goodwin's departure, the Capitol restoration idea had come to nothing. The last big APVA project on the Peninsula had been the erection of Captain John Smith's statue on Jamestown Island in 1909.

Cynthia Coleman's daughter-in-law, George's wife Mary Haldane Begg Coleman, lamented that "that first heartfelt picturesqueness was fast disappearing. There were telephones, no electricity as yet, and no plumbing, but we had two banks, one automobile, and the ox carts were not so frequently seen. The older generation felt the air of distinction was definitely disappearing. There were certainly some very disfiguring new buildings."

Fire gutted Williamsburg's colonial courthouse in 1911. Within four months the old building was renovated, and, in a manner of speaking, completed after a hiatus of 141 years. Before the Revolution, pillars had been ordered from England to put beneath the portico but were never shipped. Now columns were at last installed. That was about the height of interest in Williamsburg civic affairs in those sleepy days.

The next year the city didn't rouse itself to conduct its municipal election. Vernon Geddy, then a small boy and later a prominent Williamsburg lawyer, long remembered the lapse: "It so happened that my father was clerk of the court, and 'bout 3 o'clock in the afternoon in the day of the election he happened to remember that that was election day. They scurried around to see what could be done. Of course, no ballots had been printed. It was the election of the city council, and fortunately the charter provided that the councilmen would hold over until their successors in office were elected. The newspapers throughout the state chided Williamsburg a great deal about that event."

The *Richmond Times-Dispatch* said: "The clerk forgot to wake the electoral board, the electoral board could not arouse itself long enough to have ballots printed, the candidates forgot they were running, the voters forgot they were alive." Some editorialists tagged the blissfully forgetful city "Lotusburg."

Keeping track of time soon became more difficult. In 1913—when John D. Rockefeller, Sr.'s, wealth peaked at just under $1 billion—the city council decided it could no longer justify $50 in the annual budget for winding the town clock in Bruton's tower. So that year, the same year President and Mrs. Woodrow Wilson paid an official visit to Williamsburg, time stood officially still.

Of more immediate moment to the church was the roof Goodwin had installed. It was leaking, and the roofer was trying to default on his guarantee. The new rector, the Reverend E. Ruffin Jones, had to recruit Goodwin's corroboration of the agreement to see that it was grudgingly honored. It was hardly the only roof that leaked in Williamsburg. Places stood in disrepair all over town, and the worst of them were generally the oldest and most irreplaceable. But it turned out that the biggest threat to the survival of old Williamsburg was an assassin in Serbia.

Gavrilo Princip, one of a seven-member Black Hand squad in Sarajevo on June 28, 1914, tossed a hand grenade into a car carrying Austrian heir-apparent Archduke Franz Ferdinand and his wife Sophie. The murders were the excuse for World War I. A war requires munitions, and the DuPont Powder Company decided Williamsburg's neighborhood would be a good place to manufacture explosives for this one. The city became a boomtown.

DuPont had opened a dynamite plant about 40 miles up the James in 1911. The impromptu town of Hopewell, a lawless, wide-open, tar-paper shack and clapboard-building collection of brothels, bars, and 40,000 people, had sprung up in a money-making minute. By 1914 the plant was producing guncotton, a prime ingredient in smokeless powder. In 1915 Hopewell burned down, but the DuPont plant survived. Word spread that the company intended to build a second explosives plant on Jamestown Island to meet the demand from the European trenches. Protests against the selection were so vigorous the company announced in the autumn of 1916 that it had chosen instead a 4,000-acre waterfront site on the Peninsula's other river, the York. The C & O Railway said it would build another spur between Williamsburg and Yorktown and run three trains a day to carry workers to the plant.

Real estate speculators prowled Duke of Gloucester Street and stood on corners buying or taking options on everything in sight. Right behind them came the first of the 10,000 workers the plant would employ at its peak. DuPont built housing for 15,000 people and named the new community Penniman, after Russel S. Penniman, inventor of ammonia dynamite.

In April 1917, before Penniman production began, the United States entered the fighting in France. On the 2nd, President Wilson told a special session of Congress that "the world must be made safe for democracy," and asked for a declaration of war. He got it at 3 a.m. on April 6. The government took over the Penniman works and turned them into a naval shell-loading facility. Williamsburg came under more pressure as men flocked to Hampton Roads's expanding array of Army and Navy bases. Small

businesses and shops took over vacant lots on which had stood
18th-century homes and gardens. Subdivisions opened on
colonial farmland. Duke of Gloucester Street was paved. Room
rentals boomed.

Mary Coleman wrote that, "the old era vanished entirely.
Rumors of rising land values as a result of the advent of munitions
works, training camps, etc., battleships in the York River, soldiers'
wives seeking board and lodging, all created a chaos that one can
hardly believe now. Roads improved. There was frantic construction
of every kind. Eating houses and bootlegging establishments sprang
up everywhere."

Goodwin, almost 48 when Congress declared war,
volunteered to minister to American troops in Europe.

More than patriotism may have been involved. His mother
died in April of that year, and his eldest daughter Evelyn got
married that summer. Goodwin rented out his rectory and moved
with daughter Katherine into two rooms in a North Goodman Street
house opposite the University of Rochester. But Katherine was
spending most of her time visiting in Virginia, where son
Rutherfoord was still at boarding school. Goodwin was
mostly alone.

That July in Paris, Colonel Charles E. Stanton stood at the
tomb of an American Revolutionary hero and announced,
"Lafayette, we are here." Now Goodwin wanted to go there, too, but
the middle-aged preacher was told he could be of more use at home.
So he signed up with the YMCA and, with his vestry's approval, set
out in January on a chaplain's tour of stateside military camps.

It lasted about six weeks. His first stop was Madison
Barracks in New York; his second, Fort Dix, New Jersey. Then he
was assigned to Camp Lee near Petersburg, back in Virginia. Special
duty took him to Fort Monroe, the Norfolk Navy Base, and the
Peninsula's Camp Stuart and Langley Aviation Field.

Though there is no record of such a visit, the Virginia duty
gave him the opportunity to call on Ethel Howard, 30, who lived in
Ashland, about 15 miles north of Richmond. They had met in
Wytheville, apparently in 1917, and saw each other again that year at
the wedding of Goodwin's cousin and assistant at St. Paul's, curate
Conrad Goodwin. Conrad's bride was the daughter of the Parson's

Barely a year after this 1917 Wytheville, Virginia snapshot, romance carried Ethel Howard, here 30, to the altar with Goodwin, 17 years her senior.

uncle E. L. Goodwin, who was in turn rector of Ethel's church. Their courtship was advanced enough when winter began that Goodwin proudly sent her a copy of the Thanksgiving sermon he delivered to the Rochester Union.

Goodwin thought his Camp Lee duties were the most interesting part of the sojourn. He bunked with draftees from the western reaches of Virginia, some of whom were Mennonites and conscientious objectors. "It became my special duty," he wrote, "under the direction of the Commanding Officer, in addresses, sermons and interviews to try to quell the unrest which was being produced by their attitude and arguments throughout the military camp." Goodwin told them that war was ideally wrong, and God never intended men to organize to kill one another. But he said the divine plan of justice and liberty was threatened by the hellish purposes of the Germans, and that the enemy could be stopped only by using the same means it had chosen to fulfill its imperialistic ambitions.

It was one of the few things in his life for which he later felt cause for shame, and said so publicly. He made it the subject of a speech. He said he could still see "those boys gathered around the stoves in assembly halls. Some of them were conscientious objectors. They were not cowards. Some of them were of the wild rugged mountains. They would have fought tigers. They did not believe it was their duty to kill their fellow men. They said so. We who spoke to them were asked to <u>convert</u> them. We were told that they must be made to see red.

"How often have we repented of some of the things we told those boys! How often we have registered the determination never to do it again. We caricatured God. We did not have to draw the distorted pictures of Him which we held up to those boys. We took them right out of the Old Testament. We read what the people of old times had said God had commanded them to do. We cited passages where God commanded his people to fight. We pointed to verses which spoke of dashing the heads of their enemies' children against the rocks and letting dogs lick up the blood of their enemies. We told the horrible stories of war propaganda, of German atrocities and turned again to read and quote the Old Testament verses giving sanction to vengeance and brutality.

"Since then we have come to know that God never said these things. He could not have said them and have been God.... They

In 1917, while World War I raged in Europe, Ethel Howard spent part of her Virginia
mountain summer vacation sewing for the Red Cross.

are records of man's delusions."

    In June he returned to Virginia and on the 28th married
Ethel at St. James' Church in Ashland. She was the daughter of Mary
Howard, who had died the previous January, and James Clarke
Howard, a railroad man and a Virginia Military Institute cadet who
had fought at the Battle of New Market. Frank Ribble was, for the
second time, the Parson's best man. Goodwin, who had turned 49
just 10 days before the wedding, was starting a second family.

Purposeful in appearance, Goodwin usually affected the fashionable derby of the day when he was about church business.

Chapter Seven: **1919-1922**

Just before the war ended, Goodwin returned to the Army camps, and this time he shouldered a share of the physical risk that all soldiers assume. Disease and infection always rival bullets and bayonets as hazards to the troops, and a pandemic that swept through 1918 made the danger of death by illness especially acute. Thousands of doughboys contracted and carried home a virulent strain of influenza that, before it subsided, killed 20 million servicemen and civilians and sickened 700 million more.

Hospital camps sprang up on the American home front to warehouse and care for soldier flu victims. Goodwin volunteered for duty at the compounds in and around Rochester, and traveled to Fort Niagara to help his physician cousin Edward LeBaron Goodwin.

"I have never quite understood," the Parson wrote, "why I failed myself to contract the disease as I was with it constantly and on many occasions was ministering to men when they were dying of this disease." His cousin "was one of just a few surgeons in a camp where there were over one thousand cases of the disease," he said, "and would not stop even when the disease laid him low." Despite a fever that reached 105 degrees, cousin Edward worked until he, too, died.

With no effective means to prevent or treat viral infections, the Army could do little more than make the sick comfortable while the influenza ran its course. But Goodwin was struck by the way the military organized its operations—on and off the battlefield. The systematic efficiencies of pyramiding small units into increasingly larger commands and deploying coordinated forces across broad theaters appealed to him as the rector of a large parish like St. Paul's. Some of what he learned of Army hierarchy he thought could be useful to Christian soldiers.

Three years after publishing *The Church Enchained* Goodwin
began to compose a volume on how to set it free. It promulgated
the division of parishes into teams led by majors, captains,
lieutenants, and so on, according to neighborhood. Goodwin called
it the Group System, and he practiced what he preached. He
organized St. Paul's 937 communicants—there were 1,365 baptized
members—into platoons and companies reporting up a chain of
command to headquarters at East Avenue and Vick Park B. It seems
to have been popular with the congregation, most of which always
caught Goodwin's contagious enthusiasm for his projects and
plans. "I have never known," he later wrote, "a congregation more
responsive to the appeal of the ideal and more ready to cooperate
in setting forth the things essential in Christianity than were the
people of St. Paul's."

Titled *The Parish. Its Life, Its Organization, Its Teaching Mission
and Divine Contacts. A Handbook for Clergy and Laity,* the book was
begun in 1919 and published by a religious press in 1921. A revised
edition appeared in 1925. Goodwin accepted no money from its sales,
but his reputation profited from the timing as well as from the content.
The Parish appeared during one of the peaks in the American cycle of
religious revival, a sometimes nativist phenomena that has rolled
across the country since the first Great Awakening in the early 18th
century. This one produced the Reverend Billy Sunday, the Scopes
Trial, and Aimee Semple McPherson—whose Rochester appearance
interested Goodwin enough to preserve one of her handbills.

Moreover, the novelty of the Group System had the appeal
that nifty new methods and reorganizations tend to have for
institutions in transition, especially to establishment enterprises
reacting to the pressures of shifting cultural and economic forces.
As the 1920s opened, business was expanding, mobility was
increasing, immigration was rising, and American religion was
reacting to the impact of each.

Something of the mix of ideas these influences fathered is
glimpsed in a letter Goodwin got from William I. Haren, general
secretary of the American Bible Society in New York. Haren wrote
that "all of us are profoundly interested in whatever helps toward the
reading of the Holy Scriptures. We believe that this particular period
in the world's history requires a fresh contact with the Bible. It
seems to us that only in this way can we bring these newcomers to

our shores to an understanding of our American Civilization and keep the distinct American population with an American ancestry on the paths of its ancestors."

The postwar Episcopal Church, ever the Establishment denomination, responded with a program of institutionalized evangelism. It founded the Nationwide Campaign, an annual and highly structured America-wide crusade for increased membership, participation, and offerings. Goodwin thought *The Parish* was his best contribution, and he was flattered by requests for copies received from as far away as Africa. But not everyone shared the enthusiasm for his ideas. When Episcopal headquarters neglected to promote the book as heavily as he thought it deserved, Goodwin complained.

The Parson—or "the Doctor," as he was called now with more frequency—was never reluctant to speak his mind when he believed he was right. He was rarely intemperate, but neither did he hide his light beneath a bushel, and he attracted critics as well as admirers. As it does all men who value forthrightness above circumspection, it cost him opportunities.

Goodwin's old antagonist, High-Church Bishop Walker of the Western Diocese of New York, died in office May 2, 1917. The standing committee of the diocese's general council met 16 days later to elect his successor, and Goodwin was among the first-rank candidates. Lacking the support of the old bishop's allies and supporters, Goodwin's candidacy failed, and he was eliminated from further consideration. He congratulated himself on the defeat, because he said it attested to his unwillingness to be bound by traditional interpretations of doctrine merely to obtain a promotion. But plainly his hopes were disappointed.

The council's first selection, however, declined the office, as did a second priest chosen at a September election. In October the diocese picked the Reverend Doctor Charles Henry Brent. Former missionary bishop to the Philippines, Brent had confirmed General John J. Pershing in the Episcopal faith when Black Jack was stationed in Manila. As the United States entered the war, Pershing made Brent chaplain in chief to the American Expeditionary Force in Europe, and Brent was now in France. He accepted the New York position on the condition the diocese allow him to remain with the troops as long as he thought it was wise, and Brent did not take up his new duties until May 1919, six months after the armistice.

Goodwin promised his support and cooperation, and the pledge was more than pro forma; he grew to be the new bishop's ardent admirer and associate, and Brent returned the favor. Bishop Brent wrote the introduction for *The Parish*, put Goodwin on his executive council, and asked him to help reorganize the work of the diocese. The Doctor became head of Brent's department of missions, a member of the department of religious education, and assisted at regional and county conferences. "I shall never cease to be grateful for the coming of Bishop Brent to be our Bishop," Goodwin said. "The catholicity of his mind, the deep spirituality of his nature, his penetrating power of vision, and his genius for fellowship, endeared him to my heart and inspired in me the desire to do all in my power to follow and to further his leadership."

Goodwin's enthusiasm for the ministry grew. His correspondence was informed by a new buoyancy and eagerness, a live-wire reawakening of purpose, drive, and ambition. With Ethel he had taken up residence again in the rectory, and she contributed to his happiness by becoming the model minister's wife as well as by bearing their first son. Edward Howard Goodwin was born May 23, 1919, at Rochester's Homeopathic Hospital.

That autumn, the executive committee of the Nationwide Campaign designated Goodwin one of the denomination's 12 greatest speakers and sent him on a national speaking tour that lasted until Thanksgiving Day. Though he was more active than ever in the affairs of the community beyond the parish and in the promotion of missionary and interfaith endeavors, he won election as a delegate to the next two general conventions, the first in Detroit and the second in Portland, Oregon.

As chairman of Brent's mission department, Goodwin spoke at rural and small-town churches, and he became a popular guest preacher before other Rochester denominations. At Lent he opened his living room for lectures on church history, talks that emphasized the primacy of Virginia in the transplantation of the Church of England to America's shores. His animated rhetorical skills took him to the rostrum of such civic associations as the Rotary Club and the Chamber of Commerce, of which he was also a busy member.

Sometimes he half suspected the reason he was so much in demand was that the clubs needed someone to deliver their meetings' opening prayers. But Goodwin's standing and influence in a wide circle of associations and acquaintances furnished him allies and helped him into the stirrups of his favorite hobby horse: adding a fourth R—religion—to the public educational curriculum for the young. Since his days at Roanoke College, perhaps earlier, he had been convinced that the Bible deserved a place on the textbook list from grammar school through to college. The wall of separation of church and state had always stood in his way, but now he thought of a way to circumvent the barrier, and he recruited prominent people to help him.

Goodwin began a campaign for St. Paul's own weekday religious school to supplement the secular subjects taught in the public schools. "Secular education divorced from religious education," he said again and again, "is a menace to society." With the community's cooperation and contributions, he hired a staff, installed it in the parish house, and enrolled 150 children. The city schools arranged pupil schedules to permit attendance as if St. Paul's were an annex.

On February 26, 1921, Ethel furnished another prospective student in William Deane Goodwin, who like his brother was born in the Rochester Homeopathic Hospital. He was the 51-year-old minister's sixth child.

There came as well a pivotal addition that October to the Doctor's official family—Elizabeth Hayes, 23, of Canandaigua. She had left her job in the central office of the New York State Home Bureau at Cornell University in Ithaca. Before that she had worked in the bureau's Wayne County office. The daughter of banker Edward G. Hayes and the former Elizabeth McGill, she had attended the Shipley School at Bryn Mawr, Pennsylvania, and the Mary C. Wheeler School in Providence, Rhode Island, before completing a two-year course at the Rochester Business Institute. She replaced Mrs. John Milling, who had accepted the secretarial post temporarily after her predecessor Julia Russell imbibed the Doctor's enthusiasm for missionary work and set out for China.

Hayes caught a tram to Rochester, found the parish house, and walked down the long hall to Goodwin's green-carpeted study. He sat behind a walnut desk next to a walnut table, and she took a seat in one of his green leather chairs.

A woman of the congregation, Mrs. Levi Ward, had made a personal gift of the furnishings when Goodwin had arrived from

Williamsburg 12 years earlier. On the walls hung a painting of Bruton
Church in colonial times and engravings of ancient European
cathedrals.

"Dr. Goodwin pushed aside his writing," Hayes later wrote,
"and rose to shake hands—a broad-shouldered, dark-haired man with
brilliant eyes. He was extremely cordial, and I liked him immediately.
I had not been certain that I wanted to work with a minister, but Dr.
Goodwin was different from any minister I had known. His
cordiality put me at ease, and his description of the secretarial
needs made the position seem very desirable. I was interested in all
that he told me, and glad when at the end of the interview he invited
me to come to try it out. Besides, he was writing and editing a book,
he said, and helping to write a book was something I thought I would
like to do."

Hayes was the last secretary Goodwin ever hired for
himself. She remained with the Doctor until his death nearly 18
years later. "If I had known at that time the importance of the years
that lay ahead," she later wrote, "I would have commenced a diary
at the very first meeting." At that, her recollections and records are
the best second references for the details of the accomplishments
to follow.

Goodwin had made a beginning on his new book, the
History of the Theological Seminary in Virginia, in 1914. An assignment
from the alumni association, of which he became a director, perhaps
the book was his idea. Progress, however, had by fits and starts
come to a halt. His interest was rekindled about the time he became
a successful candidate for a vacancy on the seminary's board in the
1922 trustees' election. His marching orders were to complete the
book in time for the seminary's centennial celebrations in 1924.

In 1914 he had committed himself to furnishing a chapter,
editing chapters submitted by professors and other alumni, and
seeing through the press what would be a narrow institutional
history. As he took up the work again, he expanded the scope of the
book to appeal to a general readership. It became a fund-raising
project for the school's library. He wrote to MacMillian Publishers in
New York: "The plan which I have followed is to make the book not
alone a History of the Seminary proper, but also to show the needs
out of which the seminary grew by reciting the History of the
American Church in the Colony of Virginia during and subsequent
to the Colonial Period."

In addition to collecting and editing chapters submitted by other clergy, the Doctor undertook first-hand and time-intensive investigation. Among other things, he intended to detail the story of the founding of the church at Captain John Smith's Jamestown and to devote a chapter to the College of William and Mary. Hayes would help him prepare the manuscripts, manage the paper flow, file, coordinate contributions, attend to correspondence, correct proofs, and accompany the Goodwins on a research jaunt to Virginia. For all this she would receive $120 a month.

As the deadline crept closer, the Doctor scratched for more hours to devote to the project. At first, he regarded the literary hours as respite from daytime duties, but he was taxing his stamina. "All during week-day office hours," Hayes said, "letters were flying, calling lists were kept current, addresses and reports prepared. There was always a hustle and bustle after Dr. Goodwin's arrival at his office, which was never a languid place."

Nor did his interest and participation in civic matters abate. Like everyone, Goodwin had his opinions, but unlike most, he also had the advantage of a choice of pulpits from which to state them. Sometimes his views attracted the attention of the press. In October 1919, Congress passed the Volstead Act to enforce the 18th Amendment. Effective the following January 19, the amendment prohibited the manufacture, sale, transportation, import, or export of intoxicating liquor. A teetotaler beyond the communion rail, Goodwin nevertheless was against the amendment—though he was for enforcement of the enabling act. A year after the Noble Experiment began, the *Rochester Times-Union* invited him to explain the contradiction.

In a letter dictated to Hayes he said: "While I personally do not approve of placing the Prohibition legislation in the Constitution of the United States for reasons which I do not need here to state, I do feel that this having been made the law of the land, everything should be done to educate our citizenship to the strict observance of the law as it exists. Nothing is a greater menace to our civilization than anarchy. If the Prohibition law is not a good law, the best way to prove it, is to endorse it. I am not saying that this is not a good law, as this is not the question at issue."

His politics were almost as convoluted. "I am an independent in politics," he told a local Democratic Party functionary in 1921. "Hitherto I have enrolled under the Democratic

column because I have usually supported the National Democratic
ticket. In local politics I have, however, generally voted the
Republican ticket, as I have also done recently in state politics." The
Independent Democratic Republican had a poor opinion of
politicians in general but admired officeholders whom he believed
stood above the scrambling after votes. When his boyhood friend R.
Lee Trinkle of Wytheville had been elected Virginia's governor,
Goodwin wrote to congratulate him and praised the voter's wisdom
in choosing a man above the battle. Then he said: "Politics
throughout this nation have fallen on low plains. Their selfishness
and partisanship seem to dominate the minds of leaders. . . . Too
often the pages of our national history have been stained by the acts
of men in power who have countenanced class legislation and
iniquitous legislation solely for the purpose of enhancing their own
political advantage."

Goodwin's own performance in office, his trust as priest,
brought him further attention from the *Times-Union*. Reporter Paul
Benton wanted to see what sort of reception the city's
denominations, especially the well-to-do Episcopalians, might give to
the least of these their brethren. Benton cooked up a plan in which
he and three other scribes masqueraded as bums and separately
attended Sunday services at four Rochester churches. Benton
audited Goodwin and reported the results on Monday's front page:
"I hesitated in the cool, restful vestibule of St. Paul's looking back on
the clean, sun-bathed prospect of East Avenue, and wondered what
the next moment would bring forth when I attempted to enter and
seek a seat." No one questioned him or stood in his way. The service
proceeded, and the rector took the pulpit. "I kneeled, rose, sat with
the rest of the congregation. Dr. Goodwin's mellow charming voice
rose and fell. . . . " Benton wondered what the effect would have been
on a real derelict and concluded: "Had he come to escape for a
moment from the life material to the life spiritual, he would not have
been disappointed."

Goodwin was prospering at home and on the job. His salary
comfortably supported his growing family, permitted him to make
modest investments in the preferred stock of companies like
American Tobacco and Great Northern Railroad as well as the
common stock of Canadian Pacific, Southern Pacific, and Pacific
Oil. A vestryman, securities broker Watkin W. Kneath, supplied
financial advice. Goodwin had been able to help his brother-in-law

out with a modest loan, and early in 1922 the Doctor bought a small share in a Canadian wheat-farm mortgage. His farm in Norwood, producing too little to pay its property taxes, was the only smudge on a picture of well-being. His daughters were happily married, and he was starting a second family. But for better and for worse, Goodwin had invested too much of himself in too many activities. His prospects were about to revalued.

Julius Alvin Carroll Chandler became the College of William and Mary's 19th president in July 1919. He succeeded Goodwin's friend Lyon G. Tyler, who planned to spend much of his retirement in historical study and research. Chandler assumed all Tyler's duties immediately and began to map a vigorous expansion program. But his inauguration was delayed until October 19, 1921, when President Warren G. Harding came down from Washington, accepted a honorary degree of doctor of laws, and spoke to a crowd of Chandler well-wishers gathered in the courtyard between the western wings of the Wren Building.

Goodwin also traveled to Virginia that month, bound for Norfolk to attend an October 21st convention of the Brotherhood of St. Andrews, a national men's religious society. The records show neither when he arrived nor his itinerary, but Goodwin was within easy reach of Williamsburg at the time of the college ceremonies.

He had incentive enough to revisit his old Bruton Parish haunts. It would have been worth the short excursion just to consult with Tyler about the seminary history. But Goodwin's personal files say nothing of going back to watch the inauguration, to congratulate Chandler, to see old friends, or even to visit the graves of Evelyn and his first son William.

Such a sidetrip might help to explain the letter Goodwin got from Chandler the following February 6 offering him the posts of professor of philosophy and social service and director of the college endowment campaign.* The Doctor's salary would be about a third less than what he made in Rochester. But he would make a 5-percent commission on every contribution of up to $100,000 he raised for the endowment—and Chandler expected him to raise

---

*The date comes from a letter Goodwin wrote to Chandler's successor, John Stewart Bryan, in 1934 detailing the Doctor's association with the college. It advances Chandler's overture by about seven months from what has previously been reported. Goodwin and Hayes, however, were careful about dates cited in his correspondence, and there is no more reason to doubt the Bryan letter than the rest of Goodwin's formal reports. Nevertheless, neither Chandler's letter nor Goodwin's response remains in his personal papers. In 1957 Hayes recalled a similar letter arriving in the autumn of 1922, but there is no copy of it in the files either, and it could as easily have been a renewal of the proposition.

millions. In addition, Chandler would pay Goodwin's travel
expenses and his secretary's salary.

The overture arrived just as Goodwin was entering a period
of personal and professional stress that deepened as the year
advanced. He had buckled down to the seminary history, and he had
realized he had underestimated the demands it would make on him
and his time. "I have gotten pretty far into this work," Goodwin
wrote to an associate, "but I have now reached the point where, if I
am to carry it through, I must find some opportunity for consecutive
thought and application." One of his sons, apparently Rutherfoord,
was recovering from a December surgery, and Ethel was
recuperating from an acute and stubborn attack of rheumatic fever.
On March 4 the grippe, as Goodwin called the flu-like illness, sent
him to the sickbed; and for the first time in his Rochester ministry,
illness forced him to miss a Sunday sermon. It would be spring
before all his strength returned. While his body fought the infection,
his mind turned more to the book, and he concluded he might need
to get away for three months or more to finish the job.

Goodwin was planning to escort Ethel with sons Howard
and Bill to the home of her uncle, Judge Cardwell, in Hanover,
Virginia, that April, so they might have a vacation. But it was
Goodwin who needed a hiatus. His schedule overburdened the
energies of a man in his 50s, and as best he could recall, he had not
been out of his parish more than ten days together in the past two or
three years. He was so mentally and physically fatigued that, before
the month was out, his physician and Bishop Brent asked him to
plan a long summer rest.

Part of his weariness Goodwin blamed on not having had a
"worthy assistant" for the past three years—a curate to whom he
could entrust a share of the parish workload—since the Reverend
John K. Burleson had left to become the full-time priest at
Rochester's St. John's. Goodwin had started St. John's in a tent as a
missionary church and nursed its growth through quarters in a store,
a Presbyterian church basement, an Evangelical Church building,
and finally into a chapel built on the tent site.

In September 1921, the Reverend Roy Eltringham arrived to
take the St. Paul's curate's post, and he quickly relieved Goodwin in
the parish youth ministry. The Doctor's mind may have been eased
by the prospect of ready help and a handy vacation substitute, but
Eltringham only added, albeit innocently, to Goodwin's afflictions.

The Doctor learned from Brent on March 23 that a young man in St. Paul's congregation had accused Eltringham of some unnamed immorality with one of the parish house secretaries. Brent admonished Goodwin about the risk of the appearance of impropriety in a clergyman, and said it was always wise to dismiss a secretary at the first hint of such gossip, even if she was blameless. Brent reasoned that the church's reputation was more important than the woman's. Goodwin apparently had gotten wind of the allegation before it reached the bishop and conferred about it with Benjamin B. Chase, St. Paul's treasurer and a lawyer. Chase had advised the Doctor to protect himself from becoming the target of similar rumors.

Goodwin was probably more vulnerable to whisperings than Eltringham or less ambitious parsons. It would have been impossible for him to contribute to Episcopalian thought and literature, he said, "had it not been for the kind and considerate willingness of those who served as secretaries in the parish to shape their time and their engagements to my time and to the circumstances of my life, as much of the work had to be done at night when parish duties were ended." Chase told him: "As I think over the situation we were talking about, I am thoroughly convinced that it is absolutely essential that Miss Hayes do her typing in some other room than your private office."

Chase's fears became quickly moot; the vestry granted Goodwin a vacation from the middle of June through August, to be followed by a September trip to Oregon for the denomination's general convention. The Doctor still had to line up guest ministers for his pulpit, but he looked forward to "the first long and continuous period of rest that I have ever taken during my ministry."

Eltringham was forced to take a leave of absence, and resigned. His accuser had made his allegations official in a formal affidavit, and it looked as if the curate would have to defend himself in an ecclesiastical court if he returned. Goodwin later said, "Bishop Brent made a very careful and thorough investigation, and it was proved beyond question of doubt that the young man who had made the accusations was a liar." Nevertheless, Goodwin was again without an assistant.

On the Monday before Easter, the Doctor took his family to Virginia, spent a week at leisure, and returned to Rochester for Easter Sunday services. But he was beginning to understand that his St. Paul's ministry was coming to a close. In mid-May he wrote to

Brent "of the feeling of uncertainty which has been pressed upon me with reference to my own plans," and he declined to take part in the selection of Eltringham's replacement. Goodwin said the lack of a curate "with the duties which I have tried to perform for the diocese and the church at large, have combined to make me inexpressibly mentally tired—too tired I fear, to think clearly through any problem."

He had given the best energy of his life to St. Paul's, he said, but his disposition was to take some other work. He had in mind the rectorship of St. John's. In any case, he hoped to remain in the city. "Since the death of my first wife," Goodwin said, "I have had to try to be both mother and father to my children, and two of them are now located here, and I should like to be able to remain near them if I could. Then too, friendships have always counted far more deeply in my life than anything else, and I do very much dread transplanting." The same day he wrote to a New York City minister friend that he had never been so overwhelmed with responsibilities and duties and found himself "completely devoid of energy."

Brent asked him to come to Buffalo to talk. A few days afterward, Goodwin told an associate he had been granted an unpaid four-month leave of absence "mainly on account of my impaired health." The flu and his exhaustion had strained his nerves to their limits.

They got worse May 22, when a Ford motorcar chased him up the sidewalk beside Rochester's Baptist Seminary and knocked him down. He was almost pinned between the automobile's bumper and the school's cast-iron fence. "I was pretty badly bruised and shaken up," he told Brent, "but no bones were broken. I very narrowly escaped.... As a matter of fact, I could not come nearer being killed and escape than I did."

The next day Brent wrote to him that Eltringham's accuser had sent another bill of particular's against St. Paul's. The bishop enclosed it in his letter. What the new charges were, Brent's letter doesn't say, but he asked: "Will you kindly advise me as to the facts which he states?" The enclosure has disappeared along with Goodwin's reply.

After his brush with the Ford, Goodwin saw a physician and complained of anxiousness, twitching of an eye and the fingers of his left hand, and numbness. But he preached the following Sunday, and attended to parish duties while he prepared to depart for Virginia. Chase filed a lawsuit against the Ford's driver, which eventually produced modest insurance settlements.

Hayes also took a leave of absence from St. Paul's to go with Goodwin and work full time on the book, the Doctor paying her salary from his pocket. They set out for Virginia on a June 12th train. After a stopover in Hanover, Goodwin, Ethel, the boys, and Hayes left for Wytheville, where they moved in with Laeta, the Doctor's sister, and her husband Clarence Repass.

Goodwin and Hayes passed the months laboring long hours on the manuscript pages, mailing chapters to the Reverend E. L. Goodwin for review and editing, typing corrections, and planning more research. Occasionally the Doctor indulged in a round of golf or rambled with his small sons—nicknamed Howdy and Squinch—in the farm meadows around the house. On Sundays he worshipped at St. John's, the church his grandfather built, or preached at the chapel in Abingdon. When in August he had accomplished as much as he could in the mountains, he took family and secretary on a sightseeing and research excursion. They stopped at his Salem alma mater, Roanoke College, before heading for Richmond, where he scoured the Virginia State Library archives, called on Governor Trinkle to trade memories of old Wytheville times, and embarked on the C & O for Williamsburg.

The hospitality Goodwin's old parish showed them astounded Hayes. She remembered it in exclamation points—"Such gladness to see the Goodwins! Such joy to be in Williamsburg! Such cordiality!"—and she saw he was pleased as he could be to put his feet again on Duke of Gloucester Street. They toured Bruton Church and went to William and Mary to pursue more facts for the seminary history. Earl Gregg Swem, the school's legendary librarian, lent a hand.

On August 26th, Goodwin mailed his manuscript to Rochester parish house secretary Aida O'Connor, and two days later he headed for the Episcopal General Convention in Portland, Oregon while his family and Hayes traveled north.

There is no mention in the files of seeing Chandler on this trip either, but once more a Chandler letter would follow. It reached Goodwin after his return to St. Paul's in early October, and it asked for the names of potential Rochester-area contributors to the college. Chandler was especially interested in the descendants of Nathaniel Rochester, an 18th-century Virginian who had been a proprietor of the land on which his namesake city rose.

Of more immediate moment to Goodwin, perhaps, was finding a replacement for Sunday school superintendent John Parker, who had precipitously resigned. Then the rector was confronted by the resignations of all the officers of the senior branch of the Women's Auxiliary. He also had to break the news to the Virginia Theological Seminary that its history would require two volumes instead of one, and only the first could be ready for its centennial.

It may have been coincidence, but at this juncture, as Hayes remembered it, Goodwin took a train back to Williamsburg to confer with Chandler about his Rochester fund-raising ideas. She said that "upon his return he received a letter from the President offering him a place on the faculty . . . and the directorship."

Before December 4, when he submitted his annual rector's report, Goodwin told the vestry he was leaving St. Paul's, but he did not formally accept Chandler's offer until the following week. He told the president, "William and Mary appeals to me because the thought of training men for leadership was unquestionably dominant in the teaching of its founders and in the afterlife of many of its early students.

"As to the Endowment endeavor, I would esteem it a privilege to make use of my somewhat large acquaintance in this behalf, and would be able to enter into the work with the enthusiasm which, in all such matters, is essential to success, because not only of my conviction of what the nation owes to the College, because of what the College has done for the nation, but also because of the splendid work which the College is now doing and the still larger influence which it could exert if adequately equipped and endowed."

Hayes said, "I do not think he contemplated ending his rectorship there with anything but regret," but there was a defensive cast to his leave-taking. Goodwin told the vestry, in part: "It has been my purpose to relate St. Paul's Church to the Religious and Civic forces in our City which seek to promote the cause of righteousness and also to make St. Paul's a help and inspiration to the Church in the Diocese and to the Church at large. Too large a measure of the Rector's time may have been spent in this endeavor, but there were circumstances which seemed to call for the special measure of emphasis which these interests received at our hands."

St. Paul's vestry formally accepted his resignation at 8:30
p.m. Thursday, December 14, effective February 1. The next morning
the *Democrat and Chronicle* ran such an effusive editorial accolade to
his Rochester service that Goodwin asked for ten copies. "The
tributes of affectionate regard which came in connection with my
going," Goodwin wrote a few months later, "revealed to me a depth
of friendship and a measure of appreciation for which I then and
have ever since felt myself entirely unworthy."

Three days later he went back to Williamsburg to see
Chandler again. There was a contract to sign and details to be
settled. For one thing, Goodwin objected to accepting commissions
on endowment-fund donations. He wanted to be able to tell
prospects that he would receive nothing from their contributions,
and that every penny would go to rebuilding the college. Chandler
offered to take the commission's equivalent from a current account
instead, and Goodwin agreed. The Doctor also wanted assurance
that he would have time to finish the seminary history.

Goodwin was reluctant to give up preaching altogether; so
the day he resigned, he asked Bishop Beverly D. Tucker of the
Southern Diocese of Virginia for an unpaid assignment to a
missionary church in the Williamsburg area. Tucker was so pleased
to have Goodwin back that he gave the Doctor a token-pay post at
Grace Church in Yorktown along with responsibility for the chapel
in Toano, a few miles down the highway to Richmond.

Goodwin also took the time to explain his decision to his
priesthood associates. He told Bishop Wilson Stearly in Newark,
New Jersey: "I have felt for some time that I have given St. Paul's the
contribution which I had to give in the largest measure. . . . I also felt
that I had wanted more time for study and the opportunity of
entering college life and making some contribution to Christian
education. . . . The philosophy which I propose to teach, will be
Christian philosophy from the start to the finish, and I propose to
teach it without apology to science, falsely so called.

"I have the deepest respect for the scientific method and for
the true findings of science. But we have let science arrogate too much
to itself. We have allowed Christian faith to be cowed in the presence
of the overmastering and overbearing attitude of materialistic
psychology and philosophy. We must make the pendulum swing back.
One man cannot do very much, but he can do his best. There are
eight hundred and fifty students at William and Mary."

Elizabeth Hayes, Goodwin's secretary, became instrumental in his most noteworthy endeavors.

Chapter Eight: **1923-1924**

Doctor Goodwin took St. Paul's high pulpit for the final time as rector January 28, 1923. Like Bruton's congregation so many years before, St. Paul's crowded the pews to hear his farewell sermon. But, just as he had in 1909, the Parson wasted no words on good-byes. He delivered a lesson on God's redemptive love, taking for his text, "What think ye of Christ?"

"As I sat in the pew that day and looked around," Hayes wrote, "I found myself wondering how wise the rector was to give up this place of authority and power to go back again to the south and to the life of a small town and a struggling college." He had persuaded her to come along, at least until the seminary history was done, to help him get started at the school.

The boys choir sang his favorite anthem, Charles François Gounod's "The Sanctus," and it was over.

From time to time in the years ahead, Goodwin would return as a guest preacher, but he would never again serve as rector a congregation so large and affluent. There had been weeks of send-off dinners, resolutions of appreciation, callers, gifts, and letters. He had been entertained at a men's club banquet, a mothers' club luncheon, a Sunday school reception, and an auxiliary tea; and at each he told well-wishers he was leaving because he wanted to teach again. Sometimes he said he thought the college work might let him play a part in the preservation of more of Williamsburg's relics.

The Goodwins intended to be packed February 5 and ready to leave the 8th, but Howard had a cold, and Ethel and little Bill came down with the grippe. The youngest boy's high fever delayed them a week. They got away on the 15th, heading south for the village Goodwin had left 13 years, six months, and 15 days before with another wife and another family.

"I had only been in Williamsburg once before," Ethel said, "but I knew it from Dr. Goodwin's talking about it so much. I always thought it would be a real attractive place to live."

Her husband confided his dream of restoring Williamsburg "as soon as we came to Williamsburg from Rochester," she said. "Of course, I was intensely interested." Hayes understood him to be speaking of such a project in the days before they left Rochester. Businessman W. A. Bozarth said Goodwin presented the idea to Williamsburg's businessmen's association during a 1917 visit. Goodwin was present when Bozarth shared his recollection and didn't contradict him. Nevertheless, each of them furnished their reminiscences years after the city's restoration began, and intervening events may have colored their memories. In any case, there is no doubt Goodwin began the pursuit of his dream almost as soon as he returned.

The Doctor had leased a home from Frank and Mary Bozarth on Williamsburg's Richmond Road, just west of the college beyond Armistead Street. It needed repair, but it was roomy and within an easy lunchtime walk of Goodwin's office. Chandler had assigned him working space across from the president's rooms on the second-floor hall of the College Yard building named the Brafferton. A two-story Georgian brickpile, it was built in 1723 as a school to train Indian boys in the ministry.

Until the Bozarths' house was ready and the furniture from Rochester arrived, the Goodwins boarded with J. B. C. Spencer at the Colonial Inn, across the green from the courthouse on Duke of Gloucester Street. The once sinuous old Indian trail was a surveyor-straight ribbon of concrete divided by a median that carried utility poles through the center of town. Often called Main Street, it was busy with traffic shuttling between Richmond and Newport News. The Colonial catered to all manner of transients. In its dining room that Sunday the drummers and motorcar tourists talked about the weather, the week ahead, and the wonders archaeologists had discovered in Egypt that Friday when they unsealed Tutankhamen's tomb.

The family had a chance to look about, visit acquaintances, reconnoiter the stores, and catch up on community doings. Ethel saw that granulated sugar cost 7.5 cents a pound and coffee 33. The town was launching a rat-killing campaign; sometimes the rodents became so bold they stole fruit from the bowl on the Coleman's dining table. Most of the sidewalks were still dirt, and in February's wet weather the unprotected ground turned to thick, yellow goo. When Hayes complained, Goodwin told her: "If those mud sidewalks were good enough for Washington and Jefferson, they should be good enough for you."

Ethel said, "Some of the old people he had known here before called on us, and we felt very much at home even though we were not at home in our own house." Among them were the Peyton Randolphs, Lottie Garrett, the George Colemans, H. D. Cole, Cora and Estelle Smith, lawyer Ashton Dovell, the Van Garretts, Professor Walter Montgomery and his family, and the Morecock sisters— Pinkie, Patty, Kitty, and Agnes. Most people, including Hayes, now addressed Goodwin as Doctor. He preferred to be called *Mister* Goodwin by his friends, but they fell into the *Doctor* habit, too, and he sometimes scolded them for it.

By the 21st Goodwin was at his William and Mary job. Among the first things he did that day was write a note to daughter Katherine Buell and her husband in Rochester. "This morning I am starting out in my office in the old Indian School building," he wrote, "by sending a word of greeting to you and George and Rutherfoord. Our furniture has not come, but, as I wrote Rutherfoord, the bill has and amounts to $215.00 for transportation. If it had not been for the kindness of the people of St. Paul's, I certainly would have been swamped. Ethel likes the house."

Chandler gave him the freedom to finish the *History of the Virginia Theological Seminary* before he started teaching—three months left to get it done—but Goodwin also busied himself in preparations for his classes, and he began to raise money straightaway.

Chandler had hired him as a professor of moral philosophy and social service. But Goodwin intended to "introduce the Christian viewpoint into modern education." With the president's consent, he elected to instruct freshmen in biblical history and ethics and teach seniors a course titled "Life of the Spirit." Goodwin wanted "to be free from the responsibility of studying and propounding the metaphysical and speculative side of philosophy," and to confine himself to "practical, personal and creative" pedagogy. "Then, too," he said, "I did not care to pose as an authority

in the subject which has so greatly advanced since my college days."
Soon his academic title changed from professor of moral
philosophy and social service to professor of biblical literature and
social ethics. His designation went on mutating down the years, as
his ideas about his courses developed. Before his William and Mary
career was done, he had evolved into the head of the department of
biblical literature and professor of religion.

For help in planning lessons and selecting textbooks,
Goodwin turned to authorities like Lyon Phelps at Yale. "Modern life
has swung rather far away from its touch with Sacred Literature," he
wrote to Phelps in March, "and the mind of the average college
student is not predisposed to Bible study. The problem which I face
is, therefore, a difficult one." Goodwin said most of the texts on the
subject "are not contagious." Phelps suggested Goodwin use his
Human Nature in the Bible, and advised the Doctor to leaven his
lessons with humor. Describing Noah's flood, Phelps's book said:
"The earth needed a bath, and got it."

Goodwin wrote back: "It is good that you have pointed out
there is a place for laughter in religion. It has always seemed strange
to me that the God who made the music and laughter of the world
and filled it with sunshine and song, should have been so
extensively portrayed as an austere and melancholy personality to
be held in reserve for the emergencies of the hour of death and the
day of judgment."

Nevertheless, a state school could not require students to
study the Good Book, and Goodwin was unwilling to trust
enrollment solely to his reputation as a lecturer. Before a year
passed, he secured Chandler's approval of a "plan to make the study
of the English Bible compulsory in the College, except for those who
have conscientious objections, for whom there will be provided a
thoroughly adequate course for the testing of the strength of their
conscience." The alternative to Bible class would be a difficult
course in ethics.

Though a long-time teacher, Chandler had been
superintendent of Richmond's public schools before coming to
Williamsburg, and he was at least as interested in administrative as
academic matters. For the moment, he cared more about what
Goodwin was doing on the fund-raising front than what he intended
to do that fall in the classroom.

The goal of an endowment campaign usually is to raise

money for investments to produce long-term income, but Chandler's was intended to endow the campus with facilities. Some classes met in a barracks-like corrugated-metal hall left over from the Penniman boom. Student living quarters were scarce, and there was no proper athletic field. Among other things Chandler wanted a men's dorm, a science hall, a new dining hall, an enlarged library, a home economics building, a facility for music and art, a school of government and citizenship, and a chime tower.

Closed after the Civil War, William and Mary had staggered along after it reopened, for the college lacked wealthy alumni contributors other schools mined. Although enrollments climbed after 1918, when it became the first coeducational college in Virginia, the graduate pool was still small. Chandler and Goodwin addressed the problem by emphasizing the college's contributions to the founding of the nation, its historical setting in Williamsburg, and its connections to such colonial heroes as Washington, Jefferson, and Madison.

Pacing about his office, the Doctor dictated letters to potential donors from his earlier fund-raising endeavors, and to prospects Chandler furnished him. Goodwin understood that contributors gave money not to institutions but to people, and each message had a personal tone. For example, a note he sent in March to Mrs. Ethel Lewis of Beacon, New York: "My work here is fascinating in its interest, and I sincerely hope that you and Mr. Lewis may sometime be able to run down and see us. In addition to my classroom work, I am cooperating with the President in helping to secure enlarged accommodations, equipment, and endowment. We have an enrollment of 836 students in the College with accommodations for only about 200. We therefore have a housing problem."

Many people did come to see him, many of them northerners headed home from Florida vacations. Hayes remembered calls from, among others, J. P. Morgan, Jr., Alfred I. DuPont, Gutzon Borglum, Wade Hampton, George Plimpton, Arthur Curtiss James, R. Fulton Cutting, Robert L. Saunders, and John Barton Payne. Goodwin showed each around the town.

At night, he wrote appeals in longhand, in the artful script he had begun to practice in the Norwood schoolhouse. "Often I would see him walking across the campus in the morning," Hayes said, "swinging along in his inimitably jaunty manner, pipe in hand,

and when he entered the office he would reach into his coat pockets to toss out scraps of paper or old envelopes on which he had scribbled drafts of letters to be typed. His mind was most clear in the early morning hours when he first awoke, he said. There were no interruptions then, and so he often jotted down ideas and thoughts that came to him at dawn."

Every day, janitors Henry Billups and Alec Goodall carried up a mailbag full of replies, and Goodwin sorted through them for checks. They appeared more frequently as time passed; even the New York descendants of Nathaniel Rochester contributed.

To some it seemed presumptuous for Goodwin to solicit the patrons of the other institutions he had served. Chase, the Doctor's friend from St. Paul's, told him: "I think it unwise for you to write letters to our people for funds for William and Mary College. Mrs. H. S., I think, was somewhat provoked about it." That would be Mrs. Harper Sibley, a wealthy woman whose husband counted among his acquaintances such men as John D. Rockefeller, Jr.

Goodwin went on taking donors where he found them, raising $190,000 in his first 10 months. But he got his first big donation close to home. Chandler had suggested he see Adele Matthiessen Blow of Yorktown, who was thinking of providing the money for a gymnasium. Before April 19, Goodwin reported to Chandler that she would give $100,000 for the facility.

The donor was the widow of George Preston Blow, who had died the previous November 20. The son of a Norfolk judge, he had been an officer on the battleship *Maine* when it went down in Havana harbor. After his retirement from the Navy, he became president of the Western Clock Company and other firms. His wife was from a wealthy La Salle, Illinois, family. In 1914 the couple bought and began the restoration of the Nelson House—then called the York House—a prominent colonial merchant family's home commandeered by Cornwallis for his headquarters during the Battle of Yorktown.

Chandler had two problems with the gift. First, he wanted none of the college's new facilities to memorialize people who lacked a historical association with the school. Although George Preston Blow hadn't even attended William and Mary, his widow wanted the gym to bear his name. Chandler and his board of visitors conceded the point; but she also wanted an 18th-century façade, and that opened a subject on which Goodwin and Chandler were already at odds.

Chandler wanted his new facilities to be built quickly and as dollar-efficient and functional as the state architect could make them. Goodwin, whose fund-raising pitch was grounded on historical links, wanted architecture that embodied the school's colonial origins.

"Dr. Goodwin's idea," Hayes said, "was to have a plan drawn up to guide the college in its new growth. He advised setting up a committee of architects of national eminence, headed by Mr. John Stewart Barney of New York. Mr. Barney, a native of Virginia, had drawn the plans for Dr. Goodwin's restoration of Bruton, in which he was assisted by a group of men with outstanding knowledge of the colonial period. That is what the doctor hoped to establish at the College. He advocated that such a committee study the situation of the college, point out its present and future needs, make sure that the new buildings blended with the old, and prepare a plan which would be adequate and harmonious. The campus of William and Mary, Dr. Goodwin said, had a unique opportunity in following the pattern of Sir Christopher Wren."

Barney endorsed the idea, wrote letters to explain it, traveled to Williamsburg to push it along, and was prepared to serve *gratis*. Chandler was too impatient to wait for an advisory board to be assembled, Hayes said, and the visitors "wished to deal with only one man. They fretted that their plans would be complicated by the interference of advisors." Chandler and the board proposed Barney become consulting architect. Working out the details proved difficult.

After a disappointing session with Chandler, Barney walked with Goodwin across the yard to College Corner—the triangular intersection where Duke of Gloucester Street meets Jamestown and Richmond roads. Looking east into the city, Goodwin brought up the notion of restoring Williamsburg's houses and public buildings. Barney, the Doctor said, "was the first person with whom the Restoration thought was shared."

Hayes later said, "Mr. Barney made many valuable suggestions as to the possible scope of the plan." More than ten years after the fact, the Doctor said Barney's "sympathetic and enthusiastic endorsement contributed courage and conviction and a more determined purpose to find some means for its fulfillment." But at the time, when events were fresher in his mind, the Doctor gave the architect a larger share of the credit; he said Barney

provided the framework on which Goodwin hung his restoration
proposal. In an April 1926 draft of a letter to the rector of the board
of visitors, the Doctor said: ~~"Now the proposition is not really mine.~~
~~It~~ ∧ The proposition was outlined rather extensively and in detail by
Mr. J. Stewart Barney. I know exactly what his plan was, and would
be prepared to outline it . . . with maps and other data showing the
whole scope of the idea."

Goodwin said that plan "definitely related to the acquisition
of these homes for our college endowment endeavor" and envisioned
"that the points of historic interest be taken over and that any funds
over and above what was necessary to keep the property in order
should be used in the interest of the college, that the homes could be
assigned to the professors of the college as residences, etc., etc."

The plan had six essential points:

• Secure options on all colonial homes in Williamsburg—
"the optional right to purchase in case of sale"—and buy all the
properties on Duke of Gloucester and Francis streets. The idea was
to secure the core of the city and have first call on houses in
jeopardy of being sold to developers, but to leave them in private
hands in the interim.

• Rebuild the Capitol and the Raleigh Tavern.

• Establish a Colonial Holding Corporation to manage
the project.

• Remove Duke of Gloucester Street telephone poles; make
a park of the Palace site, replace African-American homes on Duke
of Gloucester with reconstructed colonial housing.

• Give rent profits to William and Mary.

• Have Richmond and Jamestown roads "given over" to the
college; reconstruct colonial homes to replace present structures,
and use them for faculty homes and fraternity houses.

Goodwin's chief addition to Barney's plan seems to have
been the restoration of William and Mary's Wren Building to its
colonial appearance, which brings matters back to where they
began. At issue for the moment was the campus architects advisory
board that Goodwin and Barney wanted appointed.

The bureaucracy dickered with Barney until, frustrated and
insulted, he withdrew. "My title would carry with it the duties of a
well-trained butler," he wrote to Goodwin. "I must lay upon the
'Board' any talent and skill which I may possess, arranging in the
most attractive and artistic form, garnished with the most subtle

arguments, and served with infinite tact. Those who care to come to this feast, when it does not interfere with their other engagements, may pick and choose such dainty morsels as their 'provincial digesting' might suggest. The rest of the feast I am expected to swallow along with my wounded pride and disappointments. . . .

"My advice to your Board is to employ some thick-skinned Yankee, who will make you pay every dollar, and more besides. He would be appreciated as I will never be. He would get the reward in the only language that he understands, namely, dollars and cents, and I would not be called upon to take the high and lofty position of laying up for myself treasures in heaven."

Determining the design of Blow Gymnasium looked to be beyond Goodwin's job description. But what couldn't be done one way could be done another. "Finally Dr. Goodwin conceived a plan to calm President Chandler's impatience," Hayes said. "Mrs. Blow as the donor of a large sum of money toward a building at the college stipulated in her letter of donation (the paragraph rough-drafted by Dr. Goodwin), that a designated architect or architects, recognized as a colonial expert should draw up the exterior design for the new building to be in harmony with the old buildings." Goodwin was instrumental in securing architect Claude Bragdon of Rochester to design a gymnasium with a colonial revival exterior, while the state architect designed the interior.

"Of course," Ethel said, "Dr. Goodwin was very much interested in the college, but it wasn't everything."

He liked to walk along Duke of Gloucester Street with her and the boys, especially when the honeysuckle was out, and look at the Capitol's foundations and the mulberries along Francis Street. The weekends took him farther afield.

He officially became rector of Grace Church on March 1, and he set out each Sunday for a 3:30 p.m. service for its 16 communicants. A boxy little building in decay, the church was built about 1697 and was the only surviving colonial structure in the state made of marl. Its communion silver service, the second oldest in Virginia, dated to 1649. In little more than a year Goodwin persuaded the vestry to let him undertake the church's restoration.

In the meantime, he joined his close friend, Professor Montgomery, in the work of the Society for the Preservation of the

The Blair House was the first Williamsburg home Goodwin helped preserve.

Blair Homestead, organized to lift from Dean Jonathan Garland Pollard a burden he had assumed for history's sake. John Blair had helped frame the Constitution, and Washington appointed him to the Supreme Court in 1789. Now the justice's ramshackle clapboard home on Duke of Gloucester was about to be demolished to make room for a service station or a department store. In 1921, Pollard, head of the recently revived law school, purchased the property to save it. On Christmas day 1923, perhaps as a present to the dean, the society incorporated for the purpose of conveying the property to William and Mary for use as an alumni clubhouse. Raising the purchase money was a responsibility Chandler shared with the society's next president, Goodwin. The agreement was concluded just after F. R. Savage enlisted Goodwin in another civic-minded association, this one intent on securing government funds to build a post office.

Golf was still the Doctor's chief outdoor avocation. He soon accepted membership at the Fort Eustis officers' golf club and became a charter member and director of the short-lived Williamsburg Golf and Country Club. As a college professor, he could play on Sundays if he liked.

Some Sunday evenings Goodwin preached in Toano, and he shared with Bruton's rector, the Reverend Ruffin Jones, the duty of ministering to youth groups.

Jones's father and Goodwin's had served in the same outfit at some point during the Civil War. The newest member of the Goodwin household, Ethel's father, now carried the family's Confederate standard. John Clarke Howard, recently retired from the traffic department of the Richmond, Fredericksburg, and Potomac Railroad, came to live with them. He was something of a Virginia hero. In Hayes's words: "Mr. Howard was described by his friends in an awed whisper as having been one of the Virginia Military Institute freshmen cadets called from their classrooms to charge the Union forces in the triumphant battle of New Market in 1864." He was straight, slender, and courtly now, with snowy hair, sideburns, and a dapper beard parted in the middle. But when he and the Corps of Cadets had marched through Staunton to the battlefield, they were so fresh-faced the regimental band played "Rock-a-Bye Baby."

Montgomery pitched in on the *History of the Virginia Theological Seminary*, reading proof mailed from the press by the Rochester publisher, as Goodwin and Hayes corrected and typed new chapters and sent them north. Almost all the work was done in the Doctor's study after dinner. "Page by page, chapter by chapter," Hayes said, "the book grew thicker, and at last the final page was put in the mail." Toward the end of May the first volume was coming out of the bindery. "As he opened the box and held the thick red-and-gold book in his hands," Hayes said, "Dr. Goodwin's exclamation was, 'Now we will have to go to work on volume two.'"

Goodwin mailed copies to friends like Chase, then caught a northbound train for fund-raising calls. After stopping in New York to confer with Barney, he dashed back to Arlington in time to present his history at the seminary centennial celebrations June 6. At the end of the following week, the Goodwins sublet the Richmond Road house for the summer and left town just ahead of the worst of Tidewater's sticky heat. Intending to go back to Rochester when the first half of the seminary history was done, Hayes had gathered up her job references and gotten to work on her resumé. But she found William and Mary life lively and work with Goodwin agreeable, so she decided to stay on awhile longer. She went with them.

The Doctor taught at a vacation church school, and moved on to the Southwest Virginia mountains near the Tennessee border.

He took the vacant pulpit at St. Thomas's Church in Abingdon for
the summer, and worked in a makeshift office on the rest of the
book. In July he wrote to Bishop Brent, "On Sunday afternoons I go
down into the mountains to the Church of the Good Shepherd at
'The Knobs' and minister to mountain people as primitive and
ignorant as one can find anywhere." The Knobs are a range of
heights east of Abingdon where Goodwin was as well a missionary
to the log church at Piney and at the Ivanhoe chapel.

In August the Doctor was back in Tidewater to speak at the
laying of the cornerstone for the Newport News High School. His
files are full of invitations to speak at graduations and special
occasions like this; there are few records of him turning one down
for anything but a schedule conflict or ill-health. He never asked for
a fee, and he was popular with the program committees of women's
groups and men's associations. The next spring he would give the
Memorial Day address to Confederate veterans at Appomattox,
where his father's rebel career ended, and he was constantly off to
places like Baltimore and Philadelphia to speak in behalf of the
college. Goodwin would go just about anywhere to make a speech.

Classes resumed September 17, but Chandler wanted
Goodwin to get back on the money-raising trail. "Between now and
the first of the year," the Doctor wrote to a friend in October, "the
President is expecting me to put every spare moment of time into
the effort of securing funds necessary to complete the Monroe

Goodwin, in the front row, gave the Memorial Day address to Confederate veterans
at Appomattox in 1924.

Dormitory now in process of construction on the College Campus."

Before he got started, he moved into a Wren Building office and began to work up a 48-page endowment campaign booklet. Published in January on heavy stock with a four-color view of the Wren on the cover, the *Romance and Renaissance of the College of William and Mary* was replete with photos and printed in Old English type. It devoted 22 pages to the history of the college and the region and 26 to campaign goals and fund raising. Above the Wren's picture, Goodwin printed another version of the Ruskin quote he loved so well: "Our duty is to preserve what the past has had to say for itself, and to say for ourselves also what shall be true for the future."

It was probably in conjunction with this project that Goodwin took the next step in the colonial Williamsburg campaign—the assembly of similar materials to promote the restoration plan. "Prior to sharing the thought of a restoration with the hope of securing participating interest this preliminary data was collected and systematized as far as possible in notebook form," he said. "These notes were illustrated by photographs which had been taken by a visitor to Williamsburg—Mr. Clarence A. Phillips of the Carnegie Endowment for International Peace. Mr. Phillips' photographic hobby proved of great value to us as we arranged this material in an endeavor to be prepared should an opportunity occur to present the thought of a restoration to one whose interest might be enlisted."

The kind of camera most on his mind that autumn, however, was the sort used to make motion pictures. D. W. Griffith came to Tidewater in November to shoot scenes for the silent movie *America* in Williamsburg and Yorktown. Goodwin became Griffith's volunteer assistant, making arrangements for the use of Grace Church and the campus of the College of William and Mary as sets. Shooting started at the school on the 17th. Goodwin wrote the day before to daughter Evelyn Farr: "I may appear on the campus as one of the professors and thus become immortal."

A few days later he told son Rutherfoord: "When you see this picture, which I understand is to be Griffith's greatest production, you may recognize me in the act of breaking up a fast and furious cock-fight, which was staged just around the corner of the building in which my office is located. I was Commissary Dawson, president of William and Mary, with lemon yellow stockings, black velvet

Goodwin was costumed as William and Mary's colonial president for D. W. Griffith's film *America*. His scenes, however, were cut.

breeches, bands and wig. Dr. Montgomery, Dr. Hall, and Dr. Pollard were my fellow Colonial professors. You will see the students scamper as we arrived, with fighting cocks tucked under their arms! I suggested the scene. It was thoroughly typical of the time."

He persuaded Griffith to speak to the Grace Church congregation on the educational value of films, and he struck up a correspondence with the famous director. "I never expected to be a moving picture actor," Goodwin wrote to him, "but now that you have preached in my Church, and I have played in your picture, we can consider ourselves as partners."

Since the film was in black and white, the color of the Doctor's stockings made no difference, and none of the William and Mary scenes made the final edit anyway. Goodwin's movie career ended on the cutting-room floor.

On the first day of 1924, Bishop Robert Carter Jett of Roanoke asked Goodwin to consider becoming rector of Emmanuel Church in Bristol. By return mail, Goodwin thanked him for the offer but declined, saying: "In the first place, I feel profoundly convinced that the greatest need which we face in the present is to relate education very closely and very definitely with spiritual forces and to a spiritual objective. It has been too largely related to material forces and to a material objective." Secondly, the college needed funds raised, and thirdly Goodwin wanted to work out his college course of Bible instruction and religious education. He was also busy writing lectures for each department on the relation of their subjects to "the spirit life and spiritual goals."

John Seaton Goodwin, the last of the Doctor's seven children, was born January 11th in Richmond, the birthplace of his

In this scene from Griffith's film, written by Goodwin, the young men of William and Mary re-created a cock fight.

father 54 years before. There were now six people under the
Goodwin roof. Rutherfoord was arriving from Rochester on the
25th to join the household, enter the college, and prepare for the
ministry. The Doctor made of his need for more space an
opportunity to buy his first house. The day John arrived, Goodwin
signed a contract to purchase from W. S. McGill the dilapidated
home at 124 East Francis Street at the corner of Queen's Lane. It
stood opposite the Masonic Lodge next to the Lightfoot House on
what would become the grounds of the Williamsburg Inn. There was
space for everyone, including his daughters and their families, and
in back a garage.

On February 9 he took a loan to help finance the purchase
and begin what he termed a reconstruction. It would take months of
work and much more money to make the house habitable, but the
Doctor was looking forward to the project. He intended that the
improvements give the house a colonial appearance.

Chandler, however, was anxious for Goodwin to get back on
the road. On the 26th, the Doctor left for New York "to attend the
Senate meeting of the Phi Beta Kappa and also to try to get some
money for the College."

The trip, the Doctor said, "unwittingly helped to initiate the
restoration of colonial Williamsburg."

The catalyst for what was to come was "a banquet of a large
number of the members of this Society," Goodwin wrote, "in the
interest of the proposal to erect on the campus of the College of
William and Mary a hall as a memorial to the men of the college
who on December 5, 1776 founded the Society in Williamsburg."

At the dinner, a Hotel Astor affair, Phi Beta Kappa President
Charles F. Thwing, president of Case Western Reserve, was to
present a charter for the Phi Beta Kappa Foundation. The
foundation would raise $100,000 to build an auditorium at William
and Mary to mark the society's 250th anniversary. The hall would
also contain guest rooms and a representation of the Raleigh
Tavern's Apollo Room for use of the Alpha Chapter. Hayes said, "Dr.
Chandler was anxious that the college cooperate as it had dire need
for an auditorium." He had been invited to appear but, Goodwin
said, "being unable to go delegated me to represent the college and
to speak on the subject of The College of William and Mary and its

Historical Environment."

No text of these remarks survives; the Doctor may have spoken without notes. A week earlier another clergyman had asked for a copy of a Goodwin speech, and the Doctor said, "I have come to the point where I carry the outlined notes of my lectures and of my sermons sufficiently clearly in my mind to make me independent of the necessity of making notes which would be in the least intelligible to anyone else. I generally do nothing more than write down just a few caption words which serve to suggest thoughts and lines of treatment to me."

What he said to the 130 members and guests of the society likely was similar to what he told a Richmond radio audience in a May 20, 1926, speech titled "The Historic Environment of the College of William and Mary." Rehearsing the importance of Williamsburg and the college to the nation's founding, he explained the school's need for funds. He also spoke of the Memorial Hall fund-raising campaign, the appropriateness of a William and Mary site, Phi Beta Kappa's sesquicentennial, and the society's contributions to higher education. No doubt he mentioned the honorary Phi Beta Kappa membership bestowed on him by the college in 1908. By some accounts, he went on to detail his dream for restoration of a Williamsburg stripped of its modern "excrescences" and restored to its 18th-century appearance.

Goodwin said Dr. George E. Vincent, president of the Rockefeller Foundation and "toastmaster at the banquet, asked me after my address if I had ever met Mr. John D. Rockefeller, Jr., a Senator of the Phi Beta Kappa, and kindly offered to introduce me to him. I had not until then realized that Mr. Rockefeller was in the room and when I was introduced I invited him to visit Williamsburg."

Rockefeller, the vice-chairman of the new fund-raising foundation told Goodwin, he hoped someday to visit—a remark Goodwin later spoke of as a "pledge." Years afterward, the Doctor said he had always hoped the philanthropist "might visit Williamsburg. The knowledge of what he had done and was doing furnished ground for the hope that he would recognize the great educational value of the restoration of the colonial city and become interested in making this contribution to the enrichment of life."

When he returned to William and Mary, Hayes said, Goodwin told Chandler that Rockefeller was the man, of all men, who instinctively understood the spirit of the college and of the city.

Perhaps America's wealthiest man, John D. Rockefeller, Jr., declined Goodwin's early requests for William and Mary aid.

Chapter Nine: **1924-1925**

John D. Rockefeller, Jr., paid more personal federal income taxes in 1924 than any person in America. When the accountants were done, the bill on his earnings came to $7,435,169. Second was Henry Ford, from whom the Internal Revenue Service collected $2,467,000. Ford's son Edsel was third at $1,984,000. Before the year ended, Goodwin approached all three in behalf of William and Mary's endowment fund; but for partners in the idea of Williamsburg's restoration, he looked only to the Fords.

Born to Irish immigrants on a farm six miles from Dearborn, Michigan, in 1863, Henry Ford grew up with an interest in machinery and precision. Sixty years later, he and his Model T had recontoured America's social and economic landscapes.

In 1903, with $28,000 in capital, he organized the Ford Motor Company. The enterprise grew and worked its way through eight production models until in October 1908 Ford announced the utilitarian, inexpensive, everyman Model T. "I will build a car for the great multitude," he said. The genius of the idea was in the efficiencies Ford and his engineers brought to the assembly line and in the vertical integration of the business. During the next 19 years, they built almost 16,750,000 Model Ts, just under half the world's automobile production.

In 1914, Ford announced he would pay eligible employees $5 a day, more than double the $2.34 industry average, and cut the workday from nine hours to eight. Through increasing efficiency and economies of scale, he lowered the price of a car even as he raised wages. Despite inflation, the customer invoice for a Model T fell from $950 in 1908 until it reached $290 in 1927, when Ford introduced the Model A.

He made mammoth profits on volume, but his seven major stockholders viewed rising wages and falling prices as mismanagement and an infringement on dividends. In the course of the dispute, Ford stepped out of the line of fire and made his only son Edsel the company's figurehead president in 1918. A year later Henry Ford bought out his antagonists for $126,812,134 and began an expansion that ultimately embraced operations in 33 countries. He was organizing the world's largest industrial endeavor when Goodwin approached him.

Rockefeller's wealth came from the petroleum industry. His father, a descendant of an 18th-century German immigrant, had begun to transform the business in 1863—the year Ford was born— with the a single Cleveland refinery. Through tightfisted management, hardhearted consolidation, ruthless shipping deals, and cutthroat competition, John D. Rockefeller, Sr., built the Standard Oil monopoly into an international commercial empire. In the bargain, he made himself one of the world's richest men and one of its most feared. During the Standard's prime, he said: "I have ways of making money you know nothing about."

Mr. Junior, as Rockefeller senior's associates called his only son, went to work in his father's office at 26 Broadway in New York on October 1, 1897. He took a desk on the 9th floor. To help manage the Rockefeller businesses and philanthropies, Mr. Junior hired Charles O. Heydt as his private secretary, and the Reverend Frederick T. Gates helped him bring system to the family's charitable endeavors. Gates helped the Rockefellers develop a science of benevolence that focused on grants to institutions rather than individuals. They created the Rockefeller Institute for Medical Research in 1901 and the General Education Board in 1902. Through Rockefeller generosity most of the South was rid of such evils as hookworm, and much of the planet was freed of the bane of yellow fever.

A devout Baptist, the father reared his son to the same rigorous standards of private morality he enforced on himself. The younger man's surname and reputation for personal probity led to his appointment, over his objection, as foreman of a New York City grand jury impaneled in 1909 to investigate white slavery and the corruption it caused at city hall and the police department. Both had become so open, the public clamored for reform until the politicians and judges could no longer ignore their constituents. But the anxious officeholders hoped to contain the damage. They imagined that by selecting Mr. Junior, inexperienced in wordly affairs, they could handicap the probe while mollifying voters.

With the close cooperation of Police Chief Arthur A. Woods, Rockefeller asked for 54 indictments in seven months. Afterward he carried on the anti-prostitution campaign by establishing the private Bureau of Social Hygiene.

The Rockefeller fortune was large enough to support a general scheme of global uplift. In 1913, the senior Rockefeller's wealth peaked at just under $1 billion. That year he founded the Rockefeller Foundation "to promote the well being of mankind throughout the world," and put his son and Gates in charge.

In 1917, the elder Rockefeller began a five-year transfer of his massive wealth to his philanthropies and his son, keeping for himself about $20 million. Mr. Junior's personal fortune had by then grown to about the same figure. After the war, he added to his staff former police chief—now colonel—Woods, who became his majordomo. By 1922, Mr. Junior's fortune had increased about 25 fold, to roughly $500 million, or about the same amount set aside for the philanthropies. Rockefeller benefactions became so ubiquitous they reached even into Williamsburg. The General Education Board provided $200 toward the construction of a school for black children, was awaiting a request for $300 more, and had offered William and Mary a third of the $300,000 it needed for a new science building, if the college could secure the balance by March 1, 1926.

It was with another contribution to William and Mary in mind that Goodwin first approached Mr. Junior; the college needed all the money it could find.

The Wren Building was in such disrepair a ceiling fan in Goodwin's office fell and smashed the L. C. Smith typewriter Hayes used. The college was "so absolutely destitute of funds," as Goodwin put it, it could not afford to send out Christmas cards.

As a Richmond College student 25 years before, Goodwin founded a chapter of Phi Gamma Delta fraternity. As a William and

Mary professor, he quarterbacked a campaign for a Williamsburg charter. But the application was voted down. Howard William R. Biers of the University of Virginia chapter communicated the decision. "Nothing would please me more," Biers said, "than to see William and Mary restored to her rightful place among American colleges and universities. I feel quite sure that you will agree that at present she is far from the lofty pinnacle to which her glorious history and noble traditions entitle her."

Early in June, during a trip to deliver a series of commencement addresses, the Doctor presented himself at 26 Broadway, hoping for help in refurbishing some of William and Mary's claim on noble traditions and asking to see Mr. Junior. Goodwin carried a letter describing a plan for the restoration of the Wren, the Brafferton, and the President's House. Private secretary Robert Gumbel—Heydt was now managing Rockefeller real estate holdings—accepted the letter and heard Goodwin's proposal, but that was as far as Goodwin got. On the 9th, W. S. Richardson of Rockefeller's office informed him: "The letter which you addressed to Mr. Rockefeller, Jr., and presented through Mr. Gumbel has received his consideration. He appreciates the circumstances you present, and regrets that he could not wisely make an exception to his policy in the matter of personal gifts to educational institutions. We have received most cordial expressions of interest in the work of the College of William and Mary, and regret that it is not best for Mr. Rockefeller to assist in this trying time."

Goodwin was already trying to round up allies for an approach to Henry Ford with a far more ambitious idea—the restoration of Williamsburg. He asked S. S. McClure, editor of *McClure's Magazine*, for advice on how to go after the automobile tycoon. On June 11, McClure wrote from New York: "It is absolutely impossible under any circumstances to get Mr. Ford to do anything for anyone. That I know from long observation." But on the 13th, perhaps the day McClure's letter arrived, Goodwin asked Hayes to set up her stenographic machine and, puffing his pipe, slowly began to dictate a letter to Edsel Ford, Henry's son. It was a letter, he told his secretary, that "could have consequences so far-reaching that they could be of national value for all time." It was the first time he had committed to paper the idea of restoring all the city.

"Seriously," Goodwin wrote, "I want your father to buy Williamsburg, the old colonial capital of Virginia at a time when

Virginia included the land on which the Ford factory is now located, as in those days the western boundary of Virginia was the Pacific ocean. Williamsburg is the one Colonial city left, until recently unchanged by time." He described the town's 18th-century distinctions, its colonial houses and layout, and named its historic personages.

"It would be the most unique and spectacular gift to American history and to the preservation of American traditions that could be made by any American," Goodwin said. "Other men have bought rare books and preserved historic houses. No man yet has had the vision and the courage to buy and to preserve a Colonial village, and Williamsburg is the one remaining Colonial Village which any man could buy."

Disavowing personal financial interest and offering the "deeply interested" Barney's services free, Goodwin tried to make Ford feel guilty. "Unfortunately you and your father are at present the chief contributors to the destruction of this city," he said. "With the new concrete roads leading from Newport News to Richmond and with the road to nearby Jamestown passing through the city, garages and gas tanks are fast spoiling the whole appearance of the old streets and the old city, and most of the cars which stop at the garages and gas tanks are Ford Cars!

"I am writing this letter to you with the hope that through you the letter will reach your father," he said. Goodwin invited them to visit "to see for yourself the unique opportunity which this place presents to do a spectacular thing which will attract the attention and win the gratitude of all lovers of history and of historic traditions in America." Under a separate cover he sent to both Fords copies of *The Romance and Renaissance of the College of William and Mary in Virginia.*

Goodwin also wrote to Richardson and Gumbel that day, acknowledging Rockefeller's disinterest in the college rennovations. To Richardson he said: "Of course the letter was a great disappointment to me, but we wish you would be good enough to express to Mr. Rockefeller our appreciation of his kindness in giving consideration to this matter.

"I would be glad for you to tell Mr. Rockefeller, also, that appreciating as I do the reference to personal gifts to educational institutions, I wish he would give me $100,000 in order that I might have the pleasure of giving it away and of sharing one brief moment of the satisfaction and joy which men of means have in helping where help is so greatly needed. I could give him ample assurance and infallible proof of the fact that neither any past policy nor fear of future precedent would prevent me from giving it away ten minutes after I got it."

To Gumbel he wrote: "Having heard from Mr. W. S. Richardson that Mr. Rockefeller did not feel that it was possible for him to comply with our request, I am writing to thank you for your kindness in the matter and I wish that you would be good enough to express to Mr. Rockefeller our appreciation of the consideration which he has given to our need." He invited Gumbel to Williamsburg, too.

In a dispatch to McClure that day, Goodwin agreed it was impossible to get Henry Ford to do anything for anyone, but Ford's office sent a note the 18th thanking Goodwin for the pamphlet and saying, "It will be looked over with interest at an early opportunity." McClure's and Goodwin's mutual opinion looked to be vindicated, however, when the office sent a form-letter reply July 1: "We regret that Mr. Ford's many activities are absorbing his entire attention. He is, therefore, unable to interest himself in the matter mentioned."

Nevertheless, Goodwin had opened lines of communication and gotten his ideas across. In the meantime, he would do what he could on his own to save old Williamsburg. On the 20th, as president of the Blair Homestead society, he transferred the house to the college. For the second time he had assured the salvation of one of the city's colonial structures. He had his eye on the Powder Horn next, but he still had college buildings to erect.

The next day he wrote to Gumbel on the excuse of asking for the address of a Rockefeller philanthropy in Atlanta, adding: "I hope it is not as hot in New York as it is in the College of William and Mary at present. When I think of the students working today under that galvanized iron roof of our temporary Science Hall, it makes me long for the finding of the man or the men who can help us meet the generous offer of the General Board of Education, so that we can give a Science Hall and provide some place where students can study science without having to work in a veritable furnace of Hell, as they are having to do here at present with the temperature around 86 degrees, with the galvanized iron roof just ten feet above their heads." Gumbel provided the address and thanked Goodwin for the invitation to visit a place so appealing.

The Doctor was as busy with his ministerial and his private affairs as his work for the college.

He was attempting to divest himself of two lots with flawed titles in old Richmond—"those rat holes over on Church Hill"—that had descended from his grandfather Rutherfoord. The lawyers had him tied up in red tape six ways from Sunday. The Powder Horn was again in danger of collapsing, and Goodwin was talking to the APVA about saving it once more. He persuaded the Grace Church vestry to let him restore that building, and proposed to renew the foundations, build an entrance vestibule, erect a new cupola, strengthen the roof timbers, relieve the lateral pressure threatening to destroy the walls, install windows of colonial design, panel off the east interior, restore and dignify the chancel, nail up wainscoting, and rewire. He agreed to raise all the money, line up the architect and contractor, review their plans, and direct the work.

The number of his communicants grew by one with the addition of Hayes. Raised a Congregationalist, she decided to become an Anglican, and took her catechism from Goodwin. Before her confirmation June 24th, he wrote her a note of fatherly affection. "You have very little idea how glad I am to be associated with you in the step which you are taking this afternoon in being confirmed in Old Grace Church, Yorktown," he said. "I hope it will furnish light to guide us both into richer helpfulness and enable us to do many things together in the days and years which lie ahead that will bless our own and help in the lives of others—You must always let me help you in any and every way I can."

Whenever Hayes remarked on the diversity of the Doctor's interests and activities, Goodwin liked to tell her: "Each person's life is like a violin. There are four strings to a violin—if a person plays continually on just one string he will wear it out—it will snap from tension. But if he uses all the strings, they will last longer and will make more harmony with less strain to the violin."

Overseeing the renovation of the Francis Street house, he had targeted August 15 as the day to move in. But Goodwin's builder misconstrued his order for deep mullioned windows—a colonial touch—and they all had to be replaced. Matters went more smoothly in the construction of the modern two-room backyard quarters for cook Martha Burwell and her husband. It came complete with indoor plumbing, which could not be said of every house in town. "He was very much of the opinion," Hayes said, "that white people did themselves an injustice when they failed to improve the living conditions of the negro race. 'These southern servants come into our homes, cook for us, and tend our babies and our children,' I have heard him say. 'If for no other reason it is in the interest of our white families to see that the negroes enjoy modern sanitation.'"

Martha's best dish was Brunswick stew. But she was almost as renowned for her gingerbread as Ethel was for hers, and the acknowledged expert at Goodwin's favorite dessert, "The Fabulous 'Queen of Puddings.'" He was almost as delighted by the concoction as he was by the family dog, a snow white miniature Eskimo spitz named Alaska.

Ethel Goodwin's Virginia Gingerbread

2 eggs	1 teaspoon of ginger
1 cup of butter, melted	1 teaspoon of nutmeg
three-quarters of a	1 teaspoon of cinnamon
cup of molasses	1 cup of sugar
1 teaspoon of allspice	3 and a half cups of flour
1 cup of seedless raisins	3 teaspoons of baking soda
1 cup of sour milk	

Beat eggs, add shortening, molasses and sugar. Sift flour, add dry ingredients and sift twice. Mix flour and sour milk alternately with mixture, leaving one-half cup flour to dredge raisins which are added last. Bake in shallow pan (10" x 10") at 375 degrees until a straw comes out clean—about 45 minutes.

Fabulous 'Queen of Puddings'

1 quart scalded milk	5 egg whites
5 egg yolks	One-half cup of sugar
1 scant cup of sugar	1 teaspoon vanilla
2 cups of fine bread crumbs	pinch of salt
1 teaspoon lemon extract	

Pour scalded milk on beaten egg yolks and sugar. Add bread crumbs and lemon extract. Bake in deep buttered pan in

moderate oven—350 degrees—until set, about thirty minutes or a
little more. Beat whites still, add vanilla, and one-half cup of sugar
folded in. Draw pudding to front of oven and pile on meringue,
returning to oven for five minutes or until meringue is light brown.
Serve hot or cold with cream.

Professor Montgomery joined the family circle, renting the
third-floor rooms. All the household, the Burwells included, knelt
each morning at breakfast to pray. Among the things Goodwin gave
thanks for were two gifts from Harper Sibley in Rochester that
helped pay for the new place.

Before approaching Ford again, Goodwin consulted with
Charles A. Taylor, a 1909 William and Mary graduate and
Richmond's largest Ford dealer. Taylor provided a letter of
introduction to his friend William Ford, Henry's brother, and on July
24 the Doctor wrote to Detroit again, enclosing Taylor's letter.
Goodwin summarized the restoration idea for William and asked for
his help in putting it before Henry.

"My thought is that Mr. Ford might be enthusiastically
interested in purchasing the town and turning it over to a Colonial
holding corporation," he wrote. "The distinctly modern innovations
could be obliterated. In place of the modern and tawdry buildings,
residences of distinctly Colonial type could be put up to take their
place. The old Colonial Governor's palace grounds, the courthouse
green where Indian treaties were made, the old powder horn which
marked the beginning of the Revolution, and the site of the original
House of Burgesses could all be reclaimed and beautified.

"It would do more to teach history to the American
traveling public than anything that could be done by any man."

Goodwin, who also wanted the Raleigh Tavern
reconstructed, offered to go to Detroit to outline his plan in person,
and again he invited the Fords to visit. He had seen a *New York
Times* photograph of Henry riding in an old carriage, and Goodwin
thought he might enjoy being met at the Williamsburg train station
by a coach with a driver in colonial costume for a ride through the
city's streets.

He thought the restoration would cost $4 million to $5
million, but the "rents could be used to defray the cost of

improvement. If Mr. Ford was disposed to do so he could provide that the income secured over and above what was necessary for the upkeep and improvement of the town could be turned over by the corporation for the improvement and preservation of the oldest historic College, although the endowment of the College is not essentially connected with the carrying out of the rest of the plan."

The next Goodwin heard of this letter, it had been printed, full page, in the Sunday, August 31 edition of the *Detroit Free Press* under the headline: "Henry Ford Asked to Buy Ancient Virginia Town." The Doctor may not have learned of it until September 5, the same day Taylor wrote from Louisville. "Mr. William Ford secured Henry Ford's permission to give this matter to the *Detroit Free Press* for publication," Taylor said, "which would certainly indicate that he might be interested in carrying out your proposition. Mr. William Ford informs me that the best way to handle the matter is to give it as wide publicity as possible through the press and other sources and that Mr. Henry Ford may become interested in the proposition, whereas, if it were presented to him at this time, he would, no doubt, turn it down."

Taylor concluded, "Mr. William Ford is, personally, very much interested in it and tells me that he is going to put it over with Henry, if possible."

Goodwin straightaway sent 25 cents in stamps to the *Free Press* for 10 copies of the article and wrote a letter to Briton Hadden, editor of a year-old magazine named *Time*, requesting a favorable story and explaining why. Then Goodwin asked Taylor for advice on how to get to Henry Ford directly. "If the plan which has been proposed could be carried out," the Doctor said, "there are certain seasons of the year when there would doubtless be from five hundred to a thousand people who would visit here and who would be taught, as they could not be in any other way, the lessons which history has to give and which could be given through the restoration proposed."

Goodwin the next day contacted John Stewart Bryan, publisher of Richmond's *News-Leader* and William and Mary's vice-rector, and explained the *Free Press* story and Henry Ford's supposed susceptibility to publicity. He asked Bryan's cooperation.

Goodwin's ambitions had blossomed. He told Bryan he contemplated "the rebuilding of the House of Burgesses, the old Raleigh Tavern, and the purchasing of the property on the Duke of

Gloucester Street from the college to the Capitol, and the property on the street adjacent." He wanted telephone poles removed, Duke of Gloucester Street planted with crape myrtles and roses, the Palace site made into a park, African-American homes on Duke of Gloucester replaced, and the historic houses to be controlled by a "Colonial Holding Corporation." He wanted faculty homes and fraternity houses built on Jamestown and Richmond roads, which were to be given to William and Mary within the area of the college.

A carbon copy of this proposal Goodwin dispatched to Dr. John Finlay, editor of the *New York Times*, with a letter that said in part: "With the new concrete road running from Richmond to Newport News and Norfolk, passing down the Duke of Gloucester Street, there is imminent danger of the entire obliteration of the colonial features of this most interesting colonial town in America. Gas tanks, restaurants, moving picture houses, and cheap boarding places, are fast being built up along the old street from the College to the Capitol."

A friend asked if it was true that Goodwin told Ford his motor cars were responsible for Williamsburg's plight. "There is no place in America," Goodwin said, "where there is as much of historic interest and associations as are left here. But it will not be left long unless somebody comes to the rescue. . . . I told Mr. Ford that Ford cars threatened to be the destroying agencies of the ancient shrines of this time-honored place, and that I wanted him to save the city from the ravages of his own industrial output."

Hadden declined to give *Time's* assistance, but Bryan said, "I will see what can be done to further the movement you outline." Apparently what he saw to was the submission of a story from Richmond to the *Sunday Sun* in Baltimore. It contained details Goodwin had so far confided only to Bryan. The piece appeared November 4, but the *Sunday Sun* also savaged Goodwin's idea in an editorial headlined "A Novel Proposition."

"What Mr. Ford will say to this proposition remains to be seen," the editorial said. "If he still adheres to the assertion attributed to him some years ago that 'all history is bunk,' Dr. Goodwin's suggestion may not appeal to him strongly. . . . To ask him to invest four or five million dollars in 'bunk' would seem, on the face of it, expecting too much from a man of Mr. Ford's practical turn of mind." Even if Goodwin succeeded, in the newspaper's view the reconstructed results would be pale imitations beside such originals

as Monticello and Mount Vernon. "Would he people the House of
Burgesses with wax figures . . . of the great men who gave distinction
and fame to Williamsburg of the Colonial period? Not all Mr. Ford's
dollars can bring back the grace and power of a day that is dead.

"But if some work of suggestive restoration is possible,
should Virginia be willing to sell its birthright in Williamsburg to
anyone? Is this not essentially a task for Virginians? And if they have
ceased to care, why carry through a pretense? Every relic of
Virginia's noble past should be sacredly guarded in Williamsburg
and elsewhere in the State. But the spectacle of the Old Dominion
huckstering off her ancient capital to an outsider, in order to get a
flivver imitation of departed glory, would bring a blush of shame to
the pale cheeks of her mighty shades."

Goodwin sent a five-page reply, complimenting the
editorialist on his skill and style and responding to his points. He
said Williamsburg had not offered itself for sale to anyone. "This
proposition, for better or for worse," he wrote, "originated in my
own dreams. In these dreams I have seen a city beautiful. Often,
however, as a result of what has transpired about me here, these
dreams have been turned into a nightmare." His proposition, he said,
did not envision the immediate purchase of the city's historic
houses. "As long as they are privately owned and preserved nothing
more is to be desired. My idea was to form a Colonial Holding
Corporation and to secure from the owners of these homes the right
to purchase, should the property at any time be forced upon the
market for sale."

Instead of wax figures, he was thinking of marbles and
bronzes. Goodwin "as a Southern man" deplored the lack of local
interest in preserving the homes of the past, and he faulted the
carelessness of the region in preserving historic documents and
records. "Because of these things northern scholars, with their
access to documents preserved in public libraries, have been
stimulated to write the history of this country from the northern
point of view."

From his Bruton restoration and his college endowment
work, Goodwin said, he knew how hard it was to raise funds for such
projects in the South, and he had been compelled to look elsewhere.
Anyway, he said, the land on which Ford lived had been part of
Virginia in the 18th century. "I trust that the Baltimore 'Sun,'" the
Doctor said, "will do what it can to help in the realization of this

hope. Now come to see me, and I will prove to you, on the spot, that my dreams have foundations in fact."

Goodwin sent a carbon of the letter and a clipping of the *Sun's* editorial to William Ford with another invitation to Henry Ford to come to Williamsburg. "My personal conviction is that the suggestion that it be preserved, restored, beautified, and transmitted as a city redeemed to be an inspiration to the future would appeal to any man possessed with a soul of patriotism and the means adequate to render large public service."

Goodwin may have thought that if the Fords got the negative review from him first, accompanied by his counter arguments, it might blunt the impact. There was nothing he could do to lessen the blow to his hopes that came with word of Barney's death on the 22nd. A third piece of bad news arrived a few days later; his summer church in Abingdon had burned.

He looked for things to encourage him. "Mr. Ford has not yet bought Williamsburg," Goodwin told a friend, "but Williamsburg and William and Mary College are getting a tremendous lot of good advertising and nobody knows what Henry Ford will do, not even Henry Ford himself. . . . At any rate it only cost two cents to write and tell him, and ask him to come to the rescue."

There still were other projects to pursue. He was thinking of establishing a parochial high school in Williamsburg to promote Christian education. More than ever, he believed "All education should be related to Spiritual development and the spiritual expression of human personality," and that "Learning without a Christ-like purpose is knowledge without either power or wisdom." Goodwin believed that "Some way must be found by which Religious Education can be more closely associated with all education and thus related to the ordinary process of life and of living.

"This is true because of the fact that religion does not consist primarily in simply knowing the facts about religion or about the great characters of religious life. It does not even consist in knowing the facts about the life of Christ. Religion is essentially life at its highest. It is the life more abundant. It is a power and inspiration, a vital spiritual influence which is designed and intended to enter into all of life's activities."

At home he was working up an autobiography for his family that he wanted to have finished by Christmas. Though the Doctor did much of it on his own, he turned to Hayes to help him complete it on time. When he had all the facts on paper, he wrote:

"Thus end the fragmentary notes which constitute a partially continuous record of some of my doings during a part of my pilgrimage down the narrow stream of time which lies between two eternal seas."

Nearly as soon as he got back to his office after the holidays, Goodwin wrote to William Ford, reminded him of the publicity generated for the restoration idea, and renewed the invitation to visit. Then he went about his other business.

The Doctor was trying to raise $200,000—twice what he had collected for Blow Gymnasium, or what Phi Beta Kappa was providing for Memorial Hall—from the American Bar Association for Pollard's law school. The second volume of the seminary history was done, but he was working on a second edition of *The Parish*. Ever the popular speaker, he was off January 19 to deliver a Robert E. Lee birthday speech to Confederate veterans at Stratford Hall, the general's birthplace.

Goodwin told his children: "You must learn all you can about Robert E. Lee. He was one of the greatest men that ever America produced, and perhaps the finest gentleman." In speeches such as these, Goodwin always identified himself as the son of a Confederate veteran and, like the postwar Lee, always preached reconciliation. "It is a gracious providence which makes time's soothing touch heal the scars which are inflicted in the conflict of life," he said in one address. "Bitterness like the mists of the morning, vanishes from the heart of the Free man as the clean light dawns upon the heart, and as men come to see that the things that make men brothers are more eternal than the things which for a time made them enemies. Around the old stumps of discord the honeysuckle twines itself, and the ugliness that once was is covered over with the sweet bloom of its flowery mantle."

Goodwin joined the efforts of Williamsburg boosters in the erection of a memorial plaque at Eastern State Hospital to mark it as the first public mental health institution in British America. On the tablet was inscribed the 1770 law that authorized its construction as The Public Hospital for Persons of Insane and Disordered Minds. Goodwin's chief contribution to the wording was seeing that the 18th-century term "ideot" was removed to spare the feelings of the hospital's current inmates.

February was nearly gone before Goodwin wrote again to Rockefeller. The Doctor spoke of the invitation he had made at the Phi Beta Kappa banquet, and he suggested Rockefeller come in early May. "You can bring your pocketbook, or leave it behind," he said. "We want the pleasure of having a visit from you. While you are here we could visit Jamestown and Yorktown, as well as seeing Williamsburg and the College of William and Mary."

Of more immediate concern to Goodwin was his health. Privately, he complained of neuritis in his left shoulder and mysterious outbreaks of blisters. The neuritis seemed to be a sign of age—he was 55—and the blisters turned out to be an allergy to a coal-tar-based stomach medicine prescribed by a Rochester physician.

Rockefeller replied March 6. He appreciated the invitation, wished he could accept, but could not. "Mrs. Rockefeller and I have long wanted to make a pilgrimage to this interesting and historic spot, but other plans and obligations already entered into for this spring will prevent our availing of your kind suggestion. Hoping some day to see your College, and with renewed thanks for your kind invitation, I am, Very sincerely . . ." Though the answer was still negative, it was for the first time personal.

Thanks to Ford's newspaper publicity, Goodwin's interest in Williamsburg's historic real estate was by now as well known as his restoration idea. Late in March came a letter from Marie Louise Stewart of Portsmouth asking his advice about a prime city property. "Through the death of my aunt, Mrs. Kate Slater of Williamsburg, the dwelling house on Duke of Gloucester Street commonly known as the old 'Paradise House,' has recently come into my possession," she said. "Perhaps you may remember a conversation we had about this house when we walked together down Duke of Gloucester Street about a fortnight ago? You very kindly offered to give me advice about selling the house and I remember that your idea was the same as my own: *i.e.* that the house should not be sold for any other purpose than a dwelling house.

"Now I wonder if you would be so very kind as to advise me as to the best way to advertise the house. . . . I should be so grateful for your advice before taking any definite steps as I have heard much of your keen interest in the beautifying of the old town, and the keeping up of its historic interest and I feel sure that like myself, you would not like to see the old house fall into the hands of someone who would not value it for its real worth."

It is difficult not to read between the lines of Stewart's inquiry and see an offer to sell the home—called today the Ludwell-Paradise House—to Ford at a price reflecting "its real worth." All Goodwin said in reply is that he couldn't suggest any advertising vehicle of which Stewart was not already aware.

If Rockefeller knew by now of Goodwin's plans to restore the city, he hadn't heard of it from the Doctor. All Goodwin had proposed to Rockefeller was the restoration of the three colonial campus buildings. But Goodwin was ready to give him a peek at a bigger picture, to share with Rockefeller a grab bag of the Doctor's pet projects. Chandler was pressing his fund raiser to get on the road again, and Goodwin planned a trip to New York the week of May 13 to call on such benefactors as William Rhinelander Stewart, R. Fulton Cutting, Jeremiah Milbank, Walter Case, George Gordon Battle, the Reverend Doctor Russell Davis, and Theodore H. Price, a Rockefeller acquaintance. He hoped to see Rockefeller, too.

The day before he left Williamsburg, Goodwin wrote to Rockefeller and asked for an opportunity to talk about William and Mary's hopes. Goodwin wanted as well to share some thoughts on how Southern colleges could help Southern African-Americans and, "further, to advise with you relative to working out a vital experiment in the relationship between the College and the religious life of the churches in the College center, and also with reference to the educational department and the College, and the educational life of the town in which the College is located."

There would, Goodwin said, be financial aspects to the conversation, "But it is not my purpose in asking for this interview, to ask you for money, but rather to intelligently interest you in William and Mary with a further view of anticipating your visit when we hope that you will come as our guest." If after such a visit, Rockefeller still believed there were better places for his philanthropy, Goodwin said he would not try to dissuade him. In closing, he dropped Harper Sibley's name.

A summons to 61 Broadway never came. Richardson wrote to Goodwin the day after the Doctor left New York and apologized for the delay, but said he couldn't have seen Rockefeller anyway. "We are sorry that Mr. Rockefeller does not feel that he can take up the study of the different college needs in this country," Richardson said.

"As you are quite aware, he tries to leave all these interests to be carefully considered and taken care of by the General Education Board which was established by his father."

If Rockefeller wouldn't come, William Ford did. He arrived the 23rd, bound for Charlotte and Atlanta by train. He'd arranged his itinerary to see Goodwin and his colonial village at last, and he brought Taylor with him. The Doctor showed them around the college and the community, pointing out historic sites and briefing Ford on their associations with great colonial Virginians. Ford caught some of Goodwin's enthusiasm. Taylor said that at the subsequent stops, Ford "was interviewed by newspaper men, and the thing that he talked the most about to the reporters, and also to me all through the week, was his visit last Sunday to Williamsburg. He was thoroughly impressed. . . . I feel sure that he is going to keep this matter in mind, and that great good will come from his visit some time in the future." Ford had run into Cornelius Vanderbilt in Atlanta and urged him to see Williamsburg, too.

A Goodwin letter chased them that argued the time had come when "unless something is done, the past will be wiped out by the cheap, tawdry, commercial present. This would be a distinct disaster." He spoke of the power of restorations to teach and said, "If this town could be secured as a whole, it could be converted into a visible school of history and historical associations." He hoped William would induce Henry Ford to come see for himself.

Ford's visit was the beginning of Goodwin's realization that the college's endowment drive and his hopes for the city's restoration might not be compatible. To Taylor, Goodwin confided an earnest hope "that the plan may be worked out embracing the whole town, whereas I am sure that Dr. Chandler's emphasis would be primarily upon the college, which is not the item in the program which would make the strongest appeal to Mr. Ford." He wanted to avoid bringing Chandler into the discussions for fear the president would make contradictory suggestions and create the impression "that we do not ourselves know what we want to do."

Goodwin believed what he said about the time having come to act. In July he took an option on two houses and a lot behind the Powder Horn to keep them out of the hands of developers. Two churches, a hospital, a pigsty, and a Toot-An-Kum-In Garage were among the 25 modern structures already crowding the octagonal tower. A year later he paid $1,000 for possession of the properties.

Goodwin returned to "the desecrated Williamsburg, from which the ancient glory and beauty had so largely departed." He complained about the blight of modern business on historic streets. Above are Owens Motors and the College Pharmacy on Duke of Gloucester Street; below is Williamsburg Motor on Francis Street.

In the meantime he persuaded the APVA to let him undertake the Powder Horn's restoration and to chair a committee to negotiate with the city council for control of a vacant municipal lot behind the building.

He persuaded the daily newspapers at Norfolk and Richmond to appeal for donations from their readers. The public's response was underwhelming. Goodwin wrote to Douglas Southall Freeman, editor of Bryan's *News-Leader*, "I cannot but feel that the attitude of our Virginia people towards this memorial is only too typical of their general apathy and actual indifference with reference to many of the symbols which still remain of an ancient and honored past." Though he redoubled his paper's efforts, Freeman collected just $130 in the next two weeks, "so little that we have not cared to announce the total."

Goodwin got better results that December in New York when, in behalf of the college, he made the keynote speech to the Virginia Society. He was pleased to say the endowment campaign had produced a men's dormitory, a women's dormitory, a gymnasium, a dining hall, and an auditorium. What it needed was money for the science hall to realize the General Education Board promise of matching funds. Goodwin called on society members individually, and he returned with a clutch of signed pledge cards.

Despite such year-end good fortune, the Goodwins' Christmas celebration was not so joyous as the last. Brother-in-law Clarence Repass had died, and Goodwin's sister Laeta and her daughter had to move from Wytheville to share the Goodwin home. Rutherfoord, after an experiment in lay preaching, gave up his aspirations to the ministry. He turned down an offer to head up a small industrial school in the Blue Ridge, returned in July to Rochester to work in an iron foundry, and then became a sportswriter for the *Times-Union*. The Doctor worried about the young man's fiscal responsibility. Ethel's father, John Clarke Howard, died December 6 at age 79 and was buried in Richmond's Hollywood Cemetery, a Confederate shrine. Hayes left a few days later for a visit to the north, and she was thinking again of finding another job.

Moreover, Goodwin realized he would need more detailed proposals for his restoration idea should Ford decide to act, but that he had no proper blueprint "nor the means to procure one."

Among Rockefeller's favorite Williamsburg sights was the ancient Great Oak at Bassett Hall, "a place to sit in silence and let the past speak to us."

Chapter Ten: **1926**

Williamsburg high school student Margaret Blackwell wrote to Goodwin that January to ask his opinion of their city. The Doctor mulled the question over and thought, as he often did, of its ghosts.

"My dear Margaret," he wrote, "If you have ever walked around Williamsburg late on a moonlight night, when most of the people who now live here are fast sleep, and felt the presence and companionship of the people who used to live here in the long gone years, and remembered the things that they did and the things that they stood for, and pictured them going into or coming out of the old houses in which they once lived, and remembered the things which they said in the House of Burgesses and at the old College—you would then know what an interesting place Williamsburg is. You would realize that it is about the most interesting place in America.

"There are thousands of cities in this country with Main Streets, but only one with a Duke of Gloucester Street like ours. There are many Protestant Churches, but none so long conspicuously in use as Bruton Parish. . . . when you walk around Williamsburg late on a moonlight night you can see the Indians on the Court Green, where they used to meet to make their treaties of peace . . . and you can see the agents of old Lord Dunmore, stealing the powder out of the Powder Horn, and you can hear the rattle of the horses' hoofs coming down the Richmond Road as Patrick Henry and the Hanover Volunteers ride on to Williamsburg and demand the powder be restored . . . .

"And so there are a lot of things that make Williamsburg interesting and there are a lot of things that make it uninteresting. We must cherish the interesting things, and try to get rid of the uninteresting things, in order that we may continue to have the most interesting old town in the country."

Rockefeller was interested in some haunted property in old Virginia, too. A dozen miles up the James from Jamestown, antique Brandon Plantation sits in swampy seclusion on a peninsula guarded by pine forests, cornfields, and a specter in a flowing white gown. Rockefeller was thinking of buying it.

The plantation's deed traced to a grant obtained circa 1616 by Captain John Martin, the buccaneer son of a London goldsmith. Martin died about 1632, the last survivor of Jamestown's founding. The place passed into the hands of three merchants, and in 1720 their heirs deeded the manor to the Nathaniel Harrisons. There in 1765 the Harrisons built a Palladian mansion on the farm in a design attributed to their friend Thomas Jefferson.

At the end of the 18th century, an inmate of the house, Jane Evelyn Harrison, 18, was murdered on her wedding day. A disappointed Williamsburg suitor, wedding guest Pierre Bondurant, poisoned her with the first champagne toast to the new couple's happiness. She died that night in a bedroom. By the time Bondurant's horse drew his carriage back to Williamsburg, the murderer was dead, too. Inexplicably, the bride's wedding ring was in his pocket. Jane's aunt Elizabeth Richard Harrison recovered the gold band and had it embedded in the plaster ceiling of her niece's room. Aunt Elizabeth was the first person to see Jane's white-robed ghost rise in the family graveyard and float into the mansion. A moment later, the plaster with the ring crashed to the floor. The ring now hangs from the ceiling by a wire, and the house is still haunted.

Early 20th-century historian Mary Stanard called Brandon "a place to dream in or dream about." W. Gordon Harrison's dream was to move off the remote estate, and he put it on the market. Rockefeller had by January 1925 paid him $5,000 for an option to buy and planned to look the place over in March, when he would visit Hampton Normal and Agricultural Institute about 35 miles east. As long as he was there, he thought he might stop to see Jamestown, Yorktown, and Williamsburg. He'd make it a family holiday and take his wife Abby and their sons Nelson, 27; Laurance, 16; Winthrop, 14; and David, 11.

General Samuel Chapman Armstrong of the Freedman's Bureau in 1868 founded private, all-black Hampton Institute, which counted among its graduates Booker T. Washington. John D.

Rockefeller, Jr.—whose father sponsored a Hampton scholarship in his name—had contributed to the school for 20 years. Philanthropic and religious agencies, as well as federal aid, also helped pay the Institute's bills, and in 1924 it launched a fund-raising drive among private individuals somewhat like William and Mary's. Hampton's principal, James E. Gregg, found opportunities for informal cooperation with the Williamsburg college in the cultivation of northern donors, and in 1925 the schools joined in showing a good time to touring students from the Rockefeller-funded International House at Columbia. Come April, Gregg planned to send Goodwin a party of Hampton Institute Anniversary guests for a look at the old Virginia capital.

The school, however, had been swept into the eye of a racial storm that threatened to damage its relationships with white institutions, and Gregg was holding a lightning rod. The problem centered on the Institute's Ogden Hall. Its public performances were open to all races, and the audiences were not segregated. No law required separation of blacks and whites in such places, only Jim Crow custom. But in Virginia that custom was ignored only at Ogden Hall. Walter Scott Copeland, editor and publisher of the *Daily Press* in Newport News, opened a vitriolic campaign against the practice and the Institute in 1925, after his wife Grace attended an Ogden Hall performance of the Denishawn Dancers in February. She was interested in eugenics, a racist and ersatz science dedicated to Anglo-Saxon gene-pool purity, and she was mortified by the Ogden Hall seating arrangements. Editor Copeland told *Daily Press* readers the Institute taught and practiced race-mixing social equality that would lead to "race amalgamation." Richmond's newspapers took up the campaign, and the eugenicist Anglo-Saxon Clubs beat the drums. Writers in the black press, including editor W. E. B. DuBois in Chicago, defended the Institute, which, of course, made its critics angrier.

Among others, Gregg consulted with William Howard Taft, president of Hampton's board of trustees and Chief Justice of the United States. Deciding on conciliation rather than capitulation, they hoped to ride out the debate. Gregg told editor Copeland the school had never encouraged interracial mingling "under circumstances which would lead to embarrassment on either side," and that he could not imagine "that any thoughtful person could advocate the amalgamation of widely diverse races." That satisfied few of the Institute's attackers, and counted for nothing after an

integrated audience attended an Ogden Hall chorale in November.
When the 1926 General Assembly session opened, Delegate
George Alvin Massenburg of Newport News submitted a bill
requiring racial segregation statewide in places of public assembly
and entertainment.

Taft and Gregg consulted, among others, Dr. James H.
Dillard of Charlottesville. Dillard was William and Mary's rector, a
top executive of two philanthropies devoted to black education, a
chairman of the General Education Board, and a Rockefeller
associate. The Institute's leadership saw no option better than
enlisting its friends among the philanthropies and the state's other
colleges in a campaign of reason and persuasion, recruiting some of
them to testify against the bill in legislative hearings.

When Massenburg's measure passed the lower house 63-3,
Goodwin told Taft, "I have always been intensely interested in the
negro and in the solution of the negro problem," but that "the human
fellowship is an evolutionary process. It may ultimately arrive at a
point in harmony with certain academic theories. It may not. We see
that future and the paths and processes which lead into it through a
darkened glass. In this instance it is darkened by prejudices which
are neither local nor sectional in their nature and character."

On March 9, the Senate approved the bill, 30-5, and Virginia
waited to see whether its new governor, Harry Flood Byrd, would
sign or veto. He might go either way; Byrd cared as little for the bill
as for antagonizing legislators.

Chandler and Goodwin learned a day or two before the
Senate vote—apparently from Dillard—that Rockefeller was
interested in seeing Williamsburg, its college, and the area's other
historic sites. They were delighted by the chance to cultivate a
prospect so wealthy, but the bill's passage raised ticklish questions.
Gregg put two of them to Chandler the day after the Senate vote.

First, he asked whether in view of the Massenburg bill it
would be embarrassing if Hampton's anniversary guests visited
William and Mary in April as planned. "Second," Gregg wanted to
know, "now that the bill has been passed does it seem to you likely
that there would be embarrassment either for you, or for us, or for
the Rockefellers in connection with their visit at the Institute and
their including a trip to Williamsburg as a part of their program? I
was glad to learn from Dr. Dillard last evening when talking with
him over the telephone that this idea of seeing the College of

William and Mary had already been under discussion by Mr. Rockefeller and himself. I was planning to take it up with you and am heartily pleased to know that Mr. Rockefeller is already interested and desirous of carrying it out."

Chandler asked Goodwin to telephone Gregg, and the Doctor obliged on the 12th, telling Gregg that William and Mary wanted the Rockefellers and the anniversary guests to come as scheduled. In a letter confirming the conversation, Goodwin wrote that he understood the Rockefellers were expected Saturday, March 27, in Hampton, would stay Sunday, and drive up with Gregg on Monday at 9 a.m. to see Williamsburg, Jamestown, and Yorktown. He hoped Rockefeller might address William and Mary's students. The college, moreover, would not only welcome the anniversary group but provide lunch. "We take it for granted that the party will be composed exclusively of white persons," Goodwin said. "It would otherwise occasion you grave embarrassment and criticism, which we would not be willing here at the College to bring about or be responsible for."

Gregg replied that he hadn't intended to send blacks to Williamsburg, but he doubted Rockefeller would care to call press attention to his visit by making a speech. He told the Doctor, "We appreciate gratefully your and Dr. Chandler's sharing with us the hospitality which we are all glad, I am sure, to show to our good friends from the North."

Goodwin acknowledged the letter and waited for the 29th. Reaction to Byrd's decision on the Massenburg bill had no impact on their plans. Five days before the Rockefellers reached Hampton, the governor allowed the Public Assemblage Act of 1926 to become law without his signature. Moreover, the Rockefellers made a low-key visit to Hampton that caused no adverse comment.

That Saturday, after consulting Dillard, Goodwin wrote to Gregg: "If you will telephone to me just as you are leaving Hampton, and give me some idea as to the time when you will reach the outskirts of Williamsburg, I will plan to meet you and your party down just in front of Bassett Hall—the house far back on the road on the left just as you enter Williamsburg after passing through the colored section, and just before you turn on to the Duke of Gloucester Street.

"This will enable me to show the party the points of historic interest on the way to the College, including Bruton Parish Church. It will also enable the party, after lunch, to go to Jamestown and drive straight from Jamestown to Yorktown . . . .

"So please 'phone me on Monday morning—at 150—about the time when you will reach the outskirts of Williamsburg. I will be there ten minutes in advance of the time which you name. Be on the look-out for me and pick me up."

The crowded, canvas-topped touring car pulled to the shoulder on York Street at the east end of town. Gregg may have handled the Doctor's introduction to Abby and the boys, or perhaps Rockefeller did the honors. With Goodwin as guide, the car growled away and turned at the second right.

The Doctor was taken with young David, but his mind was focused on Rockefeller and he described the occasion as if only he and Rockefeller were there. "I had the pleasure of showing him around the streets, through the public buildings, telling him about the Capitol, the Palace, Raleigh Tavern, and the homes and gardens of the city," Goodwin said. "His interest was awakened . . . ."

"We stopped at the Capitol site, at Bruton Parish Church and the Wren Building of the College, where Dr. Chandler joined us and was host at luncheon." Although Chandler had ordered Goodwin to find $68,000 in the first quarter, and allowed him to curtail his office hours to search for it, the Doctor did not ask Rockefeller for a contribution. He and Chandler thought it would be impolite to ask their guests—Gregg's guests, actually—for money.

Little David wanted some souvenir pictures, and the party stopped at Goodwin's office to pick up photographs of colonial Williamsburg buildings. The fuss Goodwin made over the boy stuck in Rockefeller's mind. After they had visited Jamestown and were motoring back to the college to drop the Doctor off, Rockefeller surprised Goodwin with an opportunity to sell his Williamsburg restoration idea, "in which, incidentally, I found that he himself was interested," Goodwin said. "It was in connection with the preservation of the old homes and points of historic interest in Williamsburg. Mr. Rockefeller was asking me about these homes and I mentioned to him the letter which I had written to Henry Ford. He immediately became interested and asked me just what plan I had in mind . . . and if there was any way by which the property could be kept in perpetuity. I did not feel free to tell him what my plan was as it would seem to open the question of the College endowment and this we decided we would not broach to him at all during his visit."

Rockefeller at first declined to undertake restoration of the College of William and Mary's Wren Building.

In another recollection of the moment, Goodwin said, "Our guest showed great interest in the history of Williamsburg and in the suggested thought that some means might be found for saving the Colonial buildings which remained and restoring those that had vanished. My heart was so full of appreciation of the priceless value of these historic shrines and my mind was so convinced as to the necessity of some immediate action to save them from despoliation and decay, that it was exceedingly hard at the time to be politely restrained in unfolding the long cherished dream without introducing the question of financial implications."

That Rockefeller expected to discuss the financial implications, the Doctor understood when he sidestepped the issue. Hayes said, "Dr. Goodwin, of course, had formulated such a plan, but he did not, at that time, feel he should present it." In fact, the Doctor still lacked the kind of blueprint needed for a detailed briefing of someone seriously interested in so large a project. Moreover, Goodwin said, "Mr. Rockefeller said that when a proposition was presented to a business man it should be clearly outlined and presented in a definite way." Goodwin wanted time.

He returned to his office elated with the conversation, while the tourists drove to Yorktown. That Thursday, the Rockefellers reached Richmond, boarded a riverboat, and steamed downstream to inspect Brandon. Rockefeller cared too little for what he saw of the plantation to pick up his option; and Robert W. Daniel later bought the place. Goodwin was anxious to make good on his new claim to the millionaire's attention. First he had to create a united front and turn the short-term-minded college president into a stay-the-course ally of a restoration proposal that didn't include his campus. Then there were the Fords to consider.

As far as the Doctor's records show, Goodwin had had no dealings with Detroit in ten months, but he still harbored hopes. Just as Rockefeller's interest seemed to be piqued by the mention of Henry Ford's name, the automaker's competitive spirit might be stoked if he knew of the oilman's visit. The Doctor wrote to Ford dealer William Mitchell of Norfolk, outlined the restoration idea and his dealings with the Fords, and asked Mitchell for help. "A few days ago," Goodwin said, "when Mr. John D. Rockefeller, Jr., was our guest here, he was deeply impressed with this opportunity. Now my hope is that something may be done to lead Mr. Ford in a perfectly natural way to find this place, and it has been suggested to me that you could doubtless bring this about by inducing Mr. Ford to visit Williamsburg with you."

Goodwin also asked Theodore Price in New York to bring up the College of William and Mary when Price next saw Rockefeller. The Doctor suggested Price mention saving Williamsburg's old houses and "my well thought out plan, which included securing these houses in connection with our Endowment Fund programme, as residences for College professors." Goodwin said, "I think he will be very much interested in this plan if I can have an opportunity, at some future time, to lay it all before him."

It was April 20 before Goodwin had Chandler's permission to make even a tentative and indirect approach to Rockefeller about the city's restoration. That day he wrote to Rector Dillard—in effect the college's chairman of the board—and shared with him for the first time the details of the restoration proposal, saying, "I have spoken to Dr. Chandler about it, and he says we should take no steps without consultation with you."

It occurred to Goodwin that Dillard or Gregg might explain to Rockefeller the cause of the Doctor's earlier reticence and tell him that "I did have a plan which had been suggested by Mr. J. Stewart Barney of New York which I should be most happy to explain to him." Goodwin would be prepared to present maps and other data "showing the whole scope of the idea."

His intent was not to ask Rockefeller to undertake the restoration "but simply to let him know exactly what I thought should be done to preserve these ancient materials in the atmosphere in which they stand." His plan included the Wren. "The fact that this building is associated with the College," he said, "is no reason why it should be excluded from the restoration and preservation plan visualized from the point of view of Williamsburg as the old Colonial capital."

He hoped Dillard might find a way to let Rockefeller "know the exact reason why I did not fully answer his questions on the occasion of his visit here." Goodwin asked Price to do the same, and to make a joke of his backwardness.

Meanwhile, Goodwin tried to put together a clearly outlined and definite proposition, as Rockefeller had put it, to present to the businessman. For one thing, he wanted a map to supplement his photographs. Chandler asked Charles Robinson of Bryan's Richmond *Times-Dispatch* to have someone prepare one to Goodwin's requirements, showing Williamsburg's streets and pinpointing the colonial houses. Goodwin wanted to designate which structures on Duke of Gloucester Street between Bruton Church and William and Mary should be removed—all except the Blair House—"to provide a dignified approach to the College." He would also delineate "the houses which should be acquired to protect the College property" along Jamestown and Richmond roads and the three colonial buildings in the College Yard. Goodwin said he could not go to see Rockefeller "without this plan as it will present the total scheme which we have in mind."

As Goodwin made his preparations, Rockefeller embarked on a similarly ambitious project at Jackson Hole, Wyoming, under circumstances that would prove strikingly similar to the Williamsburg enterprise. With the National Park Service's Horace Albright for a guide, he, his wife, and their three youngest sons visited the Teton Basin country near Wyoming's western border.

Albright and the National Park Service wanted to make a preserve of the wilderness acreage but couldn't afford it. The service approached the Whitneys, Morgans, and Vanderbilts—as Goodwin had the Fords—with the suggestion they purchase the land and hold it until the government was ready to buy them out, but the families considered the idea too ambitious. Albright hoped Rockefeller would take an interest, but he did not want to pressure his guest;

and, like Goodwin, he did not broach the subject directly during the philanthropist's visit.

When Rockefeller returned to New York, he asked Albright for maps. Albright brought section plats in person, but Rockefeller asked for bigger maps. He wanted to take on the whole project, not just pieces. To facilitate the acquisitions, he set up a corporation, the Snake River Land Company in Salt Lake City, and put Colonel Arthur A. Woods and Kenneth Chorley, a newer Rockefeller retainer, in charge. Rockefeller's involvement was kept secret to avoid driving up land values. Soon he acquired a home on the site, the JY Ranch, once a dude ranch.

Goodwin was also busy acquiring property—Williamsburg's Wythe House. Built about 1750, the two-story, hip-roofed, five-bay brick home stood on Palace Green, separated by a masonry wall from the Bruton Church graveyard. Builder Robert Taliaferro presented the house as a wedding gift to his daughter Elizabeth and her husband George Wythe. A William and Mary graduate and a lawyer, Wythe became a leading member of the House of Burgesses, served as mayor, and taught law to Thomas Jefferson, James Monroe, St. George Tucker, John Marshall, and Henry Clay. Wythe was delegate to two Continental Congresses, and he signed the Declaration of Independence. Washington made his headquarters in the Wythe House before besieging Yorktown.

In 1791, Wythe moved to Richmond, where he presided over Virginia's Court of Chancery. The Reverend James Madison, president of William and Mary—and a cousin of the fourth President—bought the house in 1792. It passed through at least five owners, a succession of renters, and decades of neglect. It was a tourist attraction during the 1881 Yorktown celebrations, and Mary King Sherwell acquired it for rental property in 1886. But 40 years later, it was vacant, nearly derelict, and, of course, haunted; and absentee-owner Sherwell was ready to sell. Goodwin said the house "was fast falling to decay and was being sought for purchase with the view of turning its spacious yard into a cemetery."

Enough of the Wythe House's appeal remained, nevertheless, to catch the eye of Boston architect William G. Perry. Shooting companion and Harvard classmate Arthur Derby telephoned Perry the second day of the new year and invited him on a motor trip to South Carolina in Derby's new Marmon. On the way back, they stopped in Williamsburg, boarded two days with Mrs.

Norvell Henley, Jr., and looked around. The Wythe, Perry said, "had been abandoned; its doors, front and rear, stood open and ajar, a window sash was missing but within, and in perfect condition, were the paneled shutters of the windows. Unfurnished and forlorn it appears to be awaiting—what? Destruction or reconstruction?" Goodwin's sister Laeta came in to see who was poking around, and told Perry that Goodwin wanted to buy the house and remodel it. But Perry didn't have a chance to meet the Doctor. He and Derby had to catch the train to Boston that day, leaving the Marmon beneath a tree at Mrs. Henley's.

A Norfolk church recruited Ruffin Jones, Bruton's rector, to be its minister; and Bishop Beverly Dandridge Tucker wanted Goodwin to fill the Bruton vacancy. Although he worried the job would conflict with his college duties, Goodwin accepted and would start officially in July. Jones told Goodwin that Sherwell wanted to sell the Wythe House and suggested its use as a parish house. Goodwin thought it would make a good place for a Sunday school, parish meetings, and student groups. Upstairs he would have a rector's office, and downstairs would be a historical exhibition. In back he would build a sun porch for an assembly room.

To acquire it, the Doctor persuaded Bruton's vestry to incorporate the Marshall Foundation, a device to allow the church to hold real estate in excess of the amount permitted the church's trustees under state law. He promised to raise the funds. Sherwell was asking $20,000, and he needed at least another $10,000 for renovations. Goodwin talked Sherwell down $5,000 and took out personal bank loans to hire contractor William J. Holland and his son Elton to begin work. Goodwin got most of the purchase price through Mrs. Walker R. Tuckerman of Bethesda, Maryland, and Mrs. W. E. Fendall of Washington, D. C., officers of the Society of Colonial Dames of America, Chapter III. "Dr. Goodwin," Hayes said, "had a genius for interesting in his projects the type of woman whose interests were broad and influential." The chapter threw a charity ball in Washington to raise money for the Wythe down payment and gave Williamsburg's Peninsula Bank and Trust a promissory note for the balance. The transfer was made in November. When all was said and done, the Colonial Dames provided $9,654.78. They walked away from an unpaid balance on the loan of $5,654.22 when Colonial Williamsburg became interested in the property. Mrs. John Rutherfoord of Washington, and New Rochelle, New York, contributed the remainder.

Goodwin asked R. T. H. Halsey, an authority on colonial homes and creator of the American Wing of the Metropolitan Museum in New York, for restoration advice. Taking up the study of colonial architecture at first hand, the Doctor toured colonial mansions on the Peninsula and ranged to Fredericksburg and beyond.

The Wythe renovations began before spring, and they may have been under way when the Rockefellers came in March. Recalling that day, Goodwin said Rockefeller "visited the Wythe House and saw what was being done to preserve and restore this ancient building . . . . The restoration of this house very strongly appealed to Mr. Rockefeller. It enabled us to point out to him the great advantage which would result if other old and historic houses in the city, fast falling to decay, could be rescued, preserved, and restored." It seems likely, however, that Goodwin's recollection was of a later Rockefeller tour.

While the Hollands worked at the Wythe House, Goodwin tended to college business. President Calvin Coolidge came May 15 to celebrate the 150th anniversary of the Virginia Resolves for Independence and accept an honorary degree. The ceremonies were broadcast, and Goodwin delivered the prayer. The Doctor was on the air again five days later when he shepherded a busload of college students to radio station WRVA in Richmond for a three-hour choral program, and delivered two speeches on William and Mary and its needs.

He was wondering if he needed to find a new secretary. Hayes, thinking of leaving, was gathering letters of recommendation and updating her resumé. For the present, she was helping Goodwin prepare a magazine story for the June issue of *National Republic* titled "Save the Historic Powder Horn." In it the Doctor invited readers to help preserve the building from collapse and secure three adjacent lots. Before summer was out, he agreed to superintend the work— which went to the Hollands—and conduct the transactions for the lots. He needed $2,900 for the land; and repairs ultimately cost $770.

It was May 23rd before Perry left Boston to meet Derby and recover the Marmon in Williamsburg. They boarded again with Henley. Goodwin appeared as they ate dinner and invited them to visit the Wythe House the next morning to see what he was doing. Derby's appendix, however, ruptured early the 25th and he was sent

to Richmond for surgery by Dr. Robert Coulter Bryan, brother of the
newspaper publisher.

"I met Dr. Goodwin later that day on the piazza of the Inn,
standing there on the historic ground of the Courthouse Green,"
Perry said later. "I can see him now in his tweeds, his black felt hat
and his ubiquitous pipe, which he was always lighting with a match,
seeming oblivious to the tobacco content; a keen man with startling,
intelligent eyes."

They walked to the Wythe House, where "the work that he had
initiated was under way." To Perry it was not restoration but "repair and
renovation for representation of the original suited to new uses."

"As we went in I said, 'Doctor, you've got a great many doors
here. I've noticed the doors, and on them are the marks of the old
rimlocks that you haven't got any more. Do you mind if I take the
dimensions of these locks?'" For 20 years, Perry had been collecting
old locks and their keys, which he kept at home in a barrel.

"On the way downstairs he said, 'We don't know how to
terminate the cornice at this point.' The front hall had never had a
cornice, but here was the cornice. 'How do we terminate it?' I had a
piece of chalk in my hand and I said, 'This way, I should suppose.' To
me it seemed to be one of the most simple things in the world. To
him it was a miracle."

Perry took measurements and outlines of all the locks and,
when he reached Boston, sent ten of his, with keys, for repair to
colonial hardware specialist W. C. Vaughan in Haymarket Square. It
was August before Vaughan telephoned Perry to say they were
ready. Perry told him to ship the lot to Williamsburg and wrote a
letter to tell Goodwin what they were and where they went.

Goodwin returned to Bruton's pulpit July 1, more than three
years after his return to Williamsburg. Chandler agreed to cut his
teaching hours by half, with a corresponding reduction in salary, to
give him time for the church. The Doctor had now three
occupations—professor, fund raiser, and rector—and carried his
restoration dream into all of them.

Cousin Mary Goodwin remembered that "after he became
rector of the church he would very often refer to the 'old city' in his
sermons." He was as apt to talk about Williamsburg's houses,
furnishings, and decorations, as about salvation from sin. "He did

this so frequently that an old lady in town who very much resented the Restoration, and was a personal friend of ours who felt she could say anything, told him one day, 'Well are you going to preach the Gospel tomorrow or are you going to preach about wall paper? If you are going to preach about wall paper, I'm not coming to church.' He was so full of Williamsburg he couldn't keep it out of his sermons." The sermons were, at least, brief. Rutherfoord said his father was an "oratorical humanitarian" who kept his discourses to 20 minutes, timing them with a silver pocketwatch. Ethel sat with Howard on a front pew, and carried a white silk handkerchief to wave if the Doctor went on too long.

William H. Baker became Goodwin's sexton, Hayes served as the rector's secretary, and for his curate he hired the Reverend John B. Bentley, a William and Mary graduate from Hampton recently returned from Alaskan missionary work. The Doctor needed all the help he could get. He was still looking after Grace Church at Yorktown, the chapel at Toano, and had begun conducting services at the Yorktown Navy base. With Bruton came the appointment as dean of the Jamestown pro-cathedral—the Robert Hunt Shrine and the memorial church—"which" he said, "is the oldest ecclesiastic position in America." The Jamestown "congregation consists entirely of tourists," he wrote. "The only human responsibility which rests upon me is the care of one lone man who acts as superintendent of the island." But Chandler expected him to pursue college fund raising as vigorously as ever, and Goodwin had to find someone to take his classes "when I am sent by the High and Mighty Potentate of the College on trips away from the institution in search of the nimble dollar."

Goodwin may still have been irritated that Chandler had required the now full-time clergyman to give up his state-provided Wren office. On the job, Goodwin was respectful of the president and, despite differences in temperament, they got on well. But Chandler could be prickly. Fannie Lou Stryker, who started work at William and Mary in 1919, said, "You might call the experience that Dr. Chandler brought to the college explosive at times, because he would fire people one day and feel sorry for them and take them back the next." She thought he became more volatile as the years wore on. The Morecock Sisters thought "he was a little bit disturbed about his job," and "probably not as tactful as he might have been." Agnes said, "he just went a little bit too far, lots of times."

Soon after Goodwin's arrival, Chandler's wife died, leaving him to raise four sons. Hayes said that "without a wife to smooth his social contacts President Chandler was seldom relaxed. 'Jac' Chandler's peppery disposition was famous at the college among both the faculty and the students, and because of it he was sometimes misunderstood, becoming the target, even, of an impassioned kind of criticism. If one wanted to compare the personalities of these two men, he would find the contrast between them in their methods of smoking. Whereas Dr. Goodwin puffed slowly at this pipe, reflectively, that is, and in a manner suggesting patience and control, Dr. Chandler's quick, nervous impatient chewing of his cigar gave the impression of an Air Force general ready to take off with his squadron of bombers."

No one, however, ever doubted Chandler's dedication to the school, and when Goodwin differed with his boss, he was forthright. "'Jac Chandler,' he would say, shaking his pipe in emphasis, 'you don't think big enough,'" Hayes wrote. "Then he would go on to reiterate his belief that to a man of large means the college should not hesitate to present an ambitious plan."

Goodwin got the chance to demonstrate what he meant when a letter arrived in early September from Colonel Arthur A. Woods.

Dillard had finally forwarded the Doctor's request for an interview. Rockefeller, Woods said, "has sent the letter to me with the suggestion that you might be willing to see me, so that I could take the matter up with him at a later date." He invited Goodwin to call when next in New York. Goodwin replied that he would give himself the pleasure sometime in October, but he procrastinated. The Powder Horn and Wythe House restorations had further persuaded Goodwin, if he needed it, of his need for outside assistance in the city's restoration. But though the Doctor went out of town for about a week on October 9, he did not call on Woods, nor did he contact the Fords.

When he got home, Goodwin wrote to Washington journalist Rhys James suggesting a newspaper story to be headlined, "Dead Virginians With Live Ancestors." The Doctor said, "I am entirely unable to understand the apathy, the irresponsiveness, combined with the complacency and pride, which characterizes the average Virginian with reference to our historic memorials. Something

certainly needs to be done to rouse them to some sense of
responsibility. Perhaps the first thing that needs to be done is to
make nine-tenths of them mad. You might be able to do this. I have
tried to, but seem not to have succeeded." But still he did not make
an appointment with Woods.

Hayes said Goodwin was organizing his presentation,
"thinking through any objections which might be raised. . . and in
forming his resolve to base his plea on the value of a restoration of
Williamsburg as a great teaching center." Perhaps the Doctor was
holding out for Rockefeller, or perhaps he wanted to be as prepared
for Woods as he could be. After his ill-fated first call at Rockefeller
headquarters in 1924, Goodwin said "it is terribly hard, when one
makes a wrong approach to a very busy man, to undo the error. It is
not because of a diminished faith in the man approached, but
because of diminished faith in oneself." Not until the morning of
Wednesday, November 24, three days before Rockefeller was due in
Williamsburg for the dedication of Phi Beta Kappa Memorial Hall,
did Goodwin appear at 61 Broadway. He wore one of his dark
weekday civilian suits and his oversize gold Phi Beta Kappa key. He
delivered a detailed narrative of the early history of Virginia and
Williamsburg, and he outlined the possibilities of using the city's
colonial buildings for education. He showed his map and
photographs, and suggested the preservation of the remaining 18th-
century homes, the restoration of the original college building, and
the reconstruction of the Palace, the Capitol, and the Raleigh.

Woods listened carefully, asked questions, studied the map
and the pictures, and expressed his personal interest, but he was, as
Hayes said, "entirely noncommittal." Goodwin told her he doubted
he had made the best use of his opportunity.

The Memorial Hall observances began in the auditorium
Saturday morning at 10:30 with a procession of dignitaries and
dedicatory speeches full of high-blown sentiments and patriotic
allusions, followed by an afternoon tour of Williamsburg. Rockefeller
and Goodwin rode in a chauffeured limousine lent by Judge Robert
M. Hughes of Norfolk, passing the Blair House and stopping at
Bruton and the Wythe, where work was still going on. Goodwin gave
him a printed sheet of facts on the house and its history; and he
introduced George Parsons, the African-American caretaker, as "a
saint." Rockefeller said he had always wanted to shake hands with a
saint and clasped his hand. Parsons pulled some discarded hand-

wrought nails from his pocket and gave them to the millionaire. Rockefeller said he would give them to his sons for mementos.

The preacher and his patron motored on through the city to Bassett Hall and walked into the woods past a gargantuan oak, a towering tree that had been a sapling when Columbus sailed. As they left, Rockefeller said, "If I come back some day, can we bring our lunch and eat it under the oak tree?" He would remember it as "a place to sit in silence and let the past speak to us."

Goodwin said, "We talked of the educational value which would come from the perpetual preservation of the buildings and the colonial greens. Then Mr. Rockefeller suggested that we walk over the ground which we had ridden over, in order to see the houses more closely and to get up an appetite for dinner." Then, by some accounts, Rockefeller asked to wander alone, to get a better grasp of the possibilities.

There was more speechmaking that night at the 6:30 Phi Beta Kappa banquet in the college refectory. Goodwin wrote that all that was said that evening was not said to the audience. "Mr. Rockefeller, next to whom I was seated, filled with the suppressed desire to recall the restoration thought, finally asked me if any further consideration had been given to the restoration idea." Hayes said, "At no time had Dr. Goodwin asked Mr. Rockefeller for money. His appeal was not for money, but to enlist interest—because, as Dr. Goodwin said, 'when interest has been aroused the gift of money becomes a spontaneous and consequent expression of this interest, which was sure to result in a deeper personal satisfaction to the giver.'"

Before the dinner ended, Rockefeller said he would commission sketches visualizing the restoration of Williamsburg and preliminary drawings showing the Wren's restoration, and he gave Goodwin the job of finding an architect. "He said that the offer represented his entire present interest," Goodwin wrote, "and that it must be understood that it should not be taken as giving any expectation or promise of further cooperation on his part." Rockefeller said his role had to be confidential, and Goodwin must for now keep from Chandler Rockefeller's interest in the Wren.

He also asked Goodwin about the status of the Wythe House, the Blair House, and the Powder Magazine, and two days later the Doctor sent him a letter detailing it all. Goodwin began by mentioning the pleasure Rockefeller's visit had given him, and asking him to return with Abby. Earlier that day, Goodwin said, he

had run into Thomas Tallmadge, a Chicago architect renowned for
his colonial expertise, in front of the Wythe. Tallmadge startled him
by proposing the restoration of the Palace and Courthouse greens,
and Goodwin offered him a month's room and board if he would
draw up the plans. They left it at that.

Goodwin told Rockefeller he was personally liable on the
Wythe House for $15,892 beyond what the Colonial Dames had
contributed. The college owed $6,000 on the Blair House, and
Goodwin still owed $1,000 on the Powder Horn lots.

"You have given me a lot to think about," Goodwin said. "But
I expect to get the major part of my rest for the next few months by
prowling around, thinking about how the 'City Beautiful' might be
built. I am convinced that from the historic point of view this is the
greatest teaching opportunity which exists in America." Hayes
would make new pictures, he said, and Lyon G. Tyler would
assemble information on each historical house.

"In the meantime I wish you would buy Bassett Hall for
yourself. It would give you a charming vantage point from which to
play with the vision and dream which you see, and it might give me
the joy of being your 'playmate' in this dreamland playground. Don't
forget to mention me to David."

Rockefeller was writing to Goodwin the same day; and on
December 2 a envelope from Room 2000 at 26 Broadway and
addressed to the college was delivered to Bentley's rectory, where
the Doctor was keeping an office. It contained two letters. One put
on paper their banquet conversation about the Wren, the other
asked for further and more detailed information. Rockefeller said
the interior of the Wren was so disjointed that he wasn't presently
interested in spending the $250,000 Goodwin thought its restoration
would require. But he agreed to provide anonymously up to $10,000
for a study of the Wren's rehabilitation on the condition that
Goodwin would not tell Chandler where the money came from and
mistake cooperation for commitment.

The second letter asked for a complete set of photographs
of every house to be restored, a sheet of historical facts on each, an
assessment of the relative importance of their acquisition, a memo
on which owners might be anxious to sell, and the financial facts on
sites Goodwin "had tied up or gotten a hold on."

Rockefeller wanted to concentrate on assembling material
around the Capitol neighborhood and the Palace green. Historic

houses from other parts of town, he thought, might be moved to those locations, but "any effort to reproduce the conditions as they existed along the main street leading to the College would be quite impossible, except where the two centres above mentioned abut the main street." He was not interested in buying isolated houses for the use of the college's professors unless they were part of these centers.

"As I said to you, this proposition would not interest me unless some complete thing could be done and so tied up with the University and its historical department as to insure not only its permanent maintenance but its permanent use as a centre for the study of American history. I feel clearly that the University is naturally by far the best organization to which such an enterprise should be attached and by which it should be maintained and operated, availing, of course, of such outside cooperation in development and management as might be deemed wise and advantageous." That afternoon Goodwin wrote two letters in reply, agreeing to everything.

Rockefeller wrote Goodwin the same day, asking for more details on the Wythe House, Powder Horn, and Blair House finances and pledging to match every dollar the Doctor raised to renovate the Wythe House. Thus Rockefeller made his first investment in a historic Williamsburg property, Bruton's parish house.

That Friday, Goodwin ran into real estate man Gardiner T. Brooks. He seems to have come away with a confused understanding of the status of the Paradise House, the home Marie Louise Stewart had been trying to sell for nearly two years. Goodwin told Rockefeller the next day that Stewart had cabled the agent to sell the house for $8,000. Brooks was willing to give Goodwin an option, "as far as he could control the sale," for ten days, but "he could not guarantee that it would not be sold by the owner." The Doctor was sending a snapshot and notes on the house. He thought the price was exceedingly low, "and that it would cost a great deal more if we had to buy it back after it was purchased by someone else." If nothing came of their plans, he said, Rockefeller could put it back on the market at little loss. "I am writing because I felt that it was only fair to share with you the information which has come to me in this matter," Goodwin said. In a postscript, he told Rockefeller that the cable in question had been sent two months before, and that the price did not include the house's new $598 roof. He also said, "Some Washington people have been negotiating this purchase."

Rockefeller bought the Paradise House—his first outright Williamsburg purchase—for the College of William and Mary in 1926.

Goodwin next drafted a memorandum titled "Suggestion as to Emergency Purchase of Property," prepared in case Rockefeller "should desire to make emergency purchases when, as in this instance, Colonial property comes suddenly upon the market" while the restoration was still being studied. Goodwin proposed he be "authorized to take title giving you, in advance, a written statement and agreement that all property purchased by me in the city of Williamsburg subsequent to December 1, 1926, and deeded to me, would, unless explicitly other wise stated, be subject to transfer to you or party or parties designated by you upon your written request. This agreement would be known only to you and to myself."

Goodwin conducted services that weekend. While waiting for a reply on the Paradise, he wrote to Blow asking for a contribution to his Grace Church restoration. He must have received Rockefeller's letter containing the Wythe House pledge that Monday. "It is an unspeakable delight to me," Goodwin wrote that day, "that, through your kind offer of cooperation, I now see my way out of this responsibility and will be more free for other things, especially the things in which you are also interested." He included a breakdown of financial details about the Wythe, told Rockefeller the renovation cost had already risen $3,200, and that the bill now totaled $30,520.15. He needed $14,532 more, and he thought the kitchen house should be rebuilt as well. Goodwin promised additional information soon about the Blair and the Powder Horn, and he prepared to leave town the next day.

It looks as if Goodwin was in Washington when Rockefeller

Rockefeller approved purchase of the antique Paradise House for $8,000 with this wire.

wired him about the Paradise. Timed 11:28 a.m. that Tuesday,* the telegram read: "AUTHORIZE PURCHASE OF ANTIQUE REFERRED TO IN YOUR LONG LETTER OF DECEMBER FOURTH AT EIGHT ON BASIS OUTLINED IN SHORTER LETTER SAME DATE." It was signed, "DAVIDS FATHER." Thus Rockefeller made his second investment in Williamsburg real estate, buying outright his first house for William and Mary. Perhaps Hayes relayed the word to Goodwin in the capital. There is no record of the Doctor's response in his, Rockefeller's, or Hayes's files, then or later, which suggests he replied on the road.

The emergency purchase arrangement became the standard operating property acquisition procedure in the buying program that followed—as did the use of the David's father code name. "During the first 18 months of the restoration," Goodwin said, "it was necessary that all of the work of the restoration in Williamsburg should be confined to my office. The name of the donor was not known. Every possible effort was being made by newspapers and others to learn from me and from my secretary the name of the person responsible for the purchase of this property. In order to conceal the identity of

---

* Sexton Baker, in a Colonial Williamsburg oral history recorded and transcribed in June 1952 by Parke Rouse, said "the telegram came" while Goodwin sat in the Page section of Bruton's graveyard on a Sunday afternoon. Baker said Goodwin "came out there right often" and was "looking down on the ground when that telegram came," and he said, "This is what I was waiting for. I want you to be with me in this thing." Baker, however, couldn't recall the wire's contents. Rockefeller's wire is dated December 7, a Tuesday, and Goodwin was in Williamsburg the 9th, a Thursday. It seems unlikely the telegram did not catch up to Goodwin until the afternoon of Sunday the 12th. In any case, there was as yet no "thing" for anyone to be in with him, and Baker's recollection makes more inexplicable the lack of any record in Goodwin's files and Hayes's memoirs of Goodwin's answer. It may be that Baker was speaking of another telegram or that, nearly 26 years later, he was mistaken.

the donor, envelopes were often addressed to men of wealth and left in conspicuous places upon my office desk and table. In consequence thereof reports were circulated the restoration was being done by Mr. Henry Ford, by Mr. Cornelius Vanderbilt, by Mr. J. Pierpont Morgan and by every other man in America who was supposed to have enough money to buy all this property. The name of Mr. Rockefeller was, however, never revealed. His name did not appear at all in my letter files. During this period he was known in telegrams and in correspondence as Mr. David."

By the time Goodwin got back to Williamsburg, apparently on the 9th, Rockefeller was writing again about the Wythe. First he pointed out a 25-cent error in Goodwin's addition of the costs—it was in Goodwin's favor—then told the Doctor he would give a lump sum $10,000, or $2,734 more than the value of his offer of the 2nd, to help relieve Goodwin of his personal obligations on the property. Goodwin, of course, accepted the change, and Rockefeller mailed the check four days later. In turn, Goodwin was writing to Rockefeller to say there was no hurry about the Powder Horn but recommending they purchase another nearby lot behind Dr. Bell's hospital on Market Square.

Then he sent Bentley to the college library to have the "Frenchman's Map" copied. Goodwin shot more pictures of the houses, using a blueprint of the town as a key to locating historic structures that could be moved into the "historic teaching centers." He told Rockefeller he might be prepared to brief him by January 15 or perhaps a little later. He had already contacted two architects, but he was somewhat hamstrung by his inability to share the secret of Rockefeller's involvement. His first choice was Tallmadge, who was too busy working on a book; his second, Charles Allerton Coolidge, recommended the Boston firm Perry, Shaw and Hepburn. Perry was William G. Perry, whom Goodwin well remembered.

Ten days before Christmas the Doctor paused to write to Rockefeller: "Your very kind letter, with check for ten thousand dollars ($10,000), enclosed, for the Wythe House restoration was received this morning. The generous contribution on your part entirely cancels every promise in full which you have been good enough to make in connection with the Wythe House restoration. It is gratefully received." Goodwin told him he had used the money to pay off the notes for the restoration, and he said, "I look forward with pleasure to the day when I may have the privilege of going with you into the Wythe House restored and beautified."

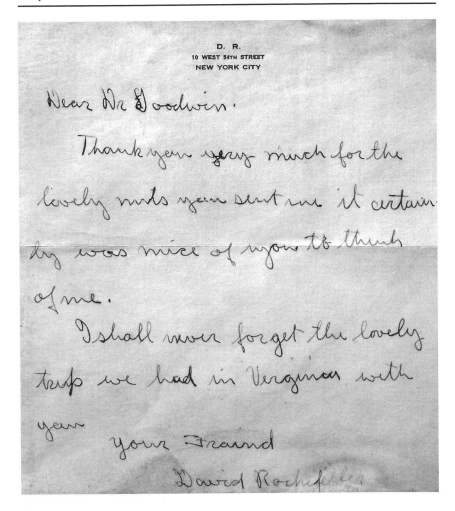

D. R.
10 WEST 54TH STREET
NEW YORK CITY

Dear Dr Goodwin.

Thank you very much for the
lovely nuts you sent me it certainly was nice of you to think
of me.

I shall never forget the lovely
trip we had in Verginia with
you.
                Your Freind
                    David Rockefeller

Eleven-year-old David Rockefeller sent Goodwin a handwritten thank you for a 1926 Christmas Gift.

Then he shipped to David's father a Christmas box of holly, mistletoe, and running cedar from the Williamsburg woods, and to young David a box of nuts. David's reply read: "Dear Dr Goodwin: Thank you very much for the lovely nuts you sent me it certainly was nice of you to think of me. I shall never forget the lovely trip we had in Verginia with you. Your Freind David Rockefeller." David's father said, "I have thought many times of that marvelous oak tree you took me to see and of the fall woods into which we looked. What a wonderful picture it was."

Goodwin had a genius for interesting in his projects women of means and
influence. Among them was Edith Tuckerman, chairman of the Wythe House Fund,
with whom he posed at a Washington charity ball in 1927.

Chapter Eleven: **1927**

In the deserted hours of a January night, a solitary figure hurried through Courthouse Square in the half-light of a full moon. It was still and eerie. He heard the murmurs of a small knot of men standing in the shadows like a crew of Goodwin's ghosts. One held a lantern, another a sword. Less than 50 wary feet from them, his eye caught the glint of something snaking along the frozen ground at his feet. It gave a jerk, and shot away in a shiny thin ribbon underlined by a clattering sort of metallic hiss. With a terrified shout, he hurdled the serpent, landed in full sprint, and dashed into the dark, as if the devil himself was in pursuit. All that followed him, however, was the laughter of the band of skulkers—as soon as they understood what had happened.

The skittish passerby had bumbled upon five fellows surreptitiously measuring Williamsburg, foot by historic foot. One of them was rewinding a steel surveyor's tape—the viper that scared him. Another, either college student Wilfred Files or classmate Upton Thomas, was using the sword, a World War I relic, to anchor one end in the soil. Goodwin commanded the squad, directing its operations by referring now and again to a copy of the "Frenchman's Map." His curate Bentley had the William and Mary library trace the chart, so they could compare what was on the ground in 1927 with what had been there 145 years earlier. The fifth member of the outfit was architect William G. Perry.

Goodwin had summoned Perry from Boston to join in a study of the preservation and restoration of "the most interesting and historic characteristics of old Williamsburg." When that was done, he wanted sketches of restorations of the Wren Building, Palace Green, Courthouse Green, Market Square, Capitol Square, and part of Duke of Gloucester Street. The Doctor made it sound all very speculative, something that might interest someone someday in some sort of restoration project. But he wanted the survey done before he left on a February fund-raising trip. Perry telegraphed acceptance immediately.

Another nasty illness forced Goodwin into a bed New Year's day. It was six months before he felt himself again, but he was already deep in restoration research. His sickroom was stocked with historical journals, and he pored over the pages for glimpses of 18th-century Williamsburg. Hayes spent her Christmas vacation in Washington at the Library of Congress studying ancient copies of Williamsburg's *Virginia Gazette*. Lyon G. Tyler, who wrote *Williamsburg—The Old Colonial Capital* in 1907, became their advisor. Goodwin was still very sick January 11 when he dictated a letter to Rockefeller about the fruits of the studies. They had found maps, turned up descriptions of the Palace, had nailed down its location, and found signs of its terraces. They also had a description and drawing of the Raleigh, and much more. The Doctor had tried to recruit Tallmadge but settled on Perry, who, he soon concluded, was the better man for the job anyway. For the first time, Goodwin used the proper noun Colonial Williamsburg Restoration.

Perry arrived two days later, took a room in the Doctor's home, and began to examine the city and the college. He needed dimensions, but Goodwin worried about attracting attention—hence the wee-hours sorties. Ethel said, "I was charmed by the night surveying parties. I think only four people in town knew what was going on and who was behind it." Actually, there were three—herself, her husband, and Hayes. Rutherfoord would join the circle later. Goodwin said other folks thought he and Perry were maniacs or demon-possessed. When anyone asked, he said he was preparing a tourist map to the historic sites and buildings. By the 19th, they had measured from Bruton to the Paradise House, all of Courthouse Green, part of Palace Green, and plotted the houses.

During the daytime, they took snapshots, donned old clothes, and, as Hayes said, "fought cobwebs in the caverns under the Wren Building." Airplanes from the Army's Langely Field near Hampton circled the city making aerial pictures for a photo mosaic—something Goodwin arranged with the colonel in command. The Doctor kept Rockefeller abreast of everything and told him, "I wish you could be here and have some of the real fun that I am getting out of what we are doing."

Perry gave 14 days to his surveys. The day before he left, Goodwin, on Rockefeller's instructions, hired him for $2,500, expenses for blueprints and drafting inclusive, to execute studies and preliminary sketches. To the list of architectural conceptions, the Doctor added a stretch of colonial homes on Francis Street that he intended for a link to the Capitol. The deadline was May. Goodwin made no other promises.

Rockefeller said that was wise. He also thought Goodwin was prudent to relay Rockefeller's mail through Gumbel to avoid tipping off the Williamsburg post office that he was corresponding personally with the philanthropist. Mr. David still was committed to no more than financing studies of Goodwin's ideas.

Nevertheless, he was increasingly ready to take risks with just-in-case acquisitions. His office found a fault in the Paradise deed and held up Goodwin's purchase, but Rockefeller decided to chance a clouded title and directed him to go ahead. Moreover, he was pushing Goodwin to acquire a Market Square lot behind the hospital before the owners built a garage on it, and he wondered if the hospital itself might be purchased. Originally a courthouse, the building dominated a strategic corner. Goodwin approached the owners and came away with an offer to sell for $14,500, if the buyer would move the building to the college or an equally advantageous site. Mr. David thought that could be done, but given the tentative state of things and the complication, he decided it could wait. "I only wish," he said, "the problem of the church on the other side were as easy of solution as the problem of the hospital."

Rather than submit piecemeal the sketches, reports, documents, and photographs he was assembling, Goodwin proposed a comprehensive presentation, and Rockefeller concurred. Another trip to the South gave them the opportunity. Mr. David and his wife Abby traveled to his father's Ormond Beach, Florida, estate in March. Rockefeller wrote Goodwin on the 24th that they planned to stop in Williamsburg on their way home. They would arrive May 21 from Atlanta and asked Goodwin to reserve Memorial Hall guest rooms. Their call could be explained by saying Abby wanted to see the Phi Beta Kappa building. "That any other significance should be attached to our visit would be obviously unwise," he said. "A day or two of rest and freedom in the beautiful environment of Williamsburg would be a real treat to both of us."

Goodwin alerted Chandler and pressed Perry. The architect

sent preliminary drawings of the Wren Building; sketches of an inn
proposed for the foot of Palace Green south of Duke of Gloucester
were already in hand. Chandler got a look at the Wren sketch and
was pleased, but Goodwin kept him in the dark. He told Perry he
had to have the other sketches May 15 to show important visitors he
did not name.

By now Goodwin had noticed the potential for conflict
between restoration pursuits and his renewed obligations to Bruton
and its parish. But he said he developed "a personal conviction
which grew more and more compelling as the work began to take
over ever increasing measure of time from other duties. It was
evident that if the restoration work was exclusively or even chiefly a
material enterprise, justification could not be found for my doing
this work while continuing to hold official connection with Bruton
Parish Church. The conviction grew, however, with ever-increasing
strength that the restoration was not primarily a material enterprise
but rather an undertaking fraught with deep spiritual significance.
        "It seemed, therefore, that the thought and time I might give
to the endeavor was and would continue to be an extension of
spiritual responsibility and ministry. It was further felt that the work
accomplished would enable Bruton Parish to exert a wider influence
and that people, drawn by the restoration of Williamsburg, would
receive impressions which would enrich their lives in deep and far
reaching ways. In this conviction I was confirmed by the opinion of
those who in the Church had authority over me."

The architect soon sent aerial color perspectives "of the
House of Burgesses Green restored" and likewise of the Palace and
Courthouse greens, along with scale drawings. He had begun
perspectives of the Capitol itself and the Wren, and he hoped to have
them to Williamsburg in time. Hayes said the Doctor admired Perry's
"complete lack of any expressed curiosity" about whom they were for.
        Goodwin and the Colonial Dames dedicated the Wythe
House restoration May 10. Nine of the keys to the ten locks Perry
had provided were stolen that day. Goodwin had to make a quick
trip out of town and leave unopened Perry's boxes of drawings, but
he rushed back to prepare for the Rockefellers' visit.

The first Williamsburg house in which Rockefeller invested, the Wythe, was where Goodwin first showed him detailed plans of the city's restoration.

He and Hayes spent the night of the 20th in his new Wythe study—the northeast room on the second floor—setting out sketches, blueprints, historical notes, and reference citations. Hayes contributed a notebook history of the city and of each colonial house, indicating each dwelling's condition and the chance of sale. "Everything possible had been done to make the display clear and attractive," she said. "At seven-thirty o'clock at night the office door was locked, to be reopened upon the arrival of the Rockefellers."

They arrived Saturday on the 9:58 a.m. train. Goodwin and Chandler escorted them from the station to their rooms, and the Doctor conducted the couple to the Wythe for a tour. They pulled chairs up to a table to examine Perry's handiwork and strolled out with the Doctor and his secretary. The party took a turn around Palace Green, stopped at the Tucker House garden, walked down Nicholson Street and up Queen between the Colonial Inn and the Paradise, then along Duke of Gloucester back to the Wythe. "Dr. Goodwin spoke in a low voice," Hayes said, "pointed out the places of interest, and Mr. and Mrs. Rockefeller asked many questions." They lunched with Chandler at the college, and Mr. David and the Doctor returned to the Wythe to get down to business. They talked into the night.

Goodwin told Rockefeller that college fund-raising
obligations required most of his time for the following six months.
Rockefeller said he had reached no conclusion about the plan,
anyway, which now envisioned restoration of the Palace Green and
Capitol areas, with a connecting link on Duke of Gloucester Street.
They composed an agenda.

The Doctor was to secure from the APVA an exclusive five-
year right to reconstruct the Capitol on its original site, in which
event the property would be deeded to the college forever.
Goodwin thought he could arrange that with John Stewart Bryan's
help. Rockefeller authorized him to buy a lot across from the
Capitol to prevent the building of yet another garage. He could have
the Paradise reroofed, and say that interested friends had
purchased the place with the intention of deeding it to the college
for a professor's residence. He could say similar purchases were
contemplated at fair prices.

Goodwin was to buy the proposed inn lot with two dwellings
on the parcel, three stores on one side, three houses on another, and
the area behind extending to Francis Street. He was also to buy the
Colonial Inn and hire the innkeeper, purchase F. Van Garrett's
house—today's Coke-Garrett House—and acquire properties on the
north side of Francis. He could pay the $14,500 for the hospital and
have it moved. If necessary, Goodwin could buy any house or lot in
the three areas to be restored to protect them from imminent sale to
others. He could also purchase properties along Duke of Gloucester
Street near the college to protect them, too, though Rockefeller
wanted to be consulted in advance about them if possible. The
Francis Street link was out. Rockefeller told Goodwin to have Perry
produce a lot-by-lot blueprint of the city, wait about six weeks, start
buying properties, and cross them off the blueprint as he went. In
addition, Goodwin would tell Perry to prepare more detailed Wren
plans for review by the best experts in colonial architecture and art.
If he had to, Goodwin could say he was trying to interest Rockefeller
in rebuilding the Wren, that Rockefeller had financed an
architectural study and come to inspect it, but that Rockefeller had
committed himself to nothing more than further study. In the other
connections, the millionaire said again and again that his name was
not to be mentioned. He took Hayes' notebook when he left.

Abby spent her evening at a program of folk singing in
Memorial Hall. During the performance, a Professor Stubbs came in

with an extra of a Richmond newspaper that said Charles Lindbergh's *Spirit of St. Louis* had landed at Les Bourget outside Paris.

The Rockefellers rose next morning to hear the Doctor preach, and they joined the Goodwins for lunch. The couple and the Doctor drove to Lottie Garrett's home so Abby could meet an 18th-century family descendant still living in its homeplace and see her antique china, silver, heirlooms, and rose garden. Lottie pinned an old-fashioned maiden's-blush rose to Abby's dress. Next was Bassett Hall and its Great Oak. Goodwin knew Rockefeller's fondness for the place and liked to tease him about it. The Doctor thought he might buy it himself. Perhaps they would have to flip a coin. "The Rockefellers wandered alone into the woods," Hayes said, "down the quiet lane, carpeted with soft pine needles and overhung by green branches." After the walk they motored on to Richmond for dinner with Bryan.

Goodwin wrote to Perry from his Wythe House office Monday to get him going on the Wren Building, and told Rockefeller: "Some day, should the plans materialize, I think I should put a tablet in this room saying that here were formulated the plans which resulted in the restoration of the historic centers and historic buildings in historic Williamsburg. . . . Should further determinations be reached it will be my desire and pleasure not only to cooperate in carrying out any wishes which you may express, but also to save you from the trouble and worry of all the details incident to the development of any plans which you may endorse or approve and present for fulfillment." Rockefeller said that Goodwin, Perry, and Hayes had done splendid work. "The conception presented of possible schemes of restoration is most carefully and thoroughly thought out and as admirably presented. The various schemes certainly offer an exceedingly attractive program. You are entitled to a tremendous amount of credit."

Goodwin said, "It will be my purpose to try, as hard as any man can try, to exercise a right judgment, and to seek to avoid making mistakes. I can clearly see that the thing most important is to avoid, as far as possible, publicity, and prevent any knowledge of what is being done from getting into the public mind which would result in increasing values and raising opposition which might rise from selfish interests. In order to avoid this it will be wise, in my opinion, to proceed gradually in the acquisition of property, and to negotiate the purchase of property through different persons, so as to avoid, as far as possible, any suspicion which might arise as to what was being done or contemplated. The question arises in my mind as to how soon it might be advisable to have it said that the College was investing certain endowment contributions which had been made in Williamsburg real estate. It would seem to me that it would not be advisable to say this at the present time, but rather to hold it in reserve as an answer which could be given when the time arrived when some answer might be necessary."

At the end of the month he entrained for Rochester and St. Paul's centennial celebration. On the way back he stopped in New York, had a 7:45 a.m. breakfast at the Rockefeller home, and showed Mr. David the aerial photos as well as Perry's scale drawing of the city.

With Rockefeller's approval, Goodwin wrote the next day to Chandler proposing to turn the Paradise over to the school and offering a peek at what was afoot. There was a possibility, the Doctor said, of gaining possession of other houses and lots that might, if the college agreed, be deeded to William and Mary to hold in perpetual trust and preserve in furtherance of a plan to restore and preserve certain historic centers. Goodwin said he proposed to secure help to rebuild the Capitol, Palace, and Raleigh Tavern, which also would be deeded to the college to be used as teaching centers or as depositories of books, documents, works of art, and objects relating to colonial history or for other mutually agreeable purposes.

Rockefeller had instructed Goodwin to take deeds in blank, signing himself and Ethel as purchasers, and send them to New York. The Doctor now asked him to consider putting the school's name on the deeds on the condition the college return them if the restoration idea was shelved. Goodwin said that would avoid the suspicion that deeds in blank created, because the college was known to sometimes buy properties for housing. He also asked Rockefeller to pay Perry at least $1,500 more and suggested the Raleigh restoration for use as a hotel.

Chandler and Dillard examined Goodwin's proposals and accepted them on the condition the gifts were conveyed with an endowment large enough to keep them from being burdens. They suggested he seek full authorization for restoration of the Wren, too, now that more plans were being drawn. As they developed, these discussions uncovered problems all around. William and Mary hadn't funds to maintain so many houses and lots; and as soon as

title passed to the school, the State Arts Commission gained
authority over renovations and alterations. The upshot was a
decision to continue to take deeds in blank for Rockefeller to hold,
"pending the agreement which he has suggested to be made between
him and the College should it be his pleasure to ultimately re-deed
this property to the college."

Goodwin returned to New York in a week to go over
procedures and plans, confer with Gumbel and Heydt, and visit
Rockefeller's office and home. He asked for an appointment of a
cooperating committee but was advised to seek privately the advice
of Williamsburg figures like Chandler, Bryan, and Ashton Dovell, the
majority leader in Virginia's House of Delegates. He had to settle for
paying Perry just $550 more.

Before Goodwin left, Rockefeller handed him a letter for
Hayes. Mr. David was delighted with her notebook. "Because you
have had such a large part in the compiling of this volume," he told
her, "because it is so important a contribution to the study of the
whole project and because you have given yourself so unreservedly
and devotedly to the work which it involves, I hope you will accept
the enclosed check as a further expression of my appreciation of
this particular piece of work, as well as of the valuable service which
you have rendered Dr. Goodwin in many other ways in connection
with this enterprise.

"If in the fall, when the Doctor is less burdened with the
college endowment problems which rest upon him, it should be
decided to go ahead with the project in its larger aspects, I should
very much hope you would find it possible to continue on in the
enterprise, in which event some definite provision for your
compensation should be made, as a part of the general expense."
Whatever thoughts she had of leaving she spiked.

Soon after Goodwin returned to Williamsburg, Rockefeller
approved transfer of the Paradise House to the college. Now the
Doctor wanted to know if Rockefeller would insure his purchases
and asked for approval in writing of permission already granted to
donate $8,000 to the fire department's drive for a hook-and-ladder
truck. He also asked permission to obtain Francis Street lots on
which to deposit modern houses removed from the historic centers.
To transact so much business expediently, Goodwin required close
cooperation from the Peninsula Bank. He took cashier F. R. Savage
into his "limited and guarded" confidence; and he told Mr. David he

might do as much with Channing Hall, president of the city council, and legislator Dovell. Rockefeller communicated no objection, but the circle of knowledge of what Goodwin was up to was growing. Bryan was next on the list.

If the Doctor was to secure the newspaper publisher and vice rector's help with the APVA on the Capitol, Bryan would want to know the reason. In an undated and confidential letter written about this time, Goodwin told Bryan he had wanted for some time to talk to the publisher about several far-reaching matters concerning Williamsburg and the college. He asked Bryan to come for a day "to get your ideas in connection with a tentative suggestion as to certain Colonial developments here which I am anxious to work out and submit to a friend" who might be willing to commit "several million dollars" and which would "greatly redound to the glory of Virginia." Mentioning Perry's work, Goodwin said the restoration of the Wren Building was possible.

Then Goodwin raised the subject of his college compensation, his devotion to the school, and said: "I am not willing, however, to continue my position with the College under terms and conditions which may be in the least embarrassing either to the President or to the Board of Trustees." Goodwin said he and Chandler agreed that the Doctor's name "should appear among the officers of the College" if he was to continue to solicit funds. He hoped Bryan would lend his influence to making the change, and asked to have Bryan's advice on "the terms and conditions under which I can best serve the College."

Bryan, of course, knew of some of the Doctor's dealings with Rockefeller and could by now have guessed Goodwin's backer and the potential for the school and the community. Perry underscored Goodwin's letter by returning with new Wren Building plans. Partner Andrew H. Hepburn came along to take a look and help with the presentation. Chandler and Dillard approved the work in short order, and Perry submitted it for review by the distinguished architects Charles A. Platt of New York, Fiske Kimball of Philadelphia, and a committee of the American Institute of Architects. Hayes thought it now must have been plain to the college's president and its rector, too, that Rockefeller was behind the curtain. "They, however, asked no questions," she wrote, "and said nothing that would lead others to guess the secret."

Goodwin's title never changed from professor and director of

the endowment fund, but when he approached the APVA about the
Capitol property, it was as the college's fully empowered
representative. President Lora H. Ellyson of Richmond was ready to
put the question to a vote of the membership, as state law required,
though it would take time. Governor Byrd assured him of the state's
cooperation in the reconstruction, and said Goodwin's plans for the
site would interfere with nothing he had in mind. In the meantime,
Goodwin began to make the purchases Rockefeller authorized in their
Wythe House meeting.

First he paid $7,000 on July 7 for the "hideous corrugated
iron" Palace Theater on Duke of Gloucester Street, acquiring it in
cashier Savage's name as trustee. The same day, he sent the Paradise
deed to Chandler. Eight days later Goodwin bought the Peninsula
Garage at the corner of England Street. Next he purchased the Toot-
An-Kum-In Garage by the Powder Horn. He decided to delay
purchases of properties above the Blair House and to limit
acquisitions below Palace Green to preemptive strikes, until he
could confer again with Rockefeller.

Goodwin returned to New York in early August and came

In August 1927, Rockefeller authorized Goodwin to option the two Lane stores that
stood on the site of the vanished Raleigh Tavern.

Behind what Goodwin regarded as the excresence of a 19th-century façade lurked the 18th-century Market Square Tavern.

home with a 12-property shopping list. He was to take options on the two Lane stores, which stood on the Raleigh Tavern site, along with the Cash Store and five houses and a vacant lot on Duke of Gloucester Street, the telephone company office on Market Square, and two houses on Palace Green.

The Doctor ran his operation from the Wythe, receiving the real-estate agents and the options there, sending the terms and details of each prospective purchase to New York. Mr. David sent cashier's checks for deals approved, and Goodwin exchanged them for deeds. The agents returned to Goodwin a third to a half of their commissions, which he deposited in an audited account to finance further purchases. Four lawyers handled the paperwork, chief among them Vernon Geddy, Sr., the commonwealth's attorney.

The Doctor's acquisitiveness began to set off speculation that blossomed into a Williamsburg pastime. "People guessed everything," his wife said. "Most people thought Henry Ford was financing the activities. The others thought there must be more than one person to undertake such an enterprise." The newspapers heard of it; and reporters, remembering the stories from summer of 1924, began asking questions. Goodwin went to the major area dailies, asked for cooperation and silence, and wrote a lengthy letter to the editor of the Newport News *Daily Press* intended, he said, to correct errors and rumors that were contrary to the public interest.

Citing his well-known and long-standing interest in

preserving Williamsburg's historic buildings, Goodwin pointed to
the Wythe and Blair houses and Bruton Church. "The historic
background and the historic memorials of Williamsburg are her
greatest asset," he said. "They belong because of their supreme
interest not to Williamsburg alone, but to the State and Nation also.
The memorials must be preserved. As far as possible the ancient
atmosphere by which the houses, which are now the windows of
history, were once surrounded must be created. They should be
made voiceful. They should be perpetuated as a witness to an
ancient greatness. They should be preserved that the future may be
strengthened and enriched by the ideas which they recall and by the
ancient sacrifice of which they speak."

Recently, he said, others who shared his interest had placed
at his disposal "a very limited sum of money which has already been
largely expended" on historic properties "with the possible view of
making the College of William and Mary the owner and perpetual
custodian of these investments." Success meant saving historic
homes from ruin, fire, "or devastating commercialism" that would
destroy the Williamsburg of the past and make the Williamsburg of
the future "a reproach to those who inherited a sacred trust and
dissipated it unmindful of its permanent value."

If speculation caused prices to advance, he said, his
purchases might stop. But he would continue to try to secure funds
to buy property offered at reasonable prices. None would be
purchased for resale profit, and he would receive no commission or
otherwise benefit financially. Property used for educational
endeavors or provided to professors for housing would leave the tax
rolls, Goodwin said, but homes the school rented out would not. He
said other Williamsburg homes would advance in value and help
make up the tax roll slack. That might pinch at property-tax time,
"but no city or individual citizen would fail to welcome a real
increase in the value of property possessed." In any case, college
rents would reimburse the purchases, and the "holding corporation"
taking title to the homes could not afford to buy them at prices that
would require such rents to be noncompetitive. Goodwin disavowed
any disposition to trample on the sentiments of people attached to
ancestral homes, and he hoped they would collaborate to preserve
the structures. He thanked individuals who had cooperated to date
and praised their "fine public spirit."

"A like spirit of cooperation may result in saving to the city and for posterity much which will be for the good and glory of Williamsburg, and much which otherwise will be irrevocably lost."

Published two days later with an interview, Goodwin's letter—apart from some careful dissembling—was a candid description of his project at that moment. It left unsaid who backed him, but obviously he had access to wealth. It might have gotten wider notice except that the nation's attention was focused on Nicola Sacco and Bartolomeo Vanzetti, the Italian-born anarchists executed that day in Boston for the murders of two men in a 1920 payroll robbery.

Goodwin told Rockefeller he had nothing to do with the press speculation, sent him the Newport News clippings, and reported the reaction from "cultured and refined" people had been entirely positive. Rockefeller wrote back: "I have read with much interest the newspaper articles which you enclosed, and think I have never seen any publicity in regard to a project so wisely and skillfully handled as you have handled the publicity of your historical project in your interview in the Newport News 'Daily Press' of August 23rd. You have taken the public into your confidence, been completely frank with them, thus disarming suspicion and capitalizing curiosity. I cannot see any flaw in your admirable interview, and congratulate you cordially upon it. You have undoubtedly adopted the wisest course."

For someone who planned to devote his summer and autumn to college fund raising, Goodwin had quite an agenda with Rockefeller. But he made time in these months, too, to finish raising the $4,000 needed for Grace Church's restoration and to dedicate the building October 23. He became a go-between in Archibald and Molly McCrea's negotiations with A. G. and Lucy M. Harwood for the sale of nearby Carter's Grove Plantation, built in the 1750s by Carter Burwell. Molly was a friend from the Doctor's days in Petersburg. Her husband, the son of the president of the Pennsylvania Railroad, was chairman of the board of the Union Spring and Manufacturing Company of Pittsburgh. The deal for the house went through with Goodwin's help the following January 21.

The Doctor attended a state church convention in Richmond and became embroiled in a peppery running dispute with the editor of a church newspaper over the content of the Apostle's Creed. When the private road on Jamestown Island became almost impassable, he complained to Governor Byrd about the "disgraceful menace," and Byrd ordered the state highway department to fix it. Then Goodwin accepted Byrd's invitation to serve on the committee that would supervise Virginia's bicentennial celebration of Washington's birth. Congressman S. O. Bland, a William and Mary alumnus and Goodwin friend, nominated him. About the only activity he gave up, and that reluctantly, was his trusteeship at the Virginia Theological Seminary.

Goodwin was at Yorktown delivering the dedicatory address to the Daughters of the American Revolution for the restored colonial Custom's House, when he got news of a decision he believed made the difference to all his Williamsburg hopes.

Hayes found Goodwin by telephone at lunchtime and said Rockefeller's office had approved his idea for acquiring six colonial homes—the Peyton Randolph House, Tazewell Hall, the Coke-Garrett House, the Brush-Everard House, the Robert Carter House, and the Barlow sisters' house—without turning out the old-line family descendants living in them. He proposed to have the homeowners sell, but retain the right to live in their homes for life. The price was reduced by the life-right's value, but Rockefeller paid for restoration, major maintenance, and repair. Heydt had come down to look around and discuss the idea with Goodwin. When he got back to New York, he approved the arrangement with modifications, authorized purchase of the Garrett, Barlow, and Randolph homes on those terms, told Goodwin to offer life tenancy to Alice and Edith Smith for Bassett Hall, asked for the prices of the Brush-Everard and Carter houses, and deferred a decision on Tazewell Hall.

In less than a week, Goodwin was in Richmond making a pitch for the Capitol site to a state APVA meeting. He described a reconstructed Capitol to be built for $100,000 and promised to set aside a room for the association's perpetual use. It took until 1929 to consummate the deal. Among other things, a state law had to be amended. But at this point, the rebuilding of the Capitol was more of a speculative proposition than a solid proposal. For Rockefeller still had made no commitment to Goodwin's restoration dream.

The Doctor preached a sermon on Williamsburg's

restoration November 13—he had made much the same address to
the Rotary Club about a month before—solicited his congregation's
help, prayers, and support, and prepared for the most important
of his Rockefeller meetings, one he had been trying to arrange for
six weeks. Five days later he left for New York to rendezvous with
Perry and Kimball and review a comprehensive report already
approved by four other distinguished architects—including
Coolidge—for presentation to Mr. David at a Vanderbilt
Hotel conference.

The proposal now embraced the construction of an inn and
a golf course; the reconstruction of the Capitol, Palace, and Masonic
Lodge, the restoration of the Wren, and the acquisition of colonial
furnishings. It addressed the problems of the two blocks of 37
businesses just below the college, the construction of housing for
African-Americans the restoration would displace, and the
relocation of the modern churches. It considered the transferring of
city property and the clearing of modern houses off leased lots on
the public squares.

Goodwin reached the Vanderbilt on the 19th, a Saturday, and
took a two-room corner suite. Perry came in from Boston before
lunch carrying an armload of oversize renderings. Some were six
feet long. One was eight, maybe nine. To get them to the suite, Perry
had to stand on top of the elevator, ride it to the floor below, and
push them through the door above. Goodwin watched. "I can see
him dancing about, enjoying every minute of it," Perry said. Kimball
came in later, approved everything, and stayed for dinner. He
endorsed the plans in a letter that stated what became the guiding
formula of the Restoration:

"Reverently to preserve every vestige of the old where it
survives, preferably on its original site; where it does not, to exhaust
first every vestige of evidence as to what the old was actually like;
where the evidence does not suffice, to work scrupulously in the
style of the very time and place, yet with artistic sensitiveness."

Kimball left while Goodwin and Perry set up the drawings.
That evening, Rockefeller sent the Doctor a note confirming their
9 a.m. meeting Monday. He invited him to attend Park Avenue
Baptist Church with the family Sunday and to lunch with them at
home—10 West 54th Street.

The Rockefeller pew was empty when Goodwin arrived. In a
few minutes John D. Rockefeller III came, and the others trickled

after. Mr. David slid in and whispered a greeting. Abby and little David were last to sit. "David slipped over to me and said, 'I certainly did enjoy the pecan nuts you sent me last Christmas,'" Goodwin wrote. "I reached down in my pocket and pulled out one large pecan nut and presented it to him, saying, 'I've brought you one of this year's crop.' I told him to plant it. Then the organ began to play." Dr. Harry Emerson Fosdick preached.

After lunch, the Rockefellers left for the laying of a cornerstone for Fosdick's new church, and Goodwin returned to the Vanderbilt. Perry showed up from a jaunt to Long Island, and they talked over the presentation. Goodwin showed him the town blueprint. He had colored in yellow the lots and properties so far acquired. Perry "was so astonished that he sat down <u>hard</u> on the bed," the Doctor wrote. "He had no idea that we had accomplished anything like that." They conferred until 1 a.m., when Goodwin asked Perry to spend the next day in his room by the telephone.

At 9:05 in the morning, while Goodwin sat reading a newspaper, Rockefeller walked in. The first order of business was the Doctor's pay. He refused any. The second was assurance Goodwin "would continue to direct the plan." Goodwin gave it. As Rockefeller perused Perry's drawings, Heydt arrived. Rockefeller estimated costs: $409,000 for the Wren, $200,000 for the Capitol, $200,000 more for the Palace, and $100,000 for an inn. Heydt took notes. Goodwin suggested buying the business blocks and renting the shops to help endow the project. Rockefeller liked the idea. The conversations lasted all day, adjourning to Heydt's office after a subway ride to lunch. That evening, Goodwin took up the business-section idea with Perry and asked for a quick sketch of what the architect imagined could be done. By 4 a.m. Perry had produced a concept of Merchants Square, two blocks of colonial-style shops generally considered the first American shopping center.

The next day, Tuesday, November 22, Goodwin collected Rockefeller, Heydt, lawyer Thomas M. Debevoise, and Colonel Woods, and they all returned to the Vanderbilt. Rockefeller explained the plans, in detail, to his associates while Goodwin listened. "<u>Mr. Rockefeller then intimated that he would be responsible for the development of the plans as they had been presented!</u>" Goodwin wrote, underlining the words himself. On the spot, Rockefeller dictated a memo of his intentions. The commitment was made at last, a decision Mr. David would back with

$68,348,354 during the next 32 years. Woods would have charge of policy, the others of their specialties. Rockefeller's identity was to remain a secret.

In instructions drafted for Woods, Rockefeller said in part: "It is my desire and purpose to carry out this enterprise completely and entirely. Such accomplishment involves in general terms the acquiring of substantially all of the property on Duke of Gloucester Street from the House of Burgesses to the College Grounds, much other property, the building of a new inn and of new buildings for business purposes, and the rebuilding of the Sir Christopher Wren Building on the College campus. The purpose of this undertaking is to restore Williamsburg, so far as it may be possible, to what it was in the old colonial days and to make it a great centre for historical study and inspiration. The purpose of this letter is to authorize my office to finance this entire program whether it costs three or four, or even five millions of dollars. . . .

"I have felt that the only way permanently to accomplish this object and to insure its continuance throughout the years would be ultimately to have the property thus acquired deeded to the College of William and Mary and controlled and operated for all time by the College."

Although the school's president had never heard his name

Goodwin paid $91,350 for the College Shop and Pocahontas Tea Room at the west end of Duke of Gloucester Street, his most expensive transaction for Rockefeller after the $265,000 laid out for the Casey family's business-district properties.

Goodwin and Rockefeller acquired ramshackle businesses like this and demolished them to build a colonial-style shopping center, Merchants Square.

mentioned in the matter, Rockefeller said, Chandler and Dillard had "expressed themselves as heartily in favor of the project and as delighted to have the College become the recipient of these properties and the trust involved."

Before leaving New York, Goodwin wrote Rockefeller a warm letter of appreciation. His patron responded a few days later. "I too am happy to be associated with you in this profoundly interesting and significant project," Rockefeller said. "In the months which have intervened since first we met, we have come to know each other and how each other's minds work to an unusual degree, in spite of the fact that we have seen each other so seldom.

"I have every confidence in your wisdom, your tact and your discretion. The loyal way in which you have observed your silent partner's wish that he should be in very truth a silent and unknown partner has also increased my confidence in you. I am happy in the thought of being able to help you in realizing the dream which you have been dreaming for so many years." He mentioned the organizational arrangement confiding control to his associates but said, "Let me know at any time if a word from me will be helpful in any of these connections."

On the way south, the Doctor telegraphed Geddy, asking the lawyer to meet him at the station. "Well," Geddy said, "it so happened that that very day I had finished the last title examinations for properties that had been purchased to date so I drove down and met the Doctor, and, as he got off the train I said, 'Well, Doctor, I'm glad to see you back and I want to tell you I have all your abstracts of titles,' and he turned to me and smiled, and said, 'Boy, you haven't started. I'm going to buy the town.'"

Almost as quickly as he reached the Wythe, the Doctor started in. He drafted a letter to Chandler saying that if the Wren was to be restored, the college and the state would have to provide a classroom building, Washington Hall, for students to use in the interim. Moreover, William and Mary would have to cooperate with him in securing the Palace site, on which stood the city's new high school and the college's old teaching laboratory, the Matthew Whaley School. He sent it to Woods for review, along with a note saying he looked forward to their collaboration. The letter to Chandler came back approved.

Not until December 3 did the Doctor consider himself authorized to tell Perry of their success and propose to retain Perry, Shaw and Hepburn "for further architectural work incident to the further development of the plans and projects under consideration." Specifically, the Doctor wanted working drawings and specifications for the Wren, Capitol, Inn, Palace, and plans for the town—projects he thought would cost a total of $897,000 when built. He also thought of a solution to the problem of custody of the completed restoration. "It might be both possible and advisable to carry out Mr. David's expressed intention of ultimately deeding the property to the College," he told Woods, "and still have the tenure and control of the property exercised under the supervision of some national organization."

By now Goodwin had corralled 47 properties, a fact a Richmond *Times-Dispatch* reporter uncovered at the courthouse December 10. The scribe began to interview people. The Doctor spoke to him thinking he had a pledge in return that nothing would be printed until Goodwin was ready, at which time the Doctor said he would give the story to all the newspapers. Why a reporter would agree to withhold a scoop he already had until his competitors got it, too, is a mystery. Goodwin may have misunderstood. The *Times-Dispatch* carried the story the next morning and the *News-Leader* that evening, followed by laudatory

editorials. The attention rattled Goodwin. Disclosure of the millions
involved, he feared, would inflate prices and damage negotiations in
progress. Worse, the newspapers had speculated about his backer,
mentioning Edsel Ford, John D. Rockefeller, Jr., and an unnamed
philanthropist. That afternoon Bryan called. He was coming down
next day for a pow-wow.

At 7 a.m. on the 12th Goodwin started down Duke of
Gloucester Street and spoke to every entrepreneur in Williamsburg
whose property he had not secured. From each he elicited a
promise of the first option on their holdings in return for a pledge of
new and better locations. Returning to the Wythe, he drafted an
open letter to the city's businessmen asking for cooperation and
promising the restoration would be good for the town's economy. To
the *Daily Press* he sent a two-paragraph notice promising to buy
nothing from speculators. Goodwin briefed Bryan on the project,
still not mentioning Rockefeller, and asked for a letter of support
that he might show his backer for reassurance. Then the Doctor
composed a long and anxious letter to Mr. David, enclosing the
clippings, saying, "I gave no information." Rockefeller downplayed
the damage and congratulated Goodwin on keeping the scale of his
activities quiet as long as he had.

This time other newspapers did take notice. The story
spread to New York, where the *Evening World* called Rockefeller's
office for comment. It had nothing to say—which, of course, said a
great deal. Bryan wrote to Rockefeller praising Goodwin's efforts,
and he, too, asked if Rockefeller was financing them. Rockefeller
said that it was good to know Goodwin's hopes were coming to
fruition. "Whomever his backers may prove to be," he told Bryan,
"they certainly have an unusually devoted, intelligent and able
representative in him. . . . Let us hope, however, that his hand will not
be further forced until he is ready to show it, and that so long as he
feels it best to withhold the names of his backers, his judgment in
the matter will be respected."

Bryan wrote to Goodwin, too, as the Doctor had asked. "It is
given to many people to dream dreams and see visions," Bryan said,
"but it is given to very few to both dream and accomplish. . . .
America has enough and to spare of factories and mines and
railroads. It has been your great privilege to preserve and extend
America's possessions in the realm of history and beauty and
imagination, and I salute and congratulate you."

The officers of the Restoration posed at Williamsburg headquarters for this picture. Goodwin is in the front row, second from the left. Colonel Arthur Woods, president, is fourth from left. In back, at top right with moustache, stands vice-president Kenneth Chorley.

Chapter Twelve: **1928**

During the first two years of the Restoration, Goodwin came within two cents of quitting, and Rockefeller, after investing more than $2 million, nearly gave it up for a bad business, too. Two cents was the price of the postage Goodwin almost put on his letter of resignation. Both had good reason to write off the project.

The Restoration spent dollars as if it had at its disposal the resources of, well, a Rockefeller. For its money, it got what Geddy described as chaos, friction, and jealousy.

Nevertheless, construction crews moved some houses, while demolition men knocked down others, and archaeologists unearthed the foundations of the 18th-century city. Architects put their pencils to colonial designs for masons and carpenters to turn into restorations and reconstructions. "This is a funny place," an old-timer said. "They tear down *new* houses to build *old* ones."

When the dust had begun to settle, the preacher told the philanthropist: "The past two years have been filled with problems which have naturally arisen out of the distinct uniqueness of this work and I am sure that we are in a much better position to proceed with the larger wisdom which has come to us through experience."

Heydt arrived early in December 1927 to advise Goodwin on, among other matters, buying business-district lots and to launch the intensive new round of buying. Perry and Hepburn came and went just before Christmas to talk over the project and look more at the Wren. Lawyers and real-estate men streamed up and down the stairs to the Doctor's study. So many Restoration transactions were conducted at the Wythe House that people called it The Shrine. Colonel Woods made his first pilgrimage just before New Year's.

Goodwin was roughly in the position of a small-town factory owner who stays on as superintendent after bargaining away his plant to a large and distant corporation. Such men have less authority than their new superiors, but a better understanding of how the enterprise was built, and what makes it run. They may wonder if they aren't better positioned to make decisions. They may be skeptical of newcomers sent by the home office, and the new management's policy adjustments. They may conclude they could produce exactly the results sought, if only they had less interference. It takes tact and mutual forbearance to keep things going smoothly.

Among the first things Woods did on his return to New York was tug at the taproot of Goodwin's operation. "You remember," he wrote the Doctor, "that we spoke about the advisability of not making any committal to the College, and you told me of what you understood to have been the situation previously, and, as I remember it, of one or two letters which you have received authorizing you to tell President Chandler that the property ultimately would probably be turned over to the College. In order to clear up this matter, and forestall any misunderstandings, would you be good enough to let me know just what was your understanding in this matter?"

Commitments *had* been made, publicly, and Goodwin told Woods so. Certainly, he wrote the colonel, the William and Mary deal wasn't done. But the excerpts of correspondence with Rockefeller, Heydt, Debevoise, and Chandler that Goodwin enclosed, along with his newspaper clippings, showed a decision had been made and widely communicated. He described ways Woods could consummate the transfer and said, "We feel that the determinations which will be finally reached by Mr. David and his advisors will unquestionably be the wisest and best which could be arrived at."

Rather than trim sails to give Woods leeway, Goodwin put on more canvas. Judge Robert Hughes of Norfolk, an ex-member of the board of visitors and one-time Republican candidate for governor, asked what he could say to associates about the college's relationship to the Restoration. Goodwin told Hughes he could say the "exact terms under which the historic property acquired will be related to the College" had not been determined, but he restated the rest of the plan point by point.

It would be hard to fault Woods if he expected Goodwin,

having at last sold Rockefeller on Williamsburg, to step a little to the
side while Mr. David's team adapted the Doctor's dream to business-
world realities. Goodwin, however, planned to devote more of
himself to the project than ever. He suspended active college fund
raising, the job that brought him back to Williamsburg, to free up
time for Restoration work.

In truth, the Restoration needed all the time the Doctor
could spare. At the next New York conference, he, Woods,
Rockefeller, and Debevoise decided to add Williamsburg's public
properties to Goodwin's acquisition program. All of it but the
streets. They wanted the Courthouse, Palace, and Powder Horn
greens. They needed the Palace site with its brand-new high school
and the college's training school and all city- or county-owned
buildings and land in Williamsburg.

The Doctor set out the deal in "The Colonial Williamsburg
Restoration Plan" and presented it to the city and county
governments January 21. In return for deeding everything to
Goodwin, his heirs, and assigns, the community would have a new
courthouse, fire station, and jail rent-free for 99 years, and a newer
high school. The public would have perpetual access to the greens;
the surrendered property would be exempt from taxation after five
years. There the negotiations opened. Some officials scoffed—
opposition to the Restoration became Mayor J. M. Henderson's
reelection platform—but bills to permit the school property swaps
sailed through the Legislature, and Byrd approved them March 16.

Heydt returned to discuss the latest private purchases and
confer about the formation of two management corporations. One,
nonprofit Colonial Williamsburg, Incorporated, would hold the
properties; the other, Colonial Williamsburg Holding Company,
would run businesses like Merchants Square and the inns. Woods
would be president of the first; legal advisor Francis T. Christy
would run the second. Goodwin would have positions in both.

Goodwin was using William J. Holland's construction
company, but Woods told the Doctor he heard good things about a
New York firm—Todd, Robertson, Todd Engineering Corporation. He
told Goodwin to ask what Perry knew about the outfit.

The home office in New York was gearing up and taking
charge. Goodwin reacted by telling Rockefeller the endeavor had

"now reached a point where it would not seem wise that the completion of the enterprise should be in any way made dependent upon any one individual other than yourself." The Doctor said he would cooperate "unreservedly and to the fullest extent until the project is completely developed." But Goodwin suggested appointment of a committee to "carry out the plan committed to my care" in case he fell ill or died. He nominated eight people, including Chandler, Dovell, Geddy, Hayes, and son Rutherfoord—all Goodwin loyalists, none from New York. As if to underscore his command of the field, he quickly secured and forwarded the college's conditional approval of the Wren renovation plan coupled with Chandler's pledge of full cooperation in the entire Restoration.

When Goodwin next heard from Woods, the colonel directed him henceforth to submit to him in triplicate all letters sent to New York about Williamsburg. Woods telegraphed February 22 saying he was sending Webster Todd, Jr., and Joseph O. Brown of Todd, Robertson, Todd to get an idea of the Restoration's scale.

Goodwin was driven to the station to collect them that Saturday morning at 10 in an early example of a Model A supplied by the local Ford dealer. The dealer was sure Henry Ford was behind everything and had the car specially assembled, so that the company's new product would be part of the new Williamsburg. H. I. Brock of the *New York Times* came on the same train to see Goodwin for a Restoration story.

The contractors left Sunday, formed the firm Todd & Brown, and won the project contract. Holland became their subcontractor. Brock's three-page story was published a month later. Christy arrived Monday with Harrison S. Dimmitt, another legal advisor. They delivered the papers to charter the Restoration corporations. For convenience, Geddy was temporarily listed as president, its first. Goodwin was named incorporator, trustee, secretary, and member.*

On Perry's recommendation and Woods' approval, the Doctor hired Boston landscape architect Arthur A. Shurtleff as town planner and designer of gardens and ornamental plantings. To the Wythe House staff, Goodwin, again with Woods' permission, added son Rutherfoord as property manager and cousin Mary F. Goodwin, uncle Edward's daughter, as historical researcher.

The Doctor asked Woods to come or send Heydt to counsel with him, Perry, and Shurtleff in March on "the selection and the

---

* By June 12, management of the still-separated corporations was unified with Woods as president, Christy as vice-president, Heydt as treasurer and assistant secretary, and Goodwin as secretary and assistant treasurer.

layout of the two areas, one for the white and one for the colored people who would have to be moved out of our territory . . . the next and the most vital matter to be considered." The conference waited until April, but Goodwin had more than enough to keep him busy.

He tried to arrange the fell-swoop purchase of the remains of Virginia's first historic city—Jamestown. Louise Barney, a Dayton, Ohio, widow, owned 1,368 acres of Jamestown Island with its buried foundations and ruins—all of it except 22.5 acres she and husband Edward gave the APVA in 1893. Barney had heard Rockefeller was buying historic Virginia properties, and she told Goodwin she was willing to sell her Jamestown holdings. Goodwin, who thought there was "nothing in America of rarer historic interest to the English speaking world," told her the Rockefeller reports were without authorization, but the Doctor might broker a sale if the asking price showed a spirit of patriotism and generosity. Barney proposed $500,000. Goodwin thought that neither generous nor patriotic. Woods asked Goodwin for background on Jamestown and told him to pursue negotiations. Barney upped the price to $547,200 and made a veiled threat to commercialize the island if Goodwin didn't come to terms. The Doctor eventually offered $102,600 and was prepared to pay $250,000, but he made no headway. He walked away hoping the state would somehow acquire the land. It remained Barney property until the federal government condemned it for a national park in 1934. Goodwin testified as an expert witness for the United States.

The Doctor had more success as Rockefeller's agent in the purchase of what is now Smith's Fort Plantation in Surry County and the Moore House in York County, where terms of Cornwallis's surrender were composed. Mr. David held the properties until preservationists were ready to take title.

Hundreds of people wrote to the Doctor trying to sell him colonial country homes, or asking for jobs, or seeking cooperation in opening Williamsburg businesses. Some correspondents offered antiques, heirlooms, and rare books. So busy was the Doctor with these matters, teaching duties, his ministry, and the Restoration, he suspended accepting speechmaking invitations. "I find that my time is so completely occupied here in the restoration work," he told one program chairman, "that I have to break most of the engagements I make. I have therefore come to the conclusion that the wise thing for me to do is restore Williamsburg and talk about it afterwards."

Most days he worked from 8:30 a.m. to 11 p.m., a tough
schedule for a man now 58. But Goodwin hung on to his
perspective, and his sense of humor. As much as the Doctor disliked
automobiles, wife Ethel didn't—and she was taking driving lessons.
Gardiner Brooks, who sold car insurance as well as real estate, heard
she was buying a sedan and offered to sell the Doctor a policy. "My
dear Mr. Brooks," Goodwin wrote to him, "You say you understand
that I have been interested in a Chevrolet car, and then wrote me a
very interesting and illuminating letter as to how much it would cost
me to insure this car, but as I have not purchased it I hesitate to
place the insurance. As a matter of fact, there isn't a car on the
American Continent that I want, or that I would have if I had to run
it, if somebody would give it to me. Mrs. Goodwin has been taking
lessons. If she doesn't get killed while she is doing it she may get a
car some of these days. The timely letter would have been one from
a life insurance agent. Good regards to you."

The minutes of the first on-site Restoration conference,
conducted the first five days in April, show how much else he had
on his plate. To Perry, Shurtleff, Brown, Todd, and Heydt, the Doctor
handed a list of 50 project questions. Among the topics was creation
of a general operating plan, the purchase of outlying properties, the
Wren renovation, zoning, an inventory of housing and stores,
population relocation, fire protection, tree surgery, Colonial Inn
improvements, a field accounting office, and a highway bypass.
They were also to discuss the golf course; relocation of churches,
banks, the hospital, and post office; dean John Garland Pollard's
desire to have the reconstructed Capitol for the college's law school;
and the rebuilding of English America's first theater on Palace
Green. The most important things, they decided, were hiring
sanitary engineers to investigate Williamsburg's water supply and
sewerage systems, selecting other engineers to plan the burial of
utility wires, and arranging another survey of the town. The session
adjourned April 10 to New York, where Webster Todd, Sr., Woods,
and Woods's assistant Kenneth Chorley joined in. They approved
the chief Williamsburg recommendations and, among other things, a
contour map, expenditure of $75,000 for a replacement high school,
and a general operating scheme. Goodwin was named local director,
and his office reported to Woods's office. Perry, Shaw, and Hepburn
reported to Goodwin. Nearly everyone else reported to the
architects or, a level down, to Todd & Brown.

Goodwin had invited Perry to lunch with him and Woods at the Whitehall Club that day and asked him to bring along Hepburn and the firm's third partner, Thomas Mott Shaw. Rockefeller appeared, and the architects finally learned Mr. David's identity. Perry said Rockefeller had injured his right arm playing volley ball with one of his sons at the family's Pocantico Hills estate near Tarrytown, New York, and had to shake hands with his left. He chatted with them through the meal and, when they were done, said: "I'd like to record my impressions. We've been working anonymously now for a year and a half, and my first impression is that I'm very grateful to these architects for not having made any inquiries as to who we are. Moreover, I believe now, from what they have done, and the pleasure I have had from meeting them, we will proceed from here."

When Goodwin returned to Williamsburg, he wrote to a French-professor friend on sabbatical in Paris. "The town will be standing on its head before very long," he said. "I can even now hear the things, or some of them, which will be said about me. Even sober people going home will be sure that they are drunk. They will leave their houses in the morning, and upon returning in the afternoon will find them moving down the middle of the street. When these days come, I think I myself will go to Paris."

Geddy said, "It was like a gigantic game of checkers. Dr. Goodwin would purchase a store down on Duke of Gloucester Street in a perfectly modern building that he wanted to wreck, so he'd move them somewhere else, then he'd go in and wreck and build something, and put them back in it. And he did the same thing with the people living in the residences. There was a continuous moving, and it was not an uncommon sight at any time of day or night to go down Duke of Gloucester Street, or Francis Street, and see one or two houses being moved up and down the street and across lots. I must say it made it terrifically exciting."

Goodwin escaped his Williamsburg duties to attend a Washington Bicentennial Committee meeting in Richmond and write a report recommending celebrations at Yorktown and Wakefield Plantation, extension and connection of federal roads to form a National Washington Highway, and employment of historians to investigate Virginia routes and houses associated with the first president. Back at The Shrine, he studied and then recommended the idea of moving colonial buildings in from the countryside. Woods told him to hold up. Everything had to be cleared by Woods—requisitions, restoration priorities, schedules, the employment of trash collectors, everything. But urgent recommendations—like the need to supply housing for displaced impoverished blacks—languished for months in New York.

Goodwin pondered his position in the new scheme of things. He wasn't sure what it was. "It will take a bit of time," he told Woods, "before I come clearly to understand my own detailed responsibility in the transition stage through which we are now passing." He understood—though he hadn't been consulted—that Perry's, Todd's, and Heydt's offices were drafting procedures to save time and streamline procedures. "I take it for granted that when these arrangements have been perfected, I will receive instructions from you or Mr. Heydt which will govern the procedure of this office."

Despite his uncertainty, the Doctor explained the new organizational chart to local employees at a Wythe House meeting—attended by Woods' deputy, Chorley, and other New Yorkers. On May 12, in accordance with the new procedures, he turned over his property account books to Robert Trimble, Jr., construction superintendent in Todd & Brown's new local office. He had spent $2,225,189.87 of Rockefeller's money.

Woods sent Chorley back within a week to work "out a definite method of procedure which would simplify the handling of matters as much as possible and yet provide for the conducting of our operations in a business-like and orderly manner." Chorley announced he was "seriously solicitous" of Goodwin's welfare and suggested the Doctor's load be lightened. Goodwin told him, "I want you people up in New York to get it out of your heads that I am a bedraggled and overburdened man. . . . I deeply appreciate all that you good people are doing to cooperate with me and to save me from the burden of detail."

What he really needed was a new ground rule for his local government negotiations. The mystery of Mr. David was impeding progress. Some townspeople grumbled about approving an agreement while the other principal party remained anonymous. They wanted to know who was buying their community before they surrendered control of the greens and public buildings. Goodwin

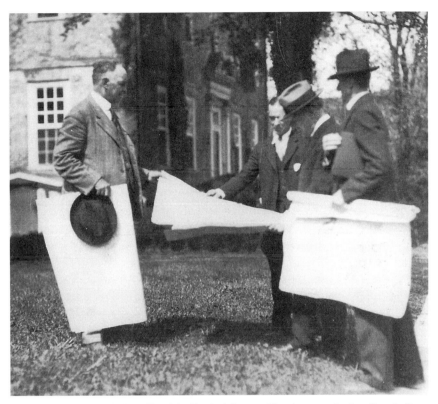

Goodwin, engineer Robert Trimble, Rockefeller, and landscaper Arthur Shurtleff (later Shurcliff) examine restoration plans at the Wythe House.

proposed to New York on May 22 that "the donor" be named, and he suggested the form of announcement.

Not that Rockefeller's connection was so secret any longer. Rutherfoord and Bentley had been told, as had Perry, Shaw, and Hepburn, as had the Todds and Brown. Hayes and Ethel had known all along. Geddy, like Bryan, had guessed. Kathryne Morecock said she found out from Fairfax Harrison, president of the Southern Railway—a friend of Goodwin's. Eventually the biggest secret would be who was in on the secret.

The argument for telling everyone became more persuasive during a May 28 joint meeting of the James City County Supervisors and the Williamsburg City Council. Goodwin and his associates got permission to improve streets and sidewalks, lay sewer pipes and waterlines, bury utility wires, doctor the trees, provide a firehouse, move homes, and pay for it all. The officials also tentatively approved the property-swap contract but deferred a decision to the citizens at large. The city would have a mass meeting in 15 days, the county meeting the day after. The Doctor would have to make his case.

That left the school board, which with the college controlled the Palace site. Goodwin wrote to Major S. D. Freeman, its chairman, about the high school. Freeman didn't care for the idea of tearing down the fine brick place he had just built.

At the next Restoration conference, a June 5 dinner gathering in New York's Racquet Club, Goodwin proposed, among other things, to reveal Rockefeller's involvement. The discussions began at 6:30 and lasted until 11 p.m., when Goodwin went to his Vanderbilt room. Twenty minutes later he began a letter to Hayes on the hotel's gray-blue linen stationary. On the first page he diagrammed the conference table seating and praised the participants. At the bottom of the second page he wrote, "It was decided to make the announcement in June at the Mass Meetings." He told her to write to everyone with whom they were negotiating property purchases to say his buying program would close at 8 p.m. June 15, precisely 48 hours after the Williamsburg town meeting began.

While he prepared for the 12th, he negotiated for Rockefeller with Mrs. Marion Carter Oliver of Shirley Plantation the $75,000 purchase of Charles Willson Peale's full-length portrait of Washington—still a Colonial Williamsburg icon.

On the afternoon of the Williamsburg meeting, Goodwin huddled with Mayor-elect Pollard, Geddy, Dovell, Council President Channing Hall, and B. D. Peachy. They wanted to be sure lame-duck Mayor Henderson, "gloriously defeated" in his anti-Restoration election campaign, had no opportunity for a veto.

There were deeper divisions in the community than the outcome suggested. Blacks had been particularly reluctant to sell their homes to the Restoration, and businessman W. A. Bozarth, a Goodwin ally, said two years afterward that the Doctor "has not had the sympathies of the people as a rule." Much later, Goodwin wrote, "There were a few conscientious objectors to the whole Restoration project. This was anticipated and, wishing to make everybody happy as far as possible, no exception was taken to these protests or to the unwillingness of a few citizens to sell their property."

But there was little reason to doubt the evening's vote. The mayor's election already had served for a referendum on the question; the losers had scant motivation to attend or make trouble.

That Tuesday night in the assembly room of the high school he proposed to demolish, the Doctor was ready to share with his neighbors the secret he had held from them for a year, seven months, and 15 days. Hayes wrote down the names of the people who filtered in—the H. D. Coles, George Coleman, Rutherfoord, Emma Lou Barlow . . . At five minutes past eight, Hall asked for quiet. "Ladies and Gentlemen," he said, "we have called this meeting in order to get an expression from the people on the subject of the transfer of the city property to Dr. Goodwin and his associates, and to give a chance for questions for free and frank discussion by citizens. I have called the meeting to order to elect a chairman."

That kept Henderson away from the gavel; Pollard got the job. At the mayor-elect's request, Hall summarized the 22-page contract Goodwin proposed and read it in full, pausing to refer the audience to a town map. The floor opened for questions. Goodwin fielded most and made a speech. He said, in part:

"It is the purpose of our associates to make this favored city a national shrine. Benefit will come in spiritual, as well as material, ways. Every business will be benefited. It should be a source of pride to you to feel that you will have here the most beautiful shrine dedicated to the lives of the nation builders. We will be the custodians of memorials to which the eyes of the world will be turned. We should return thanks that this place has been chosen as a shrine of liberty and of beauty. There will be windows built here, through which men may look down the vistas of the past. May I say that my associates do not believe in the principle of unlimited tax exemption. Without taxes there can be no fire protection, no sanitation, no police protection.

"It is now my very great privilege and pleasure to announce that the donors of the money to restore Williamsburg are"—and here he paused—"Mr. and Mrs. John D. Rockefeller, Jr., of New York." The room filled with applause. Goodwin praised Mr. David, thanked his fellow townspeople for their confidence, and said, "I'm so glad to prove to you that I was right, and that you were not wrong in your trust."

F. Van Garrett proposed adoption of a resolution of appreciation, composed beforehand and ready to read. Coleman didn't hear him and moved approval of the contract, but Freeman rose.

"It is my unpleasant duty to voice the minority side," he said in a clear firm voice. "There should be something said for both sides. If you give up your land, it will no longer be your city. Will you feel the same pride in it that you now feel as you walk across the greens or down the broad street? Have you all been hypnotized by millions dangled before your eyes? Can any of you talk back to millions of dollars? If we close the contract what will happen when the matter passes out of the hands of Mr. Rockefeller and Dr. Goodwin, in both of whom we have perfect confidence? Who will be the head? Who will control?

"I beg you to consider some things which have been overlooked. Dr. Goodwin has spoken very beautifully and poetically. But is this a philanthropic enterprise? Is it altruistic? There is no doubt but that the contract will go through, but I want you to know that there is one man who has had something to say on the other side. We will reap dollars, but will we own our town? Will you not be in the position of a butterfly pinned to a card in a glass cabinet, or like a mummy unearthed in the tomb of Tutankhamen?"

Hayes said that when he sat down "there was perfect silence." To Goodwin's mind, Freeman, "never known to float with the tide," had merely "got into the limelight and, consistently, floated upstream." The Doctor might well have asked the major, in view of his sentiments, why he had sold the Freeman home to the Restoration for $20,000 on March 28. Instead, Goodwin told the audience the state Corporation Commission chartered the Colonial Williamsburg companies, and if there had been any danger, the commission would have pointed it out. It was an answer, but, of course, the commission had no purview over considerations like Freeman's.

Pollard asked for a vote in the affirmative, and 150 people stood to be counted. Four rose in opposition—Henderson, Freeman, and Dora and Clara Armistead. A Mr. Ball asked for a secret ballot but could not find a second. Pollard called for Garrett's resolution of appreciation and, with unopposed approval, the meeting adjourned. Goodwin released a press statement describing the agreement and the Restoration plan. He cabled Rockefeller: "The citizens of Williamsburg at Williamsburg mass meeting tonight which completely filled the high school building, after endorsing agreement transferring city property passed resolution by unanimous rising vote expressing their thanks to you for your gracious and generous kindness to the city of Williamsburg. It is with heartfelt gratitude that I transmit to you this resolution."

Hayes said the county meeting, conducted the next night in nearby Toano, unanimously concurred. On the 14th the Williamsburg council formally accepted the contract. On the 15th the Wren became available for Restoration, and on the 16th the Capitol-site deal with the APVA went through. School board Chairman Freeman, however, still had a card to play. That Saturday he wrote a preemptory letter to Goodwin. He said that if Goodwin wanted the school, Rockefeller would have to pay what the site was worth to Colonial Williamsburg, including the advance in value caused by the Restoration. The Doctor told him to consult a lawyer and made a counter offer to the board's members. Outflanked, Freeman acquiesced. In November the board accepted $200,000, plus a new site, agreed to the design of a Restoration architect, and got $100,000 more from Rockefeller's General Education Board.

Goodwin told Rockefeller, "In Williamsburg the citizens are not only greatly relieved, but deeply grateful to know that it is you who is making the Restoration work possible. I told them at the Mass Meeting that you wished to have them consider themselves as your associates. I think that they were really afraid that it was Henry Ford! "

Many years later, the Doctor wrote to Mr. David: "When, with your consent, your name, as the Donor, was made known, I expressed my wish and desire to be relieved from the details of management which I clearly saw would often conflict with my duties and personal relationships as Rector of Bruton Parish Church. This relief was accorded me, for which I was then and have ever remained most grateful."

There was more to it. Ten days after pocketing the city's vote, he asked Rockefeller to meet him in Williamsburg. "While I am sure that you do not care to be concerned with the details of the work which is going on," Goodwin said, "it would certainly give me great personal pleasure to talk over with you certain aspects of the work in order that your point of view may correct and supplement my own." Rockefeller declined to come then, but he told him, "I am following with interest the development of matters and shall be more than glad when opportunity offers to discuss with you some of the problems with which you are confronted and with which you are dealing so wisely and ably."

Woods corrected and supplemented Goodwin on Rockefeller's views instead. The Doctor had passed along a gentleman's offer to sell to Colonial Williamsburg a collection of 18th-century books. The colonel said, "I don't believe we shall want to buy such things now. . . . In fact, it will be important for us to save expense in every way we can. I was talking with Mr. David yesterday as to the expense of the whole proposition, and as near as I can figure it, it will be substantially more than anything he originally thought. He was quite taken aback."

So was Goodwin. He wrote a three-page letter arguing for the purchase of antique furnishings, books, and such to complete the picture presented by the historic homes. He would, he said, rather have a Peale portrait than another half-mile of water pipe. "The soul and chief substance of the endeavor is the historic and memorial sentiment which it enshrines and seeks to perpetuate. . . . The history presented is the picture. The material improvements constitute the frame." Goodwin would sooner have a 200-year-old house trucked in with its ghosts, history, and antique charm than pay architects and contractors to build a reproduction "that might cost ten times as much." He said it was "just this side of the work that it is my duty to emphasize." He asked to confer with Rockefeller, and concluded, "I can truthfully say that since I have been intrusted by Mr. Rockefeller with this responsibility, I have tried harder to save his money than I would have tried to save my own."

A trip to New York gave Goodwin the chance to argue his views, but he did not leave satisfied. Afterward was broached the subject of a salary. Goodwin declined, though he was about to assign his Grace Church pay to curate Bentley, who was substituting in its pulpit. Rockefeller sent a check to finance a summer vacation, which Goodwin accepted to send Ethel and the boys to the mountains. He stayed in Williamsburg to work. The Capitol was being excavated. Todd & Brown built a tall safety fence around the Wren and began to dismantle the old building.

Architect Shaw and the Doctor went to take a look at its exposed brickwork one evening, and while they were absorbed in discussion, the watchman came along and locked them in. They climbed over, jumped from the top, and escaped. But Goodwin turned his leg and "sustained a severe sprain, which made me appear for a week as a wounded veteran. It is humiliating to get these reminders that one can no longer do some of the things which in other years might have been done with impunity." The knee still bothered him in December, when he had it X-rayed.

While he recuperated, Goodwin stewed. He sent Woods a confidential letter "written without a clear understanding on my part as to the exact extent of my responsibility with reference to the plans and policies and correlation of the work of the different personalities and agencies involved." He told the colonel he had no intention of "transgressing the bounds of the responsibilities, which, from your point of view, I am expected to fulfill," but he raised four issues, each amounting to a complaint that he had no role in crucial decisions made by the architects, the contractor, and Woods' office. If he was speaking out of turn, he said, it was because "the temperature down here today is at the boiling point."

A fortnight later he asked Woods that "no radical decisions be made" until they could discuss the relative importance of the phases of the work. "I feel with sure conviction," he said, "that certain changes in the plan have at least been discussed, which, if determined upon and adhered to, would produce a result which I am sure would be disappointing to Mr. Rockefeller and to many others." Though local director, Goodwin learned about these changes secondhand from erstwhile subordinates.

The same day, he asked Rockefeller for a meeting in early fall. "I have come to feel, with increasing conviction," Goodwin told him, "that it would be well for us to talk together before certain determinations which lie ahead are reached by the architects in consultation with your advisors." Rockefeller said he would come in early October for a conference. "In the meantime," he told the Doctor, "I do hope you will go away and take a few weeks of rest. You have been under a very heavy strain this past year, and yet the work is only beginning. You will need to bring to the problems still ahead calm judgment, clear vision and a vigorous rested mind, which can only be found in a rested body."

For his part, Woods assured Goodwin he was "the heart and soul of the whole scheme, and the thought that any 'radical decisions' could be reached without your intimate participation" was novel. The colonel was troubled that Goodwin suspected such a possibility and wanted an example. Goodwin replied, "Your letter gives me full assurance that completely satisfies me upon these and all other points."

Mr. David's trip would be his first to Williamsburg since Goodwin had identified Rockefeller as his partner. Weeks before he left, the *New York Herald* printed an erroneous account of his travel plans, attributing the information to Rutherfoord, who was handling press contacts. It brought the Doctor his first cross words from Rockefeller. "Please let us have it always understood," he said, "that my coming to Williamsburg is an entirely confidential matter as between you and me, and never to be made known in advance or at the time," Rockefeller said. Rutherfoord pleaded innocent; lots of people knew about the conference and were trying to get on the agenda.

Among them was Pollard, who had taken over fund-raising chores for the law school. "It would give a wonderful impetus to our appeal," he told the Doctor, if the conference gave part of the Capitol for law classes, the Raleigh Tavern for a dormitory, and three historic houses as professors' residences. The Richmond chapter of the Sons of the America Revolution said it hoped the conference would approve the purchase of Jamestown—which possibility had also reached the papers—as well as the reconstruction of its 1607 fort and five other buildings.

The conference minutes do not disclose that either proposition, or any like them, was discussed. But apart from Lady Astor's call at The Shrine, little else escaped its attention. Municipal services were discussed in detail. There were sessions on roads, squares, and stores, and so forth. Goodwin proposed the Restoration take over the Wythe House. Among the most interesting items was a decision to create an advisory committee of architects, something the Doctor had advocated since at least August. "The principal object in creating the committee," the minutes say, "is to get the interest and cooperation of the various professional bodies interested in Colonial architecture with a view to having them approve in advance Mr. Perry's plans so as to prevent later criticism." The conference also chose Robert Lecky, Jr., agent of the Merchants Fire Assurance Corporation and Richmond's former fire commissioner, to negotiate firehouse questions with the city. Lecky turned out to be something of an incendiary, but Goodwin thought Rockefeller had come to his rescue.

On the meeting's last day, William and Mary gave a dinner

for 105 people in Rockefeller's honor. Chandler did not attend; he had a sore foot. Goodwin wrote a note to Mr. David saying: "The conference which you guided us through will be of immense benefit, not alone to the program of the restoration, but to the creation of the atmosphere which must be brought to envelop this place to give it soul and the power to impart inspiration." He was pleased the "fundamental principles which underlie the work have been settled."

When Rockefeller reached his office, he replied: "I was again deeply impressed with your extraordinary versatility and with the ability which you have shown. . . . During the past year you have been working under far too high a pressure. Now that the more urgent problems have been disposed of, I want to have matters so organized that you will not be burdened with the multiplicity of things which are constantly coming to you. With that in mind, I am talking with my associates here, with a view to supplementing our organization as may be necessary in order to relieve you wherever possible. My associates will take up with you in due course the question of salary . . . . Quite irrespective, however, of the arrangement which they may make, I want the privilege of sending you the enclosed check as an expression of my deep appreciation of what you have done, what you are doing and what you are going to do in this unique and fascinating work of restoration." The draft was for a sum larger than the Doctor's salary at the church. Goodwin was to accept it, Mr. David said, in "the spirit of true friendship and warm admiration in which it is sent."

Goodwin could refuse neither the sentiment nor the generosity without the risk of giving offense. He put the check on deposit with the Security Trust in Rochester. He thanked Rockefeller and said, "I sincerely hope that you will not feel concerned with reference to any burden of work which now rests upon me." The Doctor assured him, "I have not in any way felt any burden of responsibility larger than I am glad and willing to continue to carry. I just fear that in following the generous promptings of your heart, you may incur unnecessary expense and may make provisions which will tend to cut me off from contact with the work at many points. . . . So please do not worry about me or take counsel with reference to lifting any burdens from me."

One burden of responsibility that really was troubling him was the Restoration's delay in building homes for the blacks it had displaced. He told Woods the need had become acute, and living

conditions were congested. He asked permission to encourage
outside builders to construct homes beyond the historic district for
both races, but Woods said "we certainly should not encourage
outside builders to erect houses." The problem remained.

The Doctor was almost as troubled by the houses that *were*
being built—the ones in the restored area that would be leased to
produce revenue. He told Woods that they should be considered
"from the artistic, archaeological, and historic point of view, rather
than from the rent point of view."

Geddy said that "During this time, Todd & Brown's
organization had grown by leaps and bounds, and Perry, Shaw and
Hepburn's organization had grown by leaps and bounds, and the
Doctor was still the nominal head. But unfortunately, friction and
jealousy grew up." The lawyer said "no clear line of authority was
established as between the architect, the contractor and Dr.
Goodwin's office, and frequently conflicting orders were given and
conflicting action taken." Goodwin tried to reclaim a measure of
on-site control by establishing procedures in which his office
would coordinate the work to "avoid conflict and misunderstanding
in local operations." The chief result was a feud with the
contractors and architects over the removal of the roof of Tazewell
Hall and the digging of a basement in a colonial home without
Goodwin's authorization.

Woods sent Goodwin's complaints to the architects and
contractors, who replied with counter complaints. When the fight
was over, Goodwin had less authority than before. "I hope that what
has transpired will at least result in a more complete accord and
unity of operation," the Doctor told Woods. "I would be glad to
know the nature and extent of my responsibilities in seeking to
safeguard the interests of my associates." Woods replied, "With
reference to the extent of your responsibility, we are of course
absolutely relying upon you to continue your parental relationship.
This is indispensable, and, as you and I have remarked to each
other frequently, your parental work is made easier by the good
fortune we have had in picking out the various experts who are
carrying it through their own different departments of the work. I
am certain that all are giving loyal service, and that we shall achieve
a fine result."

Whether he liked it or not, parent Goodwin would have to
accept the help of someone employed to relieve him of child-rearing

burdens. He asked that it at least be a Southerner, and Rockefeller friends recommended Lecky, the fire-insurance salesman. Heydt wrote to Goodwin on December 28 that he had signed Lecky to a year's contract as local business manager. Lecky would have complete charge of the real-estate interests in Williamsburg—not Goodwin—and Rutherfoord would work for him instead of the Doctor. "This arrangement, I believe, will bring us all much needed relief," Heydt said, "and spare us the annoyances which have troubled us heretofore."

Geddy called Lecky the general manager, which may have been a more accurate description of his portfolio. "Unfortunately," the lawyer said, "that had not been cleared entirely with Dr. Goodwin's office, and Perry, Shaw and Hepburn, and Todd & Brown, and instead of helping the situation actually it added chaos to the chaos that already existed."

Rockefeller's wealth peaked in 1928, reaching $994.7 million. His income for the year was about $50 million. On the last day of the year, he signed a contract with Columbia University to rent three Manhattan blocks for $3.3 million annually for 21 years on which to build Rockefeller Center.

Chafing under Williamsburg spending restrictions, Goodwin wrote to Woods the same day and complained "that economic considerations are often advanced which seem to be in conflict with the consideration of beauty and historic fitness." The colonel was that day promulgating a "Williamsburg Restoration Policy and Procedure" that ranked restorations, reconstructions, and new construction by historical, aesthetic, economic, and utilitarian criteria. An effort to contain costs by limiting work, it set up a hierarchy of authorizations and prior approvals.

Rockefeller was worrying over Restoration expenditures, too, and also complaining to Woods. Mr. David thought they were way too high. A year before, when he and Goodwin had considered the Restoration's cost, Rockefeller said, the estimate was between $2 million and $3 million. Now it had reached $5 million. He would go that far to complete the enterprise but no farther, and he conditioned further spending on a careful estimate of work approved and a prioritized project schedule. "Five millions of dollars," he said "is a very large sum of money."

Dressed for summer, his coat pocket stuffed with papers and his ever-present pipe in hand, Goodwin in the Restoration's hey-day.

Chapter Thirteen: **1929-1930**

About the only good news that came from New York the first week of 1929 was a note from little David thanking Goodwin for his annual present of Christmas nuts.

A New Year's Day telegram from Mr. David declined the Doctor's urgent request for a "brief personal interview in the interest of our work" to discuss "my responsibility in certain vital and far reaching matters." Rockefeller was sailing in 24 hours for Europe.

The next day the mailman delivered Heydt's letter announcing Lecky's employment. Perhaps with more hope than satisfaction, Goodwin replied, "Thank the Lord. You could not have sent me a more welcome New Year greetings. We will cooperate in every way to the fullest extent."

On the fourth came a copy of Rockefeller's $5 million-and-no-more decree. Goodwin answered, "You can fully count on my cooperation in every effort to carry this work to completion in accord with Mr. Rockefeller's expressed wishes."

Woods, Chorley, and Lecky arrived the day after for a Restoration conference. The colonel presented a prioritized budget for 26 projects. The Wren was down for $540,000. The Palace, the Raleigh, and the Capitol reconstructions totaled $389,000. Overhead would run $340,000. The new municipal buildings would require $225,000. Eight colonial homes could be restored for a combined $42,000. The bottom line came to $2,374,500. But with the spending cap, only $2 million was left. The conference deleted 13 items from the list. Nevertheless, Goodwin proposed ten more—things ranging from the restoration of all the colonial homes to buying "colonial light fixtures" for the streets—a day later.

Of the $3 million already gone, Hayes' accounts showed the Doctor and Heydt had spent $2,688,477—more than 89 percent—for property. Goodwin made the figure $2,756,835.60. His last acquisition turned out to be the December 28, 1928, purchase of the holdings of an African-American named Russell for $8,500. It was the Doctor's 38th Restoration transaction with Williamsburg's black community.

The biggest single check was written for $265,000 to the Casey family for its business district properties. The next largest was for $91,350 to buy the College Shop and Pocahontas Tea Room. The Colonial Hotel took $46,297, and the hospital closed at $15,500. The most expensive residential sale was today's Peyton Randolph House and lots, for which B. D. Peachy collected $38,600. Professor Van F. Garret's home brought $30,000, and Bassett Hall fetched $25,000, plus $5,000 for four forested acres out back that included the Great Oak Rockefeller admired. The biggest private Duke of Gloucester Street deal was with Elizabeth Coleman, who got $38,000 for her parcel. The cheapest acquisition was a $460 vacant lot.

In all, Goodwin completed 194 transactions—23 with life tenancies—at an average price of $13,858.13, exclusive of the commissions the real estate agents divided with the Restoration. He counted 37 purchases as colonial. The remainder of the deals, just under 81 percent, were for lots or modern buildings to be torn down or removed. By his estimate, the acquisition program, creating a housing shortage, doubled or tripled Williamsburg property prices.

Local Director Goodwin was still negotiating with real estate agents when Heydt directed him to step aside for Lecky and give the local business manager the $31,867.59 in the local purchase, restoration, and repair accounts. Henceforth Lecky, commuting from Richmond once or twice a week, would handle all real-estate matters. Goodwin was allotted $3,500 in revolving accounts for entertainment and office expenses, including Hayes' salary. The Doctor himself was paid directly by Rockefeller in one annual private check.

Whatever hopes the home office had that its new arrangements would bring concord to the Restoration were dead within ten days. On the 26th, "in the interest of harmony and frictionless cooperation," Goodwin asked Woods for new operating procedures. "If all those engaged in the work," the Doctor said, "could be instructed not to interfere in the work of other departments and refrain from making criticisms other than to those who are themselves concerned, a great deal that has been happening here to produce friction and ill-feeling would be avoided." Within days Goodwin was at 5600 Broadway presenting to Woods in person a ten-page *Report and Recommendations* defending his decisions and opinions, and attacking the contractors for carping. "It was my hope that the work of restoration would proceed harmoniously," the Doctor said. "There is no reason why it should not so proceed. In place of mutual cooperation and understanding there has been at times too much faultfinding and back-biting." He proposed all intramural fault-finding be typed in triplicate for official submission, and he asked for authorization to conduct weekly staff conferences.

Lecky was already having informal weekly staff conferences about which Goodwin knew nothing. The Doctor understood Woods wanted to separate Goodwin "from any situation in which I may become involved beyond a point which is advantageous to the work," but he had no reason to suspect Lecky would exclude him entirely. A few weeks later Goodwin pleaded again for the opportunity to attend such gatherings, for he needed "to be kept very much more closely in touch with what is going on." The colonel made inquiries and filled him in on the meetings.

Lecky twice asked Goodwin to change his schedule so that they might meet at the Wythe, but he neither appeared for the appointments nor canceled them. He did, however, find time to complain to Heydt about the terms Goodwin had offered in pending property negotiations—though not to consult the Doctor about them. Goodwin told Heydt: "As I have said and written, to Mr. Lecky, I would be glad to be kept informed as to the status of various matters which concern the mutual interests of us all. Concerning these matters I have been kept entirely in the dark, which is not only embarrassing, but detrimental. The desire to be kept informed does not spring from any disposition to interfere but simply to know what is going on."

Chorley, to whom Woods was delegating more Restoration responsibility, may have been unaware of the trouble brewing. He had found a quotation attributed to architect Daniel Hudson Burnham that he thought Goodwin might admire, and he sent it along. "Make no little plans," Burnham had said. "They have no magic to stir men's blood." The Doctor hit that pitch out of the park with a swing at the Restoration's new economic constraints. "It has always been my conviction," he told Chorley, "that every man should dare to dream in the terms of ideal and complete perfection, and that no plans should be compromised by either lack of faith or lack of courage. Truth and

beauty are realities in themselves. Our duty is to see them whole and
to paint our concepts on a large canvas. We contribute very little to
the beauty of a better world when we cut that canvas down to the
size of the frame which has been made by the man who has never
seen the vision and offers the frame because it is cheap. It is
unfortunate that so many people dream under the limitations of the
frames that are standardized and commercialized, and fail to dream
and plan in the terms of the ideal."

Which frame-maker the Doctor had in mind he was too
discrete to say. He was less diplomatic the next time the local
business manager crossed him. First Lecky got into a fight with
some elderly life tenants over the terms of their new residency in
their ancestral homes, then he tried to undercut the Doctor's
authority with Geddy. Goodwin told Geddy to ignore him, and
warned Heydt that Lecky was creating a community relations
disaster. The Doctor spoke of "a lack of public confidence which
follows unskillful handling of local problems" and of personal
chagrin. "At present I am in a position of having been announced
and known as the local 'director' of the Williamsburg Restoration
and am placed at the serious disadvantage of having things
constantly done and said which I am sure do not represent either
my own mind, or the mind and wish of my associates." Goodwin
said, "In the light of recent developments it has occurred to me that
in order to secure unity of operation, efficiency in results, and the
restoration and preservation of public confidence, that the
connection between your office in New York and your real estate
representative in Williamsburg might best be through my office."

Heydt, Lecky's patron, didn't budge. He told the Doctor no
change in Lecky's status could be considered without a bill of
particulars "of just what he has done to warrant your feeling that he
should be superseded." Heydt thought Lecky was doing an excellent
job "in bringing order into our real estate records and has been most
zealous in seeing that we have not been imposed upon by tenants of
our properties." So far as he knew, Lecky had performed in a proper,
upright, and admirable manner, "notwithstanding the fact that he has
been placed in a very embarrassing position at various times upon
learning that the ground has been pretty well plowed up before he
has begun his tasks." In short, Lecky was not only doing a better job
than Goodwin had but was doing it in spite of him. The Doctor fired
back copies of complaints and reports written by Lecky's only

subordinate—Goodwin's son Rutherfoord. Heydt replied that it would be improper to disrupt the chain of command to consider Rutherfoord's charges unless he communicated them through Lecky. He could not understand what Lecky could have done to arouse "such an intense feeling on your part against him."

The feeling was so intense that Goodwin told Woods he wanted to consult Rockefeller "with a view of having him determine the policy which should obtain and find expression in the Williamsburg management and further restoration." Goodwin believed "unfair, distorted, and prejudicial information" had been transmitted to New York that "misrepresents the local attitude and the local feeling." While he was at it, Goodwin wanted to hear from Rockefeller himself to what extent purely economic considerations should limit the historic, archaeological, architectural, and artistic aspects of the Restoration.

The next day the Doctor composed his resignation.

Addressed to Woods and dated April 16, the letter detailed the trust Goodwin had enjoyed until, without his knowledge, "the local management was placed in the hands of the contractor." He recited the disasters that had caused until, "without any consultation with me or with local people, Mr. Lecky was appointed." And the situation worsened. "It is extremely humiliating to have the impression given in Williamsburg and elsewhere," the Doctor said, "that I have been repudiated and have for some reason, had every duty committed to me in the Restoration taken from me and transferred to Mr. Lecky. The impression is given that I have proven myself unworthy of the confidence of my associates or have been guilty of negligence or failure to the extent that I should be removed from all position of trust and responsibility. That I have been thus dealt with is an apparent fact which Mr. Lecky seems to take evident pleasure in emphasizing by both word and public attitude.

"If Mr. Lecky is to be retained and continue to have charge of our public relations and exercise supreme authority in local management and personal contacts in Williamsburg without consultation and some measure of direction from my office, then I can perhaps best cooperate with Mr. Heydt's office by being allowed to resign as local Director of the Restoration work." As he departed, he said, he would make it clear he was not responsible for Mr. Lecky's actions nor "the mistaken policy of the local management." But he would, he promised, privately promote reconciliation. "I have

no desire to be an obstructionist, except in so far as I can obstruct
and hinder the insidious effect of uninformed and misjudged
management which is doing grave injury to the work. . . .

"I am entirely unwilling to be paid a salary and hold a title
with practically no local authority or position or duty other than to
spend my time trying to find out what Mr. Lecky is doing and in
endeavoring to try to save and build up in some measure the good-
will and public confidence which he is fast destroying."

By the time Hayes produced a fair copy of the 11-paragraph
rocket—perhaps the angriest letter of his life—the Doctor decided it
was Lecky who ought to go instead. Hayes wrote "Cancelled" across
the face of the letter and "not used" at the top; then she helped
Goodwin compose perhaps his second-angriest letter. Pulling
material from the first, it furnished Heydt more than five pages of the
specifics for which the New Yorker had asked. Among other things,
Goodwin said, Lecky employed stupid methods, bullied city officials,
was uncooperative, indiscreet, distrusted, antagonistic, dictatorial,
sycophantic, threatening, critical, and usurped Goodwin's duties—
"either rightfully or wrongfully, I do not know which."

Local hostility to the Restoration was rising. The people of
Williamsburg were quoting to one another Major Freeman's anti-
Restoration speech from the mass meeting. The Doctor hammered
Heydt with horror stories. Pollard, who was running for governor, had
complained, as had Majority Leader Dovell, President Chandler,
former state Highway Commission Chairman George Coleman, and
the chairman of the state Chamber of Commerce. All of them,
Goodwin said, doubted Lecky's reputation and regretted his
appointment. Goodwin wanted him demoted and confined to a desk
until he could be fired. To this missive the Doctor appended six pages
of memoranda, addressing subjects ranging from restorations to a
candidate for Lecky's replacement—again demonstrating the
thoroughness of the Doctor's grasp of the work. Then he went to New
York to make his case in person. Heydt was so fed up with the whole
business and frustrated with Goodwin that the Doctor felt obliged to
offer an apology, though he gave no ground on Lecky.

Goodwin's assaults on Lecky redoubled after he got back to
Williamsburg. Sometimes he addressed Lecky's character,
sometimes his competence, but he as often focused on the
doubtfulness of employing outsiders to deal with the locals. With the
possible exception of Charleston, the Doctor said, Williamsburg was

the most conservative city in the South. "Ancient traditions persist—
the super-sensitiveness of impoverished aristocracy is vitally
present—a natural pride exists among the people. They are closely
and keenly knit together. They are responsive to kindly
consideration, sensitive to criticism, appreciative of harmonious
relations but resentful of outside arrogant domination."

Not all of the fault, of course, was Lecky's. Helen Bullock,
who signed on as a researcher in 1929, said that "there was a lack of
organization and of top-level administration because too many
people had direct channels to Mr. Rockefeller, or tried to use direct
channels. There were little entities that were separate and competing
and trying to reach his ear. Dr. Goodwin by being able to go directly
through—and getting a decision on something—that really upset
efforts at planning."

In Bullock's view, Todd & Brown had no comprehension of
restoration work and thought no one but the contractors fathomed
the construction business or what it cost to keep a crew standing by.
"Occasionally they would take it upon themselves to go out and
clean up a little mess," she said. "They tore down many of the
colonial outbuildings. I think the record of destruction of Colonial
Williamsburg is as great as its record of restoration." The devastation
extended beyond the city to rural colonial structures the crews
scavenged for original materials for the historic area.

Few seemed to get along. Bullock thought fellow researcher
Mary Goodwin was inadequate, and the Doctor's restoration of the
Wythe House embarrassing. The contractors griped about the
architects. Freeman caused trouble. Heydt's methods insulted the
locals. Rutherfoord announced he would quit if Lecky were not
removed within a reasonable time. Lecky counter-complained and
publicly demeaned the architects and contractors. The skirmishes
went on until summer, when Lecky moved to Williamsburg and
Goodwin left town.

If the Doctor's position in the Restoration was less than he
wanted it to be, his standing in Virginia and his circumstances at 124
Francis Street materially improved. Governor Byrd asked him to join
the "Commission to Formulate and Carry into Effect, Plans for the
Observance of the 150th Anniversary of the Surrender of Cornwallis
at Yorktown, Virginia on October 19, 1781." In a state distinguished

Henry Ford did not accept Goodwin's invitations to Williamsburg until Rockefeller took on its restoration. Pictured here on their second visit, Ford and his wife, center, were welcomed by Restoration and civic leaders.

by pride in its past, the invitation itself was a distinction. The Doctor, however, would end up running the show.

President Charles Smith of Roanoke College begged the honor of bestowing upon its most distinguished alumnus an honorary doctor of laws degree. The occasion would be the spring graduation ceremonies and the 40th reunion of Goodwin's Class of '89. The Virginia chapter of the Sons of the American Revolution, of which Lecky was an officer, recruited the Doctor for its chaplain, a position he already filled for the Yorktown Chapter of the Daughters of the American Revolution.

In March, the Doctor ordered a $186 radio from the Stringfellow Electric Corporation in Williamsburg, and he bought a Ford for Ethel from the William Person Agency.

Henry Ford and his wife came to town May 5, taking the Doctor up on his almost five-year-old invitation for a Williamsburg tour. Goodwin showed the Fords around, arranged for a photograph, and sent the couple on to Jamestown and Carter's Grove in Rutherfoord's care. The Doctor said the industrialist pronounced the Restoration "by far the greatest and finest thing being done in America." Never one to miss an opportunity, Goodwin wrote to Ford a week later saying, "Some time, at your convenience, I would be glad to talk with you relative to certain ideas I have in mind regarding further acquisition and preservation of memorials which witness our historic past."

Apart from the Restoration, the Doctor had the church to attend to, and his part-time teaching. Hayes, who lived across the street from the Goodwins at 127 Francis, gave up many of her evenings to take dictation in his third-floor study. Fascinated by the stenographic machine, son Howard would watch the tape spill out with its mysterious symbols. The work might go on until 11. The Doctor was so busy, his William and Mary classes were sometimes better attended by his pupils than their professor. One class grew so accustomed to his absences it made up an exam and administered the test to itself. The papers went to Hayes for Goodwin to grade when he had time.

The workload was beginning to tell. The Doctor told a friend in Hampton, "this special year finds me under the necessity of conserving my strength. As you know for the past two years I have been working under great pressure and carrying a rather heavy load of responsibility, and until I get a little further out-of-the-woods I must, of necessity, refrain from doing extra things"—which extra things he proceeded to do anyway.

When the retired Bruton Parish sexton Alex Pleasants died, Goodwin took it upon himself to compose what may have been the most moving eulogy the *Virginia Gazette* had ever published for a black man. When Douglas Southall Freeman at the last moment canceled as Roanoke College's commencement speaker, Goodwin pinch-hit. When Lecky set up housekeeping in Williamsburg on June 17, Hayes took a letter from the Doctor to Woods that said: "In spite of his serious limitations, and of the well-founded convictions which I have submitted to you, I want you to know that as long as he is retained by my associates it will always be my purpose to further rather than to hinder his work. Indeed it has been largely because I have had to consider him so constantly and do so much to counteract the influence of his personality and methods, that he has given me so much trouble." When the Rockefellers motored to Williamsburg late in June with sons Winthrop and David for a two-day stay, the Doctor handled the arrangements for their accommodations at the Colonial Hotel and played host.

Winthrop drove a Nash loaded with the baggage, while his

parents and youngest brother rode ahead in another car. Its tank was almost empty when the Nash reached the outskirts of Williamsburg, and it ran out of gas just in front of the town's Sinclair retailer. Winthrop bought one gallon—enough to get him to the Standard station.

The Doctor filled up a few hours of Mr. David's schedule with his assessment of where the Restoration stood, and why it was making no better progress. John D. Rockefeller III arrived separately, looked at the sites, reviewed the plans, and confided to his diary: "Was very much disappointed when I first drove into Williamsburg but [see] now that . . . it has great possibilities. Still have a long way to go though."

Afterward the Doctor thanked Mr. David for his "deep and sympathetic understanding of the problems here" and said he was reassured. No doubt Lecky was, too, because with Rockefeller's departure, the time had come for Goodwin to go as well, at least for a time. Mr. David was sending the Doctor on a transatlantic working vacation.

A group of school children greeted America's wealthiest man when Goodwin took him to the Wythe House during one Restoration visit.

Goodwin looked forward to the break. As he packed his
trunk, he told Rockefeller, "Before leaving for Europe I want again to
express to you my cordial appreciation of your generous thought
and kindness. I will try to bring back to the work a clearer
perspective and a rested mind." He sailed from New York at 11 p.m.
July 3 aboard the *Homeric* for a three-month excursion.

Preparation for the trip had been under way since at least
June 1, when Goodwin got a smallpox inoculation from Dr. D. J.
King. He talked to Chandler, who had just spent six weeks in
examining the British archives. He conferred with Swem and the
acting head of the archives department at the Library of Congress.
He collected letters of introduction from Woods and the French and
British ambassadors to America—all of which took less time to
obtain than his passport.

Goodwin said he went "to prepare the way for intensive
research work abroad. In England the heads of the archives
departments of the British Museum, the Public Records Office, the
Bodleian Library at Oxford, the Library at Cambridge University, the
Library of Edinburgh University, the National Library of Scotland,
and other depositories of ancient records, were interviewed and
asked to give every possible assistance in search for helpful
information. This cooperation was promised and later cordially
given in every instance."

In addition to his calls, he advertised in the *Times of London*
for private papers, corresponded with prospects, and took time out
to shop and sightsee at places like the House of Lords. In August
he moved on to Paris, where he met Warren Dawson, American
Embassy attaché, who volunteered for Restoration research in
France. Colonel Woods was summering in Paris, and Goodwin
conferred with him, too. Before embarking for America on
September 11 from Plymouth aboard the *Rotterdam*, Goodwin took
delivery of a 100-year-old Indo-Persian papier-mâché box, his only
recorded private extravagance of the journey. By September 28
he was back.

The Doctor's sojourn changed his perspective on
Williamsburg and his relationship to the Restoration. He returned
relaxed, content to confine himself to contributing ideas and advice.
He had control of no office but his own, and he was ready to leave
the struggles of day-to-day decision making to someone else. It
probably helped that that someone else would not be Lecky. The

local business manager's days were numbered.

Geddy wondered if the Restoration's were, too.

"At that time the situation had grown so difficult and tense," Geddy said, "that it was very questionable whether Mr. Rockefeller would continue with the project. Mr. Heydt, I'm sure, had become quite dissatisfied with the reception he and his ideas were receiving in Williamsburg and he felt the Williamsburg people did not appreciate what we were trying to do, and we were almost at the point where Mr. Rockefeller's office was almost ready to throw in the sponge." Lecky packed for Richmond in October, three months before his contract was up, while Kenneth Chorley prepared to take over on-site management.

Many Rockefeller men regarded dog-eared Williamsburg as a place fit mainly for exile. Chorley may have, too, but he spent more time in the city than any one else from New York. He replaced Christy as vice-president of the Restoration corporations in November, and moved to Williamsburg to open an office December 1. "Had it not been for the strong intelligent hand of Kenneth Chorley," Geddy said, "I'm afraid in '29 and '30 Williamsburg may have seen the last of the Restoration. But Kenneth Chorley actually brought order out of chaos." Perry described him as "energetic, keen . . . and realistic." A later Restoration figure, Minor Wine Thomas, found him "arrogant, blunt, calculating, and ambitious." Goodwin waited until Chorley had been on the job for more than two months before he shared his opinion. The Doctor told Woods he was relieved, satisfied, even joyous. Goodwin asked Woods to tell Rockefeller the community was also pleased with the Chorley regime. Three months later, Goodwin wrote to Mr. David: "The progress of the work here since Mr. Chorley was placed definitely in charge has been not only very satisfactory, but exceedingly harmonious. An atmosphere has been created of confidence and good-will which it has given me great delight to note."

That, at least, was some good news from Williamsburg. Only a dozen days before, fire had gutted Bassett Hall, the home of sisters Alice and Edith Smith and the Williamsburg property Rockefeller most admired. "It was such a tragedy," Hayes said. "Almost like seeing a person burned. The volunteer firemen were wonderful. They rushed in and brought out furniture and doors and stair-rails, when the fire was scorching, and when the chimney fell in on them. They saved all the furnishings. Some beautiful antique furniture, priceless in value. And they also saved the woodwork in the downstairs rooms so that the house can be 'restored' fully." Chorley himself ran into the burning building, tore a banister from the staircase, and dragged it outside.

With Chorley so visibly in charge, the Doctor's mind turned to new prospects. He revisited the idea of a landscaped highway connecting Yorktown, Williamsburg, and Jamestown. He thought they might call it "Pathfinder's Road." He drafted an 11-page paper titled *The Separation of William and Mary College, Va., From State Control.* It would be a private "Cultural College," free of political control, backed by an $8 million endowment. All teacher training and vocational classes would end, and William and Mary would become an experimental school "for the purpose of developing the correspondences between the spiritual and cultural life of man, and the highest mental, moral, and spiritual environment of humanity."

For once his fund-raising timing was terrible. Ten days before he finished, the stock market crashed. It wasn't immediately apparent that Black Tuesday, October 29, meant the beginning of anything so calamitous as the Great Depression. To Goodwin, it looked more like an opportunity to buy blue chips at bargain prices. During the following 12 months, he invested heavily in stocks like United States Steel, American Tobacco, Standard Oil of New Jersey, International Harvester, General Motors, Westinghouse, American Telephone and Telegraph, Radio Corporation of America, railroads, utilities, and life insurance companies.

A month after the crash—the day Lieutenant Commander Richard E. Byrd of Virginia made the first airplane flight over the South Pole—Goodwin suggested Colonial Williamsburg invest in making William and Mary's Brafferton and its President's House part of the "harmonious whole of the Restoration." Otherwise, he was afraid Chandler would undertake the job and botch it. "Dr. Chandler," Goodwin said, "is in many respects one of the finest men I have ever known. He is very direct, insistent, devoted to his task, practical, and very inartistic."

It would take time for Rockefeller to warm to the idea, but that winter another of Goodwin's proposals produced something splendid.

Perry and his architects were committed to faithful duplication of Williamsburg's 18th-century buildings. They had historic drawings to refer to as they made plans to reconstruct the Raleigh and restore the Courthouse of 1770. But for the Wren, the original Capitol, and the Palace—signature structures—no original drawings of their early colonial exteriors could be found. The architects had to depend on written descriptions, archaeology, and conjecture.

It had been the Doctor's idea to hire researcher Mary F. Goodwin—his cousin Mamie—to help them search for data. At the State Library in Richmond during February 1929, her attention was called to a guide to early American history manuscripts in London, Oxford, and Cambridge. In the Virginia section, she saw a reference to an engraved copper plate in a collection at Oxford's Bodleian Library. The entry said the plate showed a group of buildings in Virginia or North Carolina. At once she thought there could be a Williamsburg connection. In October she and companion Kate Cannon embarked for England to pursue that and other research leads.

They presented themselves at the Bodleian the afternoon of December 21, checked the catalog, and called for the plate. The attendant thought they were wasting their time and his. But Mamie insisted, and he disappeared into the dimly lit stacks. He returned with the wrong plate, and Mamie sent him back. When he reappeared he held a 12- by-15-inch sheet of copper so dirty and corroded she couldn't make out the figures. Engraved about 1740, apparently to illustrate a book, the plate looked to have never been used. She took it to a window, held it to the light, and began to see a corner of the President's House at William and Mary. Then she saw the Wren, the Brafferton, the Capitol, and the Palace. Perspective engravings, they showed precisely how the structures appeared early in the 18th century. "No such representation of these buildings had been seen for nearly two centuries," she said.

Mamie shared the importance of her discovery with the library and arranged to have pulls—as such prints are called— produced before returning to London. She kept the news for her Christmas present to the Doctor, waiting until the 24th to cable word of the find. On Christmas morning the Doctor opened a telegram and read: "Found copper plate showing buildings of college, front and rear view, Palace and first House of Burgesses. Buildings all about two inches square. Have ordered pulls sent to you. Merry Christmas, M. F. Goodwin."

Because of the holidays, it took about two weeks to secure the prints. She sent a radiograph of one to New York. Though the images were blurred, they were good enough to show Perry that he had the roof lines wrong on the wings of the Wren. Work at the college stopped. The pulls reached the Wythe at 11:30 a.m. January 19, 1930, a Sunday. "I wish you could have seen the ceremony with which the strings of the package containing the prints were cut," Hayes told Mamie. "Dr. Goodwin almost had a prayer-meeting over the package, he was so excited. As soon as the prints were produced, Rutherfoord and the doctor each took one and sat in deep silence for at least an hour studying the pictures." Goodwin cabled her that morning, and wrote to her that afternoon. "Hurrah for you!" he said, "The pictures are marvelous. It happened that Col. Woods and Mr. Chorley were both here, and also Mr. Perry. . . . They just went wild about them as did Dr. Swem and Dr. Chandler. Mr. Perry says it is the greatest find ever made in American research work."

Mary F. Goodwin and Kate Cannon pose with the copperplate they located in the Bodleian Library.

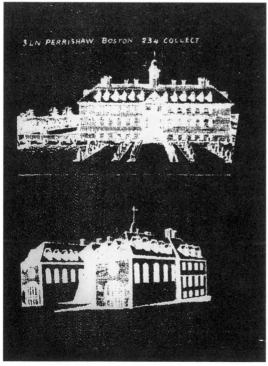

The Bodleian plate,
perhaps engraved in 1740
to illustrate a book,
showed at top the College
of William and Mary, next
Williamsburg's Capitol, the
rear of the Wren Building,
the Governor's Palace, and
an assortment of Indians,
plants, and fauna. Mary F.
Goodwin sent copies of
the drawings from London
to Boston by radiograph.

The Rockefeller men began to deal with Goodwin as a kind of guardian of the educational and inspirational principles that underpinned the project. He became a sort of Restoration senior statesman. He liked that, and the freedom. "As the Restoration work has progressed," he told Woods, "your own wise judgment in not assigning me to the chairmanship of any department of work, but leaving me free to relate myself to the various departments, activities, and problems of our endeavor as occasion requires or suggests, has been increasingly appreciated. It gives me opportunity to get unofficially mixed into everything and to emerge upon the surface to say what I saw, to report findings, and make any number of free-lance suggestions, and, I trust, some constructive criticism."

He submitted his views on the need to stock the Restoration with Southern, as opposed to Northern, antiques and on the "vital importance of providing for the proper interpretation of the restoration" through a guide bureau. Both ideas became Colonial Williamsburg fundamentals. He advised Perry on the need for unity in the architectural and artistic treatment of the Palace Green, Woods on the need for closer supervision of clean-up crews. He proposed construction of log outbuildings, an Indian relic house, and the employment of African-Americans to represent colonial servants. He reported on poor archaeological practices and suggested again the restoration of the Brafferton. At year's end, he submitted what he titled an "annual report," a 19-page critique of the performances of Restoration officials and departments that took up problems as disparate as gutters, boxwood, housekeepers' toilets, and establishment of an archaeological lab.

His interests, however, embraced more than Williamsburg. When an electrical utility proposed to dam Gotten Pass in distant Rockbridge County, Goodwin wrote to Byrd protesting against the scenic damage it would do. "We of the present are trustees of the heritage which we have received from the past," he said. When the Universal Film Corporation made a bullfighting film called *Men Without Fear*, he wrote a letter in his dog Alaska's name protesting against the studio's cruelty to animals. "I am just a dog," it began. When a custodian denied black tourists admittance to the APVA's Jamestown enclosure, Goodwin protested against that, too, though rather more gravely. He told the APVA's president he couldn't believe it would exclude "any American citizen from the grounds," and if such a policy applied to blacks, it should be canceled. He even dabbled in linguistics and acoustical phonography. When Columbia University fielded a team with a record-making machine to capture regional accents, Goodwin turned his Wythe House office into a studio, recruited a dozen friends, and spent two days recording the Restoration's first oral histories in the mellow speech patterns of Tidewater.

"Dr. Goodwin," Rockefeller said, "is an extraordinarily interesting man, is he not?" The admiration was mutual. The Doctor adopted a suggestion made by Roanoke businessman Edward L. Stone that the General Assembly officially thank Rockefeller for the Restoration, lobbied Dovell, and drafted a legislative resolution of appreciation himself. When the American Institute of Architects proposed to accord honorary membership to Goodwin for the Williamsburg work, he insisted Rockefeller be included, too. Byrd composed a private paean to the priest. "When I think of all you have done for the state," the governor said, "what little I have been able to do seems very little indeed. No man has left his work more indelibly impressed upon future generations than you have in the restoration of Williamsburg."

Goodwin hoped at least that future Williamsburg generations would be more impressed with his Restoration than some of the city's present denizens. Despite his professions to Woods, he was troubled by local attitudes. "Fundamentally the old town remains very much the same," he wrote to a former resident.

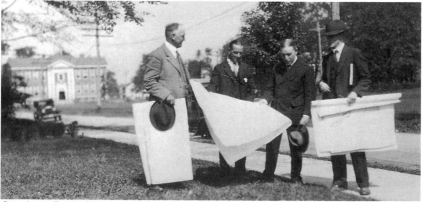

Goodwin, Rockefeller, and company confer in the Wythe House front yard on Restoration blueprints. The high school in the background was marked for demolition; it stood on the Palace site.

"Whatever the Restoration may do, I think it is safe to say that it will not reconstruct, alter, renovate, or change, the disposition of the people here to vigorously contend for the wrong thing, and to contend with equal vigor against the things that should be. I have, however, some ground for hope and encouragement arising out of the fact that so far I have not found anybody who is opposed to moving the School from the Palace Green, and rebuilding the Governor's Palace, and I think that there is very general approval of the rebuilding of the old Capitol. One, however, feels very sure that when the work is finished all those whose opinions are worth anything will approve what will have been done, even though many may not find the courage to say so."

The work, however, was a long way from finished. To a sightseer's eye, Rockefeller hadn't much to show for his $5 million. Bruton Parish and the Wythe House, neither of them Restoration properties, were the only buildings open to the public. Only the exterior of the Raleigh had been finished, and the Wren had been reduced to an ancient brick shell with an incongruous modern steel skeleton. Restoration of the Paradise, which the college deeded back to the Restoration on June, 24, 1929, had barely begun. Nothing had been done on the Capitol or Palace. Many modern buildings, however, had been removed from the historic section, and many of the smaller colonial homes reconstructed for private dwellings. Later in the year the Travis House would open as a tea room. In the meantime, the Doctor got going on his next big endeavor.

Rockefeller built the Mathew Whaley School to replace the high school the Restoration demolished. In the middle ground at left stands the Timson House, one of Williamsburg's oldest homes and a property Goodwin would buy for himself.

As the high school sank in a pile of rubble, the reconstructed Governor's Palace
rose behind it.

William E. Carson, chairman of the Virginia Commission on
Conservation and Development, wanted the federal government to
preserve some of the state's chief colonial sites as national
monuments. He won the backing of Byrd, Governor-elect Pollard,
Chorley, and others, and interested U. S. Representative Louis
Cramton of the House Interior Committee. The congressman and
his wife visited Richmond to discuss the idea, traveled to Jamestown
and Yorktown, and stopped in Williamsburg to confer with Goodwin
and company at the Wythe House.

"I made what I thought was quite an original suggestion," the
congressman said. "Later I learned they'd thought of it very
definitely before I ever got here." Cramton, a Michigan man, shared
with the Virginians his opinion that the colonial period began at
Jamestown, ended at Yorktown, and that Colonial Williamsburg was
in between. "This should be the Colonial National Monument," he
said. Cramton also got the impression it was his idea to build a
parkway to connect all three. The ideas, no matter whose they were,
dovetailed neatly with plans for the Yorktown Sesquicentennial
celebration. They would enhance the observance's standing as a
national commemoration.

Carson drove around the state enlisting Virginia's newspaper

Excavation of the Capitol grounds, leased from the APVA, revealed the old foundations.

editors in the cause and persuaded Cramton to introduce the necessary legislation in January 1930. Fifty congressmen came in April to see the sites for themselves. That summer, Congress authorized creation of the United States Yorktown Sesquicentennial Commission and approved "An Act to provide for the creation of the Colonial National Monument in the State of Virginia." Before the year was out, the President of the United States proclaimed the borders of the Colonial National Monument: all of Jamestown Island, the colonial parts of Williamsburg, the Yorktown Battlefield and Gloucester Point, and 20 miles of linking parkway.

Claude A. Swanson, chairman of the United States Yorktown Sesquicentennial Commission, authorized a Yorktown Sesquicentennial Association to plan and finance the observance. Representatives of the 13 original states conferred at Yorktown on October 19 and elected Goodwin the association's president. He was in charge of raising local, state, and national enthusiasm, as well as funds for the celebration.

"For the next year," Hayes said, "he concentrated all his energies on developing the celebration in Yorktown . . . and on advancing of the restoration program during these important early phases in Williamsburg."

Goodwin on a golfing holiday at Swannanoa with friends in 1932.

Chapter Fourteen: **1931-1933**

With the Sesquicentennial added to his schedule, the Doctor was obliged to put in 14-hour workdays. He could have put aside any of the Colonial Williamsburg duties he gave himself, but he didn't. Nor did he stint his ministry or approach his college work with less energy.

When he could, he pulled his old golf clubs out of the closet for a round of "swing, miss, and spit." Once he paid son Howard a dime to caddie. The boy was so proud for the honor of toting his father's clubs that he secretly slipped the coin back into the Doctor's pocket. His father's game may not have been much to admire, but the Doctor was someone to look up to.

Howard's younger brother Bill sought and was granted the honor of changing his name, and he registered himself at the courthouse as William Archer Rutherfoord Goodwin, Jr. The Doctor loomed as large a figure to friends, associates, and even to opponents, as he did to his boys. He was physically and mentally prepossessing. Geddy said he had a "powerful physique as well as powerful mind. He was a heavy set man, strong, very handsome, distinguished looking with a twinkle in his eye. One who always smoked a pipe and either had it in his hand or in his mouth most of the time. And when he talked to you he'd come right up to you and usually catch you by your lapels, and he kept swaying from one foot to the other while he talked to you. He was so convincing that I was certain myself that anything he might undertake he could accomplish."

For a small-town preacher, he was downright outspoken. He got fed up with the Prohibition debacle, put together an 18th-century style broadside calling for repeal, and mailed it to newspapers and public officials. The handbill proclaimed the 18th Amendment had failed of its object, that prohibition wasn't a proper subject for the Constitution in the first place, and that instead of promoting temperance, the liquor ban had "resulted in widespread disrespect of Law and consequent anarchy which all good citizens deplore." He recommended giving Congress authority to regulate the manufacture, transportation, and sale of liquor and narcotics. He offered the same program to a national group of businessmen and academics who periodically surveyed prominent Americans for ideas on Depression problems. Moreover, he suggested graduated reductions in salaries and wages, advocated military budget decreases, and proposed to cut war debts in half, to cut tariffs in half, and "to cut all politicians in half."

Whatever people thought of the Doctor's opinions, it was hard not to admire his principles, the generosity of his spirit and soul, his ability not to take himself too seriously, and his readiness to speak up for the things he believed were right. Evolution was a generally good subject for Southern preachers to avoid, especially when they had liberal opinions. Goodwin had "no objection whatsoever to accepting the term evolution, properly defined and described by and through which the eternal God works out and unfolds His own divinely conceived plan." He resented those who believed that view "less spiritual and less loyal than the views held by the so-called fundamentalists." When the troublesome Major Freeman put his modernist notions on the subject into a pamphlet, the Doctor thought the booklet so well reflected his own ideas he bought 50 copies and sent them to clergy and lay people with a flattering endorsement.

If a priest ever needed a curate, it was the overburdened Reverend Doctor Goodwin, and in Bentley he at last had found a first-class aide, a keeper. But when Bentley got a crack at a church of his own in Alaska, the Doctor encouraged his ambition and helped him secure the promotion. Four years later, Bentley was a bishop. Without Hayes, the Doctor had no staff at all, but he urged her to summer in Europe as a vacation chaperone to Governor Pollard's daughter and four other young women. She was away for three months when he needed her most.

It was his job to minister to his Bruton Parish flock, of course, but he was attentive as well to the needs of folks he never met. He heard from housemothers, painters, hostesses, carpenters, preachers, and professors asking his advice on employment in the

Restoration or at William and Mary. Teachers, social service
workers, school principals, and city managers sought his
endorsement for positions with the city. He helped every
correspondent he could, apologized to those he couldn't, and
replied to everyone.

Friends of friends asked him to book hotel rooms for them,
and complete strangers appeared unannounced at the Wythe
expecting personal walking tours. He almost always obliged. There
were incessant speaking invitations from churches, civic groups,
clubs, and schools—in part because he charged nothing. "I beg to say
that I have never been accustomed to make any regular charge for
my lectures beyond the cost of my travel expenses and
entertainment," he told one program chairman. "Any question of
honorarium has always been, and is in this interest, left entirely to
the wish of those who ask for the lecture." He accepted more
engagements than his constitution could handle. On one of the rare
occasions he declined, he said, "I am at present carrying a weight of
responsibility which is taxing my strength to a point where two
physicians have urged me to curtail my efforts."

People sought his counsel on matters so diverse as
architecture, colleges for their children, real estate, and genealogy.
Goodwin, whose ancestors included a Mayflower family, said, "I am
not a genealogist. In certain spare moments I have tried to trace
these sinuous family lines through the dim vistas of the distant past
and have found, either along the lines relating to my own or
collateral ancestors, at least three of them dangling from the ropes
of the gallows. This you must admit was somewhat discouraging. The
only compensating thought being that they were hung for being
what we now regard as distinguished patriots."

Some of the patriotic societies who sought his and Ethel's
affiliation required an application with a family tree. He usually
turned the chore over to cousin Mamie. "I am not by disposition a
'joiner,'" he said, as he gave her one of the forms, "and yet I am
willing to help forward efforts which are designed to perpetuate
ancient traditions, if I can do it without too much trouble and too
much expense." For a man who was not a joiner, he had a
remarkable list of memberships. Among other groups, he belonged
to the Masons, the National Economic League, the Mediaeval
Academy of America, the Virginia Academy of Science, the Rotary,
the Association of Biblical Instructors, the Virginia Garden Club, the

American Association of University Professors, and A Citizen's Committee of One Thousand—an arm of the Virginia Commission on Interracial Cooperation. He even kept up his dues with the Country Parsons in Rochester.

Preservation projects up and down the coast—in Annapolis, Maryland; at New Castle, Delaware; the Decatur House in Washington; and Washington's Mill in Pennsylvania, to name a few— asked Goodwin to interest himself in their work. In one or two cases, they seemed as interested in Goodwin's access to Rockefeller as in his heritage expertise, but he turned down none.

As the Depression deepened, the Doctor received with increasing frequency letters from scores of desperate individuals, and a few charlatans, begging him to appeal to Rockefeller for their relief or to slip Mr. David their sometimes heartbreaking explanations of their need for money. Goodwin's stock reply was that the gift of the Restoration was so generous he had promised to ask Rockefeller for nothing more. Nevertheless, he passed especially touching entreaties on to Woods.

He was generous with his own pocketbook. Each Christmas he sent a small gift of cash to a man in Arkansas who claimed to be disabled and in need of assistance raising a brood of children—a brood that seemed to grow no older year to year, only larger. He loaned money to hard-pressed relatives, friends, townspeople, and even the landlord of the Buckroe Beach cottage Ethel liked to rent in the summer. He was, he admitted, an easy touch and a sucker for a tramp with a hard-luck story. He also had a soft spot for penitent prison inmates.

The Doctor sought executive clemency from Governor Byrd for "a colored convict named Joe Britt, whose number is 19640" whom Goodwin knew from the Sunday services he conducted at the prison camp between Jamestown and Williamsburg. He pestered governors Pollard and George Peery for the release of State Penitentiary inmate James Wilson. He knew Wilson—prisoner 15356 serving life on a 1918 Norfolk murder conviction—only from the prisoner's annual letters begging the Doctor's intercession. But he told Pollard, "If this colored Brother's behaviour since his incarceration, or since his coming to Repentance, has been as satisfactory as the conduct which he pledges in the future, you might save the state some expense by letting him out on parole." Britt may have been freed, but Wilson stayed behind bars.

Goodwin also endorsed the plea Judge Frank Armistead made in behalf of Cyrus Jones, the aged former slave of Williamsburg's Saunders family. At Armistead's behest, the Doctor asked W. E. L. Saunders of New York City to help support Jones in his last days. "As you will recognize there are very few of the old family servants of slave times who are still living," the Doctor wrote, "and those who are living can not be expected to survive more than a few years longer. . . . I feel that we all want to do everything we can to make their exit graceful and as comfortable as possible." He also befriended a young African-American named Garland Stewart, whose mother had been the Goodwins' housekeeper during his first Bruton Parish rectorship. Emotionally disturbed, a paraplegic, and sometimes violent, Stewart needed institutional care hard to find for blacks in 1930s Virginia. But Goodwin prevailed upon a series of private and public asylums to accept the youth, and he bought a wheelchair for him, too. A woman who had been governess to his children before the move to Rochester in 1908 had since lost her sanity and turned into a wandering and impoverished paranoiac. She peppered him with long and crazy letters that were sometimes insulting and sometimes threatening. But year after year he sent her small sums, arranged for parish relief, steered welfare workers her way, and tried to persuade her relatives to take her in and keep her.

Six of his own—wife Ethel; sons Howard, Bill, and Jack; sister Laeta, and niece Ella—depended on the Doctor's breadwinnings. But a typical Goodwin income tax return lists donations to 34 charities—ranging from hundreds of dollars for Bruton Parish and its missionary funds to the single greenback he contributed annually to the Humane Society in Alaska's name. In the leanest years the gifts totaled more than 4 percent of his gross income and came on top of nondeductible private generosities—sometimes to people who should have been sending *him* money. The tenant of the Norwood farm got along on Goodwin's willingness to take annual losses on the place. Though the Doctor was out of pocket every year for seed, taxes, and such, he was not disposed "in this time of depression to turn him off the farm," and the sharecropper stayed on until he found a new situation.

The Depression—which had cut Rockefeller's fortune in half by 1934—pinched the Restoration, too. The reconstruction of the Capitol and the Governor's Palace was spread out, though the advertised purpose, despite the Bodleian discovery, was "the hope that our research workers in France, England, or America may find some old document or print which may throw some additional light upon certain details of these two buildings." It looked to Goodwin as if it would be three or four years before the buildings were finished. Long before then, the Doctor volunteered for a 10-percent reduction in his Restoration pay to help out, though the offer was declined.

William and Mary's finances went sour, too. So did the investments of Bruton Parish, the income from which helped pay Goodwin's salary. Chandler had a deficit of $110,000 and needed to reduce his payroll by at least $30,000 in 1931. He asked for Goodwin's help. "I offered to teach for nothing," Goodwin said, "but Dr. Chandler felt that it was not wise for the College to have unpaid professors engaged in the regular academic work."

To a friend vacationing in Paris he wrote: "You may have, perhaps, heard rumors of a certain depression which is said now to exist. There must be some truth in this rumor as, among other things, it has led me to take a year's leave of absence from the College to keep Dr. Chandler from having to drop some other professor, and it has also resulted in the default in the interest on all of the investments in Bruton Parish Church Endowment Fund. So it looks as if I were being divinely called to minister to the rest of the depressed people, by reason of the sympathy and understanding which has come to me as the result of the things that have happened."

One of the Doctor's own investments failed, one especially dear to his heart. The Williamsburg Golf and Country Club, Incorporated, of which he was a director, went belly up. He sent the certificate for his worthless share in the enterprise to Rutherfoord with a note that said, "This certificate, so beautifully executed and adorned may also serve to remind you to conserve your resources and not invest them as I did in corporations and institutions which so soon have nothing to show for themselves other than such beautiful and such worthless certificates." The Doctor had socked away another $15,256.78 in securities the year before. Apparently not all of them had performed as well as he had hoped.

Goodwin was reluctant to ask or accept much for himself other than sympathy and understanding. When friends suggested to Woods that the Goodwins should have the chance to live in a Restoration house, the Doctor headed them off. "Mr. Rockefeller has contributed such unmeasurable happiness and gladness to my life through what he is doing here," he told Chorley, "that I should feel deeply humiliated to have any suggestion ever made to him either directly or indirectly that I expect him to do anything for me personally." Ethel said, "We never lived in a Restoration house."

*

The Doctor retained the title of director of William and Mary's endowment campaign, but his fund raising was now merely casual and opportunistic. His leave of absence was extended year to year, until 1935, when he returned to part-time teaching for one last academic year. Goodwin's workaday connections would never again be as strong to the college after the layoff, but his interest in the school as a "cultural college" never flagged. He pursued his plan for William and Mary's privatization almost to his dying day and with almost the same sense of urgency that he brought to the scheme in 1931.

In person, by letter, and on the telephone, he prodded Rockefeller early in the year about the "<u>possibility of securing the interest of a selected group of men in providing an endowment sufficient to justify the College of William and Mary in securing a separation from the State and equipping the College for the fulfillment of a distinct cultural mission.</u>" The underscoring is Goodwin's. Though Rockefeller would not finance the takeover, he tried to help Goodwin recruit other backers. "I will not forget the matter," he told the Doctor.

It may have been the Doctor who was becoming forgetful. It is hard to believe, but dedication of the $514,000 Wren Building restoration, the project on which his association with Rockefeller was founded, appears to have slipped his mind. It could be that he had decided it was not important, though that is equally hard to believe. In any case, he missed it. Perhaps some of the facts are lost, but on the face of the record that survives, the circumstances are these:

Ethel went to Atlantic City, her favorite beach, late in August. "It is her yearly fling," the Doctor told a friend. "One of her cousins and one of her friends is with her." Leaving Hayes in charge of the office, he left for a general convention of the Episcopal Church in Denver. He traveled by way of Yellowstone, where in the days before the meeting he vacationed with a cousin employed by the Park Service.

Three days before the Wren's grand opening, Chandler sent a telegram to Goodwin's hotel in Denver, reminding the Doctor of the event and asking when he would return. Goodwin replied by letter, saying he wouldn't be there. "You know, I am sure," he wrote, "how greatly I regret not being present at the ceremonies as it is the first completed major project of the Restoration which is being set aside for the use for which it was originally designed." Two days later, Goodwin wired the college: "It is with great regret that I find that it is impossible to be present at the ceremonies incident to the dedication of the Wren Building, restored. Congratulations and all good wishes."

Rockefeller had agreed in January to spend $26,000 on the restoration of the Brafferton and the President's House, but he did not attend the dedication either. The program started at 11 a.m. September 16. Chorley read a letter from Mr. David, Perry presented Chandler with the keys, and Douglas Southall Freeman delivered the dedicatory address.

Nothing in Goodwin's personal files except his well-documented enthusiasm for the church's conventions explains his decision not to return. But the Wren work had been troubled by recurring squabbles among state officials, restoration architects, and the college's administration. Forty-one years later, as William and Mary prepared to bestow on him an honorary degree, Perry said "negotiations regarding the 'Wren Building' were by no means as simple as they might well have been; we burst in from the North and such an incursion would perhaps have been simplified if the Wren Building had not been so high on the list and was, therefore, one of the first bastions to be in the path of the invasion. Dr. Goodwin, of course, smoothed the precipitous way and soon the reasonably good intentions of the Restoration became recognized for what they were." Perry said he himself was "a target and became gradually a type of battering ram, but with a vulnerable solar plexus. 'All's well that ends well.'"

There is another aphorism that says what is well begun is half done, and preparations for the Yorktown Sesquicentennial Celebration were well begun indeed. Ten months before the four-day extravaganza, Goodwin published a prospectus—a promotional document like the ones he crafted for the college endowment

campaign in 1923 and Bruton's restoration in 1907. Designed to
encourage the governments of the 13 original states to join in
underwriting the event, as well as to solicit private contributions, the
booklet emphasized the national flavor of the celebration of the
150th anniversary of Washington's victory over Cornwallis.
Congress had appropriated $200,000 for the sesquicentennial.
President Herbert Hoover would be on hand. The Colonial National
Monument would be inaugurated. General John J. "Black Jack"
Pershing was expected.

Hoover underlined the federal stature of the affair less than
a month later by signing the national monument bill and authorizing
the Colonial Parkway—the idea Goodwin proposed to his
congressman more than two decades before. The participation of
the French government, in honor of the part Rochambeau,
DeGrasse, and Lafayette played in the Battle of Yorktown, put an
international imprint on the festivities. Lafayette's great-grandson
was invited.

The officers of the Virginia-chartered Sesquicentennial
Association, the Doctor wrote, were organizing the observance in
behalf of America without "salary, commission nor financial
remuneration of any kind." The Old Dominion, of course was
furnishing its share of the expense, and there was a paid staff to ride
herd on the details.

Goodwin planned a combination state fair, military
exhibition, and historical pageant. Along with exhibits on
agriculture, industry, and history, there would be parades of soldiers
and sailors, battle reenactments, and an array of dreadnoughts at
anchor in the York River. His immediate personal responsibility was
to help secure the ceremonial and financial participation of the
other states.

Goodwin hadn't really wanted the association's presidency,
but he tackled the job with customary energy. The celebration would
cost $625,000, and there was $312,500 left to raise. He gave five and
six hours a day to the work through the spring, often more, at home
and away. He delivered a March sesquicentennial address to a joint
session of the Pennsylvania legislature in Philadelphia. The following
day he gave it again to a joint session of the Massachusetts
legislature in Boston.

He did not return from the West until less than a month was
left before the sesquicentennial opened. But that was time enough to

see to last-minute details and put the final touches on his essay in
the souvenir program.

"The celebration bids the nation pause and take inventory,"
he wrote. "It seeks to light a torch at which many altar candles may
be rekindled. If Yorktown could speak its message to the souls of
men, it would fain transform politicians into statesmen, preachers
and priests into prophets, blindness into vision and selfishness into
self-devotion. The memories and aspirations which the celebration
will recall will be enriched and fulfilled by time. Out of the nation's
memory and aspiration and experience, wisdom, that lingers long,
will come. Then, last of all and greatest of all, love will come, the
love that kills hate and creates and preserves international
fellowship."

The sesquicentennial began October 16 against a backdrop
of naval might spread across the York. Among the American and
French vessels was the just-recommissioned *U. S. S. Constitution*,
oldest warship in the American fleet, and the *U. S. S. Arkansas*,
which would be the oldest American battleship to fight in the war
looming over the horizon. The combined fleet rode above the hulks
of British men-of-war sunk in 1781 and still rotting on the muddy
bottom. Contingents of the Army, Marines, and National Guard
drilled on the parade ground and tented where Continentals and the
troops of King Louis XVI had a century and a half before.

In the French delegation was Marshal Henri Petain, an Allied
hero of the First World War who would be a Nazi collaborator in the
second. Governor Franklin D. Roosevelt led the contingent from
New York. At 10:30 a.m. Horace M. Albright, National Park Service
director, dedicated the Colonial National Monument.

On the second day the dirigible *Los Angeles* flew in, and
there was a military and naval pageant "depicting through historical
scenes the planning and execution of the Yorktown campaign,
including preliminary battles." Grandstands were provided for the
spectators' comfort. The third day was given over mostly to religious
exercises and to the dedication of commemorative tablets, not least
among them one attesting the affection of Virginia for the mother
country despite the Revolution.

President Hoover, to whom the College of William and Mary
was presenting an honorary degree, arrived by battleship the final
day. He witnessed a re-enactment of the surrender of Cornwallis's
forces, followed by a portrayal of a dinner the defeated general gave

for Rochambeau and Washington. That was followed by "a Masque
dealing in symbolic or allegorical form with the great developments
after the events of Yorktown with main motifs of Peace, Liberty, and
Democracy." The British flag was raised from a British redoubt, and
there was a Grand Military Review featuring all the armed forces.
Goodwin delivered an invocation, and the President made a
patriotic oration.

Nothing better captures the flavor of the day, and of the
times, than the description written by Major Raymond Bottom, the
new editor of the *Daily Press* in Newport News:

> On the very ground tread by the feet of the stalwart
> legions of Washington these distinguished visitors, surrounded
> by thousands of our own people, stood in respectful reverence
> for the impressiveness and importance of the occasion.
>
> None who were present at Yorktown on Monday,
> October 19th, 1931 can ever forget the marvelous spectacle. The
> benign Providence which orders things to its plan crowned the
> day with all the glory of fall. The sun was brilliant and the sky
> cloudless. Across the rolling slopes of Surrender Field great banks
> of trees in their yet-green dress of summer formed a perfect
> backdrop for the soul-stirring spectacle that moved in ever-shifting
> brilliance before one's eyes. Events succeeded one another in
> orderly and unhesitant succession. Thousands upon thousands
> of brightly caparisoned troops marched by to the stirring strains
> of martial music from scores of bands. They thrilled the soul with
> their martial steps and the precision of their lines. Prancing horses,
> flashing in the sunlight the glittering sabers of their riders; rumbling
> artillery and its caissons bearing their immovable cannoneers;
> tattered and non-descript companies of representations of the
> brave regiments of Washington and Lafayette—all in well ordered
> arrangement passed in impressive succession, coming from one
> knew not where and disappearing, one might think, into some
> huge chasm that engulfed them after they had completed their
> performance.

By every account, the sesquicentennial was a stirring
success. For his work, the association presented the Doctor with a
silver coffee service, a silver water pitcher, and a dozen silver water
goblets at a testimonial dinner that December in Richmond. John
Stewart Bryan was the toastmaster, and Governor Pollard spoke. The
next July, H. R. Taylor of the Cosmopolitan Club of Newport News,

notified Goodwin the group would bestow on the Doctor its gold medal for "distinguished service as the Peninsula's first citizen in civic affairs for the year 1931." He accepted it October 7 at a Hotel Warwick banquet.

Restoration expenses had long since overrun Rockefeller's $5 million limit, passing $7 million by the end of 1931. Nevertheless, administrators were confident enough that the work would now go on that they decided to invest in an official seal to decorate Restoration stationary.

Perry drew an emblem with a view of the Palace set in a wreath with a floral device above. A ribbon below carried a Latin rendering of the motto "What was lost is safe." He sent it along to Chorley, Woods, and Goodwin with a list of alternative slogans, also in Latin, with translations: "For the perpetual remembrance of the thing; Honor and Protection; Be thou perpetual; To remember these things hereafter will be a pleasure; Nothing new under the sun; Give precedence to age; Truth never dies; and Posterity will admire." Woods covered the letter with a memo and passed it on to Rockefeller. Mr. David was on his way out of town but paused to scrawl in the top margin: "I know nothing of the background of a seal. What is it for? Why is it needed? I like the motto 'truth never dies' the best. Can we discuss the matter on my return?"

Two weeks later at a New York conference, the Capitol was substituted for the Palace, and Rockefeller suggested the mottoes "Let the past teach us" or "Forget not the past." Goodwin offered "Preserve the past for the future" or his line from Ruskin, "It is our duty to preserve what the past has had to say for itself." The Ruskin sentiment was approved, ordered translated into Latin, and sent to the engraver. Rockefeller, however, had the last word. Chorley told Woods in February that Mr. David now preferred "That the future may learn from the past" or "Preserve the past for the future." Anxious to order the stationary, they agreed on Rockefeller's first choice without further debate.

Another motto and historic structure had become the motifs in a less-decorous debate over the lessons to be learned from Williamsburg. On Palace Green stood an obelisk raised in 1908 with much fanfare and $1,500 in public funds. The expense was born equally by city and county tax coffers and a subscription fund created by the Williamsburg chapter of the United Daughters of the Confederacy. The tall stone shaft, protected by a wrought-iron fence, rose on a square base in honor of local soldiers and sailors who died in the War of Northern Aggression. On it was carved the maxim "Lord God of Hosts, Be with us yet, Lest We Forget, Lest We Forget."

The contract the Restoration, Goodwin, and the city signed in 1928 conceded to the Daughters the rights to the monument's ground as well as free access to and an unmolested view of the memorial. But by late 1931, the early 20th-century cenotaph had become an anachronism in a neighborhood being restored to its 18th-century appearance.

The Daughter's appointed a committee—Mrs. W. F. Luck, Agnes Morecock, and Ethel Goodwin—which proposed the shaft be moved. The destination was the Confederate plot in the city's Cedar Grove Cemetery, providing the city council agreed and the Restoration provided the labor and hauling. One day—on whose orders isn't clear—Restoration workmen took down the fence. The presumption was that it needed repair. The chapter approved the committee's idea December 3, 1931, reaffirmed the decision January 7, and secured the council's agreement January 14. Many citizens bitterly objected and promised to fight. But with unexpected swiftness and no notice, a week later the Restoration trucked away the monument before the opposition could coalesce. The obelisk was put on its side, in pieces, in the graveyard. The next morning a black-draped cross appeared on the green, but it was snatched away before most people saw it. That morning's *Daily Press* called everyone's attention to the Restoration's handiwork with a story headlined "Williamsburg Citizens Aroused at removal by Restoration workmen of Palace Green Shaft."

The argument roared through the rest of the winter and into the spring, dividing the city into three or four snarling factions. There were petitions and accusations, letters to the editor, formal replies, and requests for official legal opinions. Perhaps the only thing on which everyone agreed was that the Restoration's relationship with Williamsburg had been damaged.

The monument's removal had become emblematic of the question Major Freeman asked at the 1928 town meeting. Whose town was Williamsburg? Who had rights to its past? Did they belong to its people or to Restoration outsiders? The dispute made its way to court, and an out-of-town judge, Don Halsey of Lynchburg, was assigned the case in the interests of impartiality. Goodwin, at least publicly, took a nonpartisan stance, but he favored a compromise proposal endorsed by the Daughters, the city, and the county. Why not install the obelisk at the new, Restoration-provided courthouse? The site was nearly as public and prominent as the original. But it was *not* the original, so the battle rumbled on. Privately, Judge Halsey asked the Doctor to try to reconcile the disputants. After talking "with friends as interested in peace and unity as we are," Goodwin advised the judge it was impossible to satisfy all sides, and that the courthouse proposal was "the nearest expression of civic unity which it would be possible to secure by any action which we might take or by any effort which we might make." A Norfolk construction company put the monument up in the east yard of the courthouse May 9, but the Confederate Monument was still a sore point 65 years later.

From the outset, Colonial Williamsburg guarded its image by limiting access, insofar as it could, to Restoration information. It could not stop newsmen from asking questions about policies and operations, but it could try to control the answers. "Authorized information" came only from designated central office spokesmen. It was standard public relations policy among American corporations, and no one understood better than Goodwin its advantages. Nor, from the beginning, did anyone seem as conspicuously prone to run innocently afoul of it.

As he moved away from a central Restoration role—his current title was resident director—he became less an organization man and more a goodwill ambassador or semi-official host. That was the function he performed when visitors asked him for tours. It was the function he performed when he invited the General Assembly to Bruton Church in February to celebrate Washington's birthday. What he had to say to anyone hardly touched on topics more sensitive than his sermon to the legislators: "The Influence of Williamsburg in the Life and Service of Washington." When reporters asked him questions with self-evident answers—like how many floors of the Capitol were finished—he saw little point in declining to respond.

In late April a rumor circulated through Richmond that the Depression would force the Restoration's suspension. A *News-Leader* journalist telephoned Goodwin's office. The Doctor did his best to knock the rumor down. He said little more than he did to the National Conference of Governors, when it visited a few days

The National Council of Governors visited Bruton Church to hear Goodwin speak.

later: "The work has now been in progress for about five years. It will doubtless require two or three years more to bring it to completion. Approximately $8,000,000 has been expended to date, in the acquisition of property and in the work of restoration." The *News-Leader* story, of course, included information gathered from other individuals.

The piece annoyed Woods. "In the ordinary course of events," he wrote to Goodwin, "I have received clippings quoting you as saying things that I know you did not say with reference to plans and facts about Williamsburg. Owing to the great likelihood that no matter how careful one may be, one is so apt to be misquoted and exaggerated, don't you think it would be well if we should adhere to the custom which I think we instituted sometime ago of having information given out only through our office in Williamsburg?"

It was a mild rebuke, but it demonstrated that the father of the Restoration was not authorized to speak to reporters about it. It is also the first sign in the record of the reopening rift between the Doctor and the Restoration's upper management. The governor's meeting, another visit from Henry Ford and his wife, and a local Restoration conference kept Goodwin from composing a prompt reply. But when he got time to dictate, he denied having said anything objectionable. Though his tone was upbeat and friendly, there was a hint of sarcasm. The experience, he said, "gives me a gladly welcomed further excuse for not even telling newspapers that Williamsburg is located on the peninsula of Virginia." Moreover, he thought a good purpose had been served in that he was solely to blame, and "the Williamsburg Holding Corporation is entirely exempt from any responsibility in the matter, for which I am very glad."

The Shrine had become an island off the Restoration's shore. A letter Goodwin sent to Chorley two weeks later shows how big the gulf was becoming. It wasn't that he was "personally sensitive," the resident director wrote to the vice-president a few blocks away, but he had learned only secondhand of important architectural changes in the Capitol reconstruction plans. He wanted to be kept better informed. Goodwin sent a copy of the letter to Woods, and he complained to Perry, too.

Chorley wrote back: "As you know, ever since I came to Williamsburg I have endeavored in every way to keep you posted on all matters pertaining to the Restoration. It has, however, not been physically possible to do this at all times." In this instance, he blamed Goodwin. Chorley recalled that the Doctor had asked to be shown only material likely to be of interest. Deciding what Goodwin might be interested in was a process prone to human error. Chorley suggested Goodwin draft a memo for the architects on "all matters about which you would like to have . . . copies."

Goodwin it appears, went to Rockefeller. He may have asked again for reassurance about his status; only Mr. David's reply is in his files. "Your deep interest in this undertaking," Rockefeller said, "and your brooding care over every detail means much to the enterprise. No one can ever stand in the same relation to it that you occupy."

There are echoes of the Lecky fracas in a personal and confidential letter the Doctor posted July 13 to Woods in New York. It was not that he was "personally sensitive"—that phrase again—but Goodwin suggested he could be of real service if he was consulted about personnel selection, especially of people hired to deal with tourists. Goodwin said he and Mrs. Rockefeller agreed it was important to have Southern women hired as hostesses. Chorley, born in England and reared in upstate New York, had hired hostesses without that credential. Goodwin knew "full well, how natural it is for those responsible for the efficient management of this enterprise to select persons of their own acquaintance and persons with whom they perhaps have had some previous experience." But the Doctor said it was essential to have Williamsburg interpreted only by people who understood its history and traditions and would be "recognized by cultured visitors as belonging here." The emphasis is his.

The employees in question were three women temporarily

employed for the opening of the Raleigh Tavern, the Restoration's first exhibition building. Woods agreed with Goodwin's premise, said the Restoration would be glad of his hiring counsel in the future, but let the temporary selections stand.

The dedication ceremonies began at 2 p.m. on September 16 before a smallish crowd seated on wooden folding chairs in front of a speaker's stand. Among the guests were at least two Williamsburg residents who had been in the original Raleigh before it burned in 1859. A reconstruction of an eating, drinking, and sleeping establishment famous for its associations with Virginia's 18th-century patriots and Phi Beta Kappa's founding, the new Raleigh stands on the original foundations. Before the Revolution the first Raleigh had competed with places kept by Henry Wetherburn and Christiana Campbell along the avenue.

Goodwin was on the dedication platform, but he gave another local minister the privilege of delivering the benediction. His prayer seemed to thank the Messrs. Rockefeller senior and junior along with the deity: "God bless the father, the son, and the Williamsburg Holding Corporation." Colonel Woods handed the tavern key to the Doctor, and Goodwin opened the door for the first guest, Governor Pollard.

Chorley stopped by a few days later to listen to one of his hostesses explain to tourists the significance of the place. As she led them through, she said, "This is the famous Apollo Room where Jefferson danced with his fair Belinda, where Phi Beta Kappa was founded, and where Washington often dined, and afterwards went across the street and slept with Mrs. Campbell." Chorley was nonplussed.

Nearly six years had passed since Rockefeller had come to Williamsburg for the dedication of Phi Beta Kappa Memorial Hall and agreed at dinner to finance Perry's restoration studies. Each day Goodwin had seen more and more of his vision translated to reality, but each day he watched from a greater distance.

"Dr. Goodwin's star was on the wane in the early thirties," researcher Bullock said, "and it was too bad because he had the emotional and spiritual dedication about it. It had been a thing that he had dreamed of and then other people, as it got to be a bigger and bigger operation, took it over and took away more and more of

Goodwin unlocked the Raleigh's door to admit Governor Pollard at the tavern's dedication in 1932.

the authority and direction."

But with the professional historian's disdain for amateurs, Bullock thought it might have been for the best. "I think if left to Dr. Goodwin's direction," she said, "you would have had the same kind of unprofessional thing you had when he so-called 'restored' the Wythe House." He had copied the pineapple motif from the door at the Westover plantation mansion "and put this large pretentious door on a small townhouse. He was no worse than the people who made a weaving house out of the law office. It's just a question of degree, if you are a historian. He had romantic ideas about it, and many of his ideas weren't founded on valid research foundations. He often got emotional over things, making a thing difficult instead of having it be decided on an impartial basis.

"He was weak in the area of research, because he felt that Miss Mary's research was so tremendous, and that hers was essentially a major contribution. He thought that our efforts to demand certain standards in the form of notetaking and so on were a kind of unattractive quibbling in order to inconvenience her, a kind of heckling, almost inspired by envy. Extraordinarily enough, in all this time, I managed to get along with him."

Goodwin and Chorley seem to have patched up *their* dispute by early October, though it would prove to be temporary. His enthusiasm rekindled, perhaps, by the Raleigh opening, he helped organize a committee of nationally known historians to advise the Restoration and insure its credibility. Inspired by what Ford had done at Greenfield Village in Dearborn, Michigan, he urged Woods to ponder the creation of a Colonial Williamsburg trades and crafts program. The very next day he sent the colonel a five-page letter detailing his ideas for reorganizing the Williamsburg corporations.

He did not confine his contributions to paper. As 1932 ended, Goodwin shuttled between meetings with the governor, the highway department, the National Park Service, the Williamsburg airport authority, and Rockefeller's office to help break a bureaucratic logjam that had delayed construction of the historic district bypass since 1928.

Another road, the government's Colonial Parkway, posed a more difficult problem. As the federal highway engineers mapped it, the cheapest and most efficient route between Yorktown and Jamestown would divide the Williamsburg Restoration in half. To get from one side of town to the other, visitors would have to cross a busy, scenic road. In July, Goodwin proposed to Rockefeller the construction of a tunnel. "I never heard of a crazier idea in my life," Rockefeller said.

Chorley thought it was "a very ingenious scheme" and discussed it with Woods and others as well as the Park Service. None of Rockefeller's other lieutenants would recommend it, and the Park Service was opposed. "It seems," Chorley told the Doctor, "that there is nothing for us to do but drop it." But Rockefeller had second thoughts and grew to admire the idea. He invited Harold Ickes, Secretary of the Interior, to Williamsburg for the weekend to sell him on it.

Chorley said, "Mr. Rockefeller was driving the car and the secretary was sitting in the front seat, and I was in the back seat. He was selling the idea to Secretary Ickes so the government would pay for it. As you know, Mr. Rockefeller was completely successful, and there's a tunnel. Completely Dr. Goodwin's idea."

The Doctor was having more trouble divining solutions to two pressing personal problems—his health and the impact of the Depression on his wallet. In the pattern of an earlier illness, in 1933 he fell sick in February. He was too weak to leave his bed even to go to Richmond for treatment. He had Hayes write a letter canceling an appointment with his physician—who somewhat superfluously ordered him to take bed rest.

Goodwin stayed out of the office for at least two weeks, and was advised to get away from town altogether for awhile. "For some time I have been quite under the weather," he wrote to a South Carolina cousin late in March. "The doctor tells me that I have been going too hard. He wants me to go away from Williamsburg for a rest."

Since the Crash of '29, Goodwin's income had dwindled by a third and was still slipping away. In 1935 he would earn but 53 percent of what he made in 1930. His obligations, however, remained the same. To cut expenses, he was eliminating even the smallest luxuries. In his sickness, he thought of the economic collapse as a kind of national financial illness. "A good deal of poison has gotten into the body politic," he told an old friend. "It has to be eradicated. The political and economic system must be purged. Alcohol rubs and turkish baths have been tried and proven ineffective. There must be some surgery. I hope that it will be wisely done. There is no question but that for a long time the values which have dominated the minds and wills of men have, in many instances, if not in most instances, been in direct conflict with moral and spiritual values. They have been weighed in the balances and found wanting. We must now take inventory, have a good house cleaning, and set up a new order upon new foundations."

Before the week was out, Goodwin was confined to a Richmond hospital for two days of treatment and tests. What the diagnosis was isn't recorded, but Ethel said, "Dr. Goodwin's health began to fail soon after the Sesquicentennial at Yorktown that he took on. That, in addition to everything else, was a little bit too much for him. A few months after that he had his heart condition, and the doctor said that the muscles of his heart were just worn out. From that time on he was never well, but he did a lot."

The physicians now demanded he take a vacation and rest. Goodwin caught the train to Philadelphia for a week's stay with daughter Katherine, but he returned little mended. A church in Hopewell, less than 30 miles away, invited him to speak at the end of the month. He accepted on the condition of the use of a hotel room upon his arrival, so that he could rest before the address. "I have been quite ill for the past few weeks," he said. "It will be necessary for me to conserve my strength."

If he had to restrict his activities afield, there was, at least diversion in Williamsburg. Painter William Steene of New York showed up on the doorstep and asked the Doctor to sit for a portrait. Goodwin liked the result enough to pay for it, and to recommend the artist to Governor Pollard. It is not, however, an agreeable likeness, perhaps because it reflects the state of Goodwin's health at the time.

More flattering was a surprise Hayes had been working on— an almost-finished manuscript titled *The Background and Beginnings of the Restoration of Colonial Williamsburg, Virginia Compiled From Dr. Goodwin's Files And From her Contemporaneous diary notes; by Elizabeth Hayes, Secretary to Dr. Goodwin*. A typescript work of nearly 300 pages, it relied heavily on Goodwin's correspondence, which she had carefully tended and preserved. Her diary notes appear now to be lost. The first history of the Restoration's seminal years, *The Background and Beginnings* is still the most authoritative. Highly complimentary of the Doctor, it earned pages of his praise in the afterword he contributed. The work of restoration, he said, "has

Goodwin and Hayes at the dedication of a Bruton Church sundial provided by
William and Mary men in memory of a classmate.

now progressed to a point where its beautiful completion is in sight."

Presumably, Chorley had copies of the Doctor's Colonial
Williamsburg correspondence since the Restoration's incorporation,
and Hayes had forwarded to his office in March some letters from
Goodwin's 1927-1928 files. Clearly, there was a valuable cache of
material still in Goodwin's control. Six weeks after Hayes finished
the manuscript, Chorley requested Goodwin to turn over all the files
from the days when they ran the Restoration.

"I beg to say," Goodwin replied, "that this matter is being
given careful and continuous attention." He had been, he said,
"responsible for all correspondence relating to the transfer of
property, deeds, insurance, repairs, upkeep, rent, financial accounts,
purchase of antiques," letters to Restoration officials and
contractors, and "the general correspondence growing out of the
public interest in the Restoration." There was quite a lot of material,
and he and Hayes were going through it to isolate what Chorley
should have. The Doctor thought the procedure would "prove the

most satisfactory to all interests concerned." Four days later, Hayes sent the first batch, the Woods correspondence, and gave over the Henry Ford files six months later. More followed, Hayes saving carbon copies as she went.

Goodwin's illness lingered into the summer. He still had not recovered his strength in August, when he asked the Virginia Trust Company to redraft his will and send him a copy in Mountain Lake, Virginia, where he was going on holiday. After he returned to Williamsburg, the Doctor asked his brother-in-law to relieve him of the Norwood farm worries. He told a Baltimore friend, "Since my illness during the past spring and summer, I have been compelled to make engagements to do my work in accordance with the recommendations of my physicians."

Three weeks later, Goodwin sent Chorley his resignations as secretary of the Williamsburg Holding Company and Colonial Williamsburg, Incorporated. He remained, however, a member of the board and resident director, and he was just as eager to share his ideas on how the companies should be run and just as enthusiastic about the future of Colonial Williamsburg.

His next Bruton Church sermon started out as a lecture on civic responsibility, but turned into a plea for the congregation to support the Restoration. Then he prepared for Woods four monographs on Restoration plans and problems that underlined his proprietary feeling for the project.

Chorley chided him for feeling perhaps too proprietary. Goodwin, he had been told, had made a public announcement in church about taking people through the unfinished House of Burgesses reconstruction, "conducted a large pilgrimage, composed mostly of Williamsburg citizens, through the Capitol," and told them the Restoration's public relations man would take them through the unfinished Palace. "I think we ought to all refrain as much as possible from encouraging people to go through these buildings until they are finished," Chorley said. "Don't you agree?"

With the Capitol and Palace nearly done, Goodwin's mind moved further down his Williamsburg agenda. The monographs he sent to Woods dealt in pages of detail with restricting automobile traffic through the historic district, the restoration of ten more colonial homes, and reconstruction of the colonial theater and printing office. On his own, free of Colonial Williamsburg fetters, he intended to undertake a second restoration of Bruton Parish Church.

Neighbor and sculptor Edward Field Sanford created this bust of Goodwin four years before Goodwin died.

Chapter Fifteen: **1935-1937**

Nearly a month before he stood on the stage of Constitution Hall in 1934 and described his vision of Williamsburg restored, Doctor Goodwin sat in his study and outlined a plan to do for the country something of what he had done for Virginia.

Early in March he sent to D. M. Bates of Philadelphia, deputy governor general for Delaware of the Society of Colonial Wars, a three-page letter that sketched an idea for the creation of a National Historical Commission. A federal agency, the commission would create a policy and develop a program for the protection of historic sites and monuments across the country. Goodwin proposed a conference of America's patriotic societies in Williamsburg to work out the details, but he already had in mind a general blueprint for a commission that would "make a careful study of this whole situation and perhaps create a fund or an endowment which might be used to preserve or to assist in preserving those things most typical of the past which if not safeguarded will vanish before the march of commercialism and materialism." He thought the panel should be organized somewhat like the Restoration, with advisory groups and such, but operate on a continental scale.

Nothing properly describable as a conference ever came off, but a series of small meetings at Williamsburg and elsewhere produced a plan Goodwin himself intended to present to President Roosevelt and the National Park Service. The Doctor was never quite admitted to the Oval Office either, but it is likely he outlined the idea for Eleanor Roosevelt when he and Ethel lunched with the First Lady that May at a DAR function in Yorktown. In any case, he put it on the desks of Interior Secretary Harold Ickes and Park Service Director A. B. Cammerer, and he showed the members of the House Public Lands Committee around the Restoration after the idea was communicated to Congress.

   With the Roosevelt administration's support, the help of
now-Senator Byrd, and Chorley's endorsement, the Doctor's idea
became "A bill to provide for the preservation of historic American
sites, buildings, objects, and antiquities of national significance, and
for other purposes." In August 1935, with the president's signature, it
became Public Law 292 of the 74th Congress, commonly called the
Historic Sites Act.

   The Doctor had spent months shuttling between Richmond,
Philadelphia, Charleston, and Washington to help write, promote,
lobby, and testify for the measure, and he was delighted with the
outcome. But he was dejected that Ickes did not appoint him to the
11-member Advisory Board of National Parks, Historic Sites,
Buildings and Monuments the act created.

   It was probably just as well that Ickes did not add to Goodwin's
workload. Despite his heart condition, he was still an advisor to the
Restoration and rector of Bruton Parish. And he was spending much of
his strength and energy on Bruton Church's next overhaul.

   As it began, the project was less a second restoration than a
completion of the first. Goodwin wanted to reproduce the original
transept galleries—for which there had been no need or money in
1907—and to improve the lighting. He also proposed to repair
gravestones and landscape the churchyard. All the work, he said,
was to be "the responsibility of Bruton Parish Church and its friends
throughout the country." Goodwin asked Rockefeller to cooperate
only "to the extent of having his Restoration architects and
landscape architect make a study of the situation" and give advice.

   But the project became as ambitious as a handyman with a
new set of saws. As long as we are at it, Goodwin and his vestry
decided, why not add an organ gallery? The walls ought to be
replastered and repainted, too, and the furnace and ventilating
system should be replaced. It was about time as well to pull out the
mahogany-stained benches installed nearly 30 years earlier and put
in colonial-style square pews painted dark red.

   A likely way to obtain the money, they thought, would be to
deed the Wythe House to Colonial Williamsburg—which Colonial
Williamsburg wanted—and seek a replacement building along with a
cash contribution to the church restoration fund. In short order,

Chorley, the Doctor, and the vestry were engaged in a tedious and occasionally acrimonious three-legged negotiation. The third or fourth time the church changed its terms, Chorley dug in his heels. The talks stalled. Only the offer of a personal donation from Rockefeller, conditioned on a contract between the Restoration and the church, got the bargaining unstuck.

Bruton had underestimated what the project would involve and cost, and Goodwin overestimated the potential sources of gifts. He had been especially disappointed in the response of organizations that had profited from reconstructing the town. "Confidentially," he told Chorley, "I feel that those who have so largely benefited financially from the Restoration done in Williamsburg would instinctively feel glad to contribute to this effort to build old Bruton up to the standard of the Restoration of the city." In this instance the Doctor had in mind Todd & Brown, but his words could have applied to most businesses and people in town.

The Restoration had put money in everyone's pockets. "We are all very grateful for what Mr. Rockefeller has done for us here in Williamsburg," Goodwin told the congregation of First Baptist Church. "In addition to what he has done in Restoring our Colonial City, he has been a God-send to us through the hard times of the years of depression. What would have happened to us if it had not been for the work he gave to us during the hard times nobody can tell. While people all over the country were out of work, hungry and often homeless, the Restoration work, carried on by Mr. Rockefeller has kept things going here, helped the stores, the Bank, the working people and the Churches."

The occasion for his remarks was the dedication of the roof Rockefeller had provided for First Baptist, the most recent of his gifts to the city. When Goodwin paused to tally how much work there had been, he wrote a memo to his files that said: "As of May 18, 1936, 470 buildings wrecked, 59 colonial buildings restored, 8 colonial buildings repaired, 91 reconstructed colonial buildings, 19 modern buildings moved out of colonial area." Included in the totals were the Wren, the Powder Horn, and the new local government buildings. By 1939, Rockefeller's expenditures on the project had ballooned to about $27 million.

Goodwin had raised $34,526.82 to add to the Bruton restoration account, and with $15,000 more from Colonial Williamsburg, the work began in 1937. But while the interior

renovations were under way, workmen discovered the exterior walls
would have to be restored again, too. There was not nearly enough
money. The Doctor set out to raise another $20,000, and he quickly
secured $10,000; but it became clear still more would be required.
He had to go back to Chorley.

After letting him wait awhile for a reply, Chorley composed
a letter enumerating Goodwin's mistakes in the undertaking,
pointing out historical inaccuracies in the Doctor's plans and
crediting himself for their systematic discovery. After more than a
page of such boorishness, he came to the point. The Colonial
Williamsburg board of trustees had agreed to take over the Doctor's
project entirely, he said, if the Restoration was given complete
authority and control. There was a distinct tone of gloat in Chorley's
good news, but the Doctor took it to the vestry and in two days
secured its assent. Because of his uncertain health, Goodwin had
wanted to resign Bruton's pulpit just as soon as the work was well
started. Ethel said that "the vestry wanted him to continue to be
rector until the restoration of the church was completed . . . he held
on as long as he could until he had to give it up."

Giving up was not the Doctor's strong suit. His inclination
was to see through the things he started. There might have been far
fewer buildings on the William and Mary campus otherwise and no
Restoration at all. By the terms of the new Social Security Act being
implemented in Washington, he was three years past retirement age,
and he was no longer central to the day-to-day operations of the
institutions he had served so well and long. But his aspirations for
Colonial Williamsburg, like his hopes for the college, only grew, and
he became only more determined to help shape their futures as his
distance from them grew. He was holding on to his dreams.

By the terms of his agreement with Chorley in 1933,
Goodwin's last day on the Restoration payroll would have been
February 1, 1935. Despite the Doctor's hints that he would have
liked to have been asked to stay, the pages had fallen from the
calendar without hint of a reprieve. At February 3rd's services,
Goodwin announced his retirement from the Restoration's
management, and five days later he gave a statement to the
newspapers. He remained a Colonial Williamsburg trustee, the
Doctor said, and would continue to provide advice, but he was

disassociating himself from the Restoration's business affairs to have more time to minister to Bruton's congregation and the college's students. It may not have occurred to him that he was, once more, making unauthorized statements involving the Restoration. That did not escape Chorley's attention, nor the fact that they were premature.

The Restoration wanted the Goodwin home on Francis Street to make way for construction of the Williamsburg Inn. Though Chorley did not make it clear to Goodwin until the following November, he had decided to keep paying the Doctor, but not Hayes, until the Francis Street sale was closed.

Designed to resemble an English lodge, the hotel would be the fulfillment of another of the Doctor's dreams. He had told Rockefeller that on-site accommodations were essential if they expected tourists to take a day to see the town and linger on its streets into the evening. "It is in the twilight hours and while wandering around under the stars," Goodwin said, "that people are most apt to meet and commune with the ghosts of the past."

The Restoration did not obtain the deed to the Goodwin house until June 1, 1937, and only on that date did the Doctor finally conclude "my official connection with the Restoration is now terminated." For the present, however, he closed out his Restoration office expense account, submitted a $224.43 check for the balance of his entertainment fund, and prepared a speech for the testimonial dinner at which Williamsburg would honor him. The site was William and Mary, the date February 15, 1935.

He accepted the gift of a scroll and a sum of cash, and he told the crowded room: "When one day I shared with my good friend Dr. Chandler, then President of the College of William and Mary, my dream and hope of the Restoration, he said, 'Goodwin, that is a fine idea, but if it is started the people of Williamsburg will run you out of the city before it is finished.'" The Doctor credited Mr. David for everything that had been accomplished since. "Surely history records the name of no man who has, under God, been a more generous student of wealth than Mr. John D. Rockefeller, Jr., and his venerable father," he said. "To him is due the praise of fulfillment which he came to share, which he enlarged, and which he has beautifully consummated."

He acknowledged Chorley, "who has so efficiently served as Mr. Rockefeller's business representative in Williamsburg for the past four years," and had "proved himself amply able to direct the business of the Restoration." Anyone who knew Goodwin's attitude toward business efficiency in the Restoration's inspirational affairs understood how sharply those remarks contrasted with the acclaim he bestowed on Elizabeth Hayes, his unsung associate in all his Williamsburg achievements. The Doctor devoted more of his speech to praising her than to anyone else.

In March, she helped him close his books on the William and Mary Endowment Campaign, and the Doctor accepted a final commission check.

To people who asked about his new relationship to Colonial Williamsburg, Goodwin said, "My work with the Restoration now is only in a consultative capacity. It is a joy to me to see the Restoration work reaching its fulfillment so perfectly." He faithfully attended board of trustee meetings in New York and Williamsburg, and he went on sharing with Chorley and Rockefeller his ideas for the Restoration's enhancement. To Chorley, the Doctor's ideas were sometimes unwelcome.

Goodwin and other long-time Restoration hands were concerned about what they perceived to be commercialization creeping into Colonial Williamsburg, and their dissatisfaction grew as Chorley's administration lengthened. Cousin Mamie said later, "Dr. Goodwin didn't see beyond what he had visualized at first to the involved business of interpretation and education. I think . . . he felt that the Restoration had gotten out of hand in a few places. He was very loyal. He wouldn't actually say so, but if you pinned him down to it he would avoid answering the question." He was not so reticent with the board and Rockefeller, though he generally embodied his criticisms in constructive proposals.

To address the commercialization problem, he submitted to his fellow trustees the idea of creating a Williamsburg-based committee or commission "apart from the commercial management of Colonial Williamsburg that would tend to the problems of the perfection, preservation and interpretation of Colonial Williamsburg from an educational and cultural viewpoint." Chorley, who became Colonial Williamsburg president that October and had run the project for the past five years, would be stripped of much of his authority. It was annoying. He began to tell friends the Doctor was getting in his hair. But the perception that Chorley shortchanged the inspirational side of Goodwin's dream was shared by people like Rutherfoord, architect Orin M. Bullock, Jr., and Harold R. Shurtleff, another architect who had been the Restoration's director of research.

Shurtleff had taken a leave of absence to go to Harvard and sharpen his history skills. Rutherfoord took over the research post and quickly came at loggerheads with Chorley. He would not get in line with Chorley's program. The dispute led to the tender of Rutherfoord's resignation, but the Doctor asked Shurtleff to go down from Boston to New York to see if the situation could be saved.

Shurtleff called on Chorley and reported to Williamsburg: "I have a feeling that 'wisdom' will prevail in the long run, though it is bad sledding just now. Possibly the problem is somewhat one of educating the people at the top as to what their own best interests are. They are not certainly in the direction—as they tend to be so largely now—of so commercializing something that is educational and idealistic by intention that an onus may attach itself to the donor's name." The next time Shurtleff met Chorley, he submitted his resignation, too. "He was at his best, which, as you know, is mighty good," Shurtleff told the Doctor. "He took my statement that I wanted to sever all connection of any sort with the Restoration because I did not approve of some of their policies or of their set up—and because I told him exactly what I told you about the need of a different type of trustee, and of a museum and not a business set up in Williamsburg—very calmly." Chorley, however, persuaded Shurtleff he could have more influence by maintaining a connection than by leaving, and Shurtleff, a few days later, agreed to remain in an advisory role. Rutherfoord, who quit Colonial Williamsburg four times in his career and was thrice rehired, finally left in 1947.

Bullock, historian Helen's husband, told the Doctor, "There were times in the early days of the Restoration when I thought that some of your dreams and ideas were impractical, but the passing of the years have brought me ever closer to the broad and sympathetic understanding of what and how things should and might be that have been your fundamental thoughts since I have been privileged to know you. It is too bad that the high ideals of the Restoration could not have endured. The fine work that has been done might have a so much deeper and more vital spiritual value than the present trend seems to indicate."

Goodwin's disenchantment grew more vocal. He composed a five-page letter to Rockefeller which, without naming anyone, made a more direct attack on Chorley's management. To illustrate his points, he attached four pages of letters from Shurtleff. Once more, Goodwin proposed creation of a board of academics superior to Chorley's business-oriented office. It was to time to re-appraise and reorganize the administration and operations to save the Restoration from commercialism, the Doctor said, and to reemphasize educational and spiritual values. He thought the situation had become so acute, and morale had fallen so low, that Rockefeller himself should conduct an inquiry into the state of affairs; and he decried what he considered to be generalized employee fear of a threatening and imperious president.

"Those who seek to serve the highest ends and ideals of the Restoration should not be dominated even by an efficient business management," Goodwin told Rockefeller. "The ultimate Commercial soundness of this endeavor can best be promoted by an idealistic control and direction. If fear must exist it were better that this fear should reside in the hearts and minds of those responsible in the business and commercial side of the endeavor."

Rockefeller thanked the Doctor for his frankness but said he did not fully understand what the Doctor meant. He asked Goodwin to confer with the Restoration's new vice-chairman, John D. Rockefeller III. Goodwin said he would be glad to and assured father and son "that my only purpose is to help do those things which will give the largest measure of security, enrichment and permanence to what you are so graciously doing here in Williamsburg."

Goodwin was not a bitter man, nor vindictive. Like any person who dared to dream—as he liked to put it—the Doctor was a romantic, more imaginative than practical, more visionary than pragmatic. Ideas interested him more than dollars, sentiment more than sinecure. He tended to think of himself in reference to his relationships to others. A small and somewhat symbolic incident serves for illustration.

On July 26, 1935, Goodwin could not find his gold Phi Beta Kappa key, which represented so much in his life. The next day he sent to editor J. A. Osborne of the *Virginia Gazette* an advertisement for its return with the offer of a reward. "I am exceedingly anxious to get it back," Goodwin said, "not primarily because of the value of the key, as a new one could easily be bought, but because it was given to me by Dr. Van F. Garrett who was then senior warden of Bruton Parish Church and presented [it] to me at the time of my initiation into the society." He thought of the key not in terms of how it had linked him to Rockefeller, and opened the door to the Restoration, or even as a totem of personal achievement; he thought of the old friend from whom he had accepted it in 1908.

At Christmas, the Doctor was always as delighted as a child. This year's was among his most memorable. He had told Rockefeller in a Yuletide letter eight years earlier that he had a plan to one day plant evergreens throughout town, link them all with wires, and string each one with Christmas lights. The idea echoed an 18th-century custom of illuminating a community to celebrate occasions like the arrival of a new governor or the king's birthday. This Christmastide, Colonial Williamsburg put on its first Grand Illumination. Candles, electric and wax, twinkled and winked in windows all over town.

The night before he and Ethel would gather with the boys to open their presents, the Doctor sat looking out a parish-house window, smiling at the lights, and thinking. He got an envelope out of his desk, decorated it with five Yuletide stamps, and embellished it with the handwritten address of sculptor Edward Field Sanford, his Francis Street neighbor. Sanford was an unbeliever, a rationalist more interested in concepts like time and space than miracles and heaven. Goodwin added to the envelope the words "Wishing you a happy Christmas," and folded inside a letter that said:

> My dear Sanford:
> Tonight I am in the Wythe House waiting for the hour to strike for the midnight Christmas-Eve Service, when I will be thinking of you, as I am now. One is not alone here. The Ghosts of the past are my gladsome companions in the near midnight silence.
> As I muse the spirit of this night is playing with my heart and mind. Tonight I distrust my mind. It is no fit instrument for receiving what Christmas Eve has to say in the silence. Imagination and Emotion and Fancy and Faith—their child—have sway. Faith has many parents, and many children. And this may be said of Faith's offspring: they are more beautiful and more creative and more alluring than the children of austere reason. And so:—

'Tis Christmas-Eve! Old Santa Claus is breaking all of Reason's laws. His rein-deer sleigh leaps through the air, while Science frowns in grim despair. 'Tis Christmas Eve! Dim candle light gleams out upon the snow tonight, and Christmas trees, illumined, tell of mystic realms where angels dwell. On Christmas Eve they hover still above the Earth, and, if we will, we too, may hear them sing, and feel the restful calm they bring.

'Tis Christmas-Eve! Love is awake! She calls to Faith and bids her take a Christmas Candle in her hand, and fearless pass into the land where struggle lies and where death dies in giving birth to life transcendent and in a timeless spaceless realm eternal.

'Tis Christmas-Eve, and in the silence here one feels the beckoning Spirits near. One sees them smile and fain would linger with them here awhile. They speak of art and say it is a part essential of the life of creative spirits there where life is free from all the limitations which a space world sets. They tell of Artists who will dream untrammeled dreams and weave their fancies into free fulfillment; for in that spaceless timeless realm spirits, who have found release through conquering Courage, will work with flawless skill to give to earthly dreams the consummation which the world of time and space have harmed and hindered.

Yes 'tis Christmas-Eve! And the night is still, And in the stillness here for you I crave that Faith which is the Artist's great creative and compelling inspiration—the Faith which gives him power to see with unclouded vision the complete and perfect form and beauty which he, within a world of time and space, can not as yet make perfect and complete, but which, with an illumined soul, he visions as perfection—unrealized and unattained.

And on this Christmas-Eve I think of the Great Artist Dreamer who came to mould the clay of which men are made into the form and beauty of the ultimate perfect man. The finish of the dream of this great Artist of human destiny is the consummation to which all creative forces move. As yet we but feel the fire of the furnace in which the potter's clay is purified. We feel the tension of moulding process. We catch faint glimpses of what, in the end, may be the perfect beauty of the Artist's dream fulfilled.

We who have worked with Time and space limited materials know how they hinder the fulfillment of our dreams.

You know Sanford, if I were a God with the chance to make a universe and a man I would plan it so that his Christmas Eve dreams and hopes would some day somewhere find fruition and fulfillment. Wouldn't you?

And so tonight I am trusting my dreams and cherishing

my dim faiths, and am holding on to my Christmas Candle—I
believe in it. And somehow one feels very sure that the path it
illumines is the surest path for a man to follow because it is the
candle of the Eve of an unborn tomorrow. Human life is the Candle
of the Eve of an unborn tomorrow.

Now if you have lived through this that I have written
you will surely live forever.

I have shared with you the light from my Christmas Eve
candle. I have set it in the window of my soul which faces the
house where you dwell.

Sincerely your Friend,
W. A. R. Goodwin

Sanford sculpted a bust of the Doctor a few years later. A
bronze cast from it sits in a niche just inside Bruton's door. A
wandering syndicated newspaper columnist had come by, before
Sanford went to work and captured Goodwin's likeness in words.
The story appeared under the byline Ernie Pyle. It said:

Williamsburg, Va.—The restoration of Williamsburg wasn't
John D. Rockefeller Jr.'s idea.

The man behind the scenes, the man who thought it up
first, the man who sold Rockefeller this $14,000,000 package—He is
the one who interests me.

He is an Episcopalian minister. Dr. W. A. R. Goodwin is
his name. I liked him. He looks like—well, I don't know, like an Army
colonel in mufti, I guess. He is about 60, a nice looking well built
man, who wears a gray suit and smokes a pipe, and talks in a soft
voice, very rapidly. He believes in ghosts. . . .

Some Williamsburg people have opposed the restoration.
Some want things left as they are. Others think it's just too silly.

"It was our object," Dr. Goodwin says, "to make everybody happy. I think we have done that. The happiest ones were the
people who kicked hardest. It gave them something to do."

Dr. Goodwin is distressed because people rush in to
Williamsburg, rush through the buildings, and rush away again. He
says you don't get anything that way.

He loves to see people strolling through the gardens and
greens early of a morning, quiet and thoughtful. He says he didn't
learn about Williamsburg from its streets in the daytime; it was
alone in the starlight, strolling in the night, talking with the ghosts,

that he learned about Williamsburg.

"I wouldn't give a hoot for anybody who doesn't believe in ghosts," says Dr. Goodwin, and he laughs.

People wrote to Goodwin afterward to ask him about those ghosts. A woman in Pittsburgh said she understood there were three in the parish house and wanted to know what they were like. "With reference to the ghosts who frequent the Wythe House at their will," the Doctor replied, "may I say that they are very elusive ghosts and refuse to be delineated or described within the limits of any paragraph that might be written. The only way to come to know these spirits is to come here and hold communion with them."

He told a New Yorker, "The spirits of those unseen influences must somehow be sensed if what is being done here is to meet with any full measure of appreciation." To a 10-year-old girl in Norfolk, he wrote: "I wonder if you have learned when you visit very ancient places to shut your eyes and see the gladsome ghosts who once made these places their home. You can learn to call them back if you will. You can train yourself to hear what they have to say."

The meaning Goodwin attached to the word ghost may be most closely approached, perhaps, in something he shared with an old Wytheville acquaintance. He said he was sure God spoke through spirit influences that "although unseen, are felt in the emotions of the heart which come to us from the other side."

There was, of course, a nonspiritual side to the Doctor. He had opinions on everything from liquor-by-the-drink to low-flying airplanes. After Prohibition's repeal, he sent a three-page letter to the Liquor Control Committee of the General Assembly opposing the sale of spirits in hotels and restaurants. To him that meant a return to the drink-evil saloons. It was his opinion, moreover, that the proceeds from the sale of liquor in state-run package stores should be used to finance a statewide temperance education campaign. He sent copies to Governor Peery, Majority Leader Dovell, the *Times-Dispatch*, the *News-Leader*, and the *Daily Press*.

Ethel had a new Chevrolet, a 1934 sedan, but Goodwin never warmed enough to the motorcar to learn how to drive. He walked most everywhere, and he thought Williamsburg's visitors should walk more, too. "Our chief problem now," he told a Bruton

Church meeting of the American Institute of Architects, "is to find ways by which we can banish motion and menace and noise from these streets that there may dwell more of silence here, that in quietude the loveliness of the place may be seen, and opportunity given for listening ears to hear the voices which speak out of the past to create the hope and purpose of a richer more beautiful future." Out of concern over highway fatalities, he asked Senator Byrd to introduce federal legislation prohibiting the manufacture of automobiles capable of going faster than 50 miles per hour, trucks faster than 40 miles per hour, and police cars faster than 60 miles per hour. "Objections to such a law will doubtless be offered," the Doctor said.

He shared his views on New Deal politics with *News-Leader* editor Freeman: "I feel, very strongly, that unless the two major parties in our government make provision for a larger measure of social security and crime prevention, that these parties are surely destined to be supplanted by parties very much more radical. This we should seek to prevent by encouraging the enactment into law of reasonable social security measures which, if not now promoted and enacted by our present conservative party or parties, will be seized upon by radicals and used by them as means to place them in power when they would use their power to enact much more radical social and economic legislation."

He never flew in an aircraft, and he kept a wary eye on the rubbernecking pilots who buzzed the Restoration. To the aeronautics instructor at the college he wrote: "I am frequently reminded of you by certain things that I see over Williamsburg, which I am sure you would not do; namely, flying an airplane so low that it threatens to knock the steeple off Bruton Parish Church. . . . In view of the fact that I am working very hard at present to restore Bruton Parish Church I do not want to be *particeps criminis* with some pilot who knocks the steeple off my church, and so I am waiting to go up until I can be taken care of by a safe and wise pilot."

To the readers of his final book, he gave advice on living. "There must be release from the spirit of hurry," he said. "Our age needs redemption from the tyranny of haste. This habit is so deeply ingrained in American life that it has become a distinctly deteriorating influence upon the character of the people and the nation. It creates impatience and nervous tension. It prompts the taking of short cuts and results in action directed by immature, imperfect and distorted thought processes. Hasty generalizations are made resulting in the mutilation of truth by superficial thinking, and the result is unbalanced life. Out of this haste complex come ill-digested economic and industrial decisions and the disasters produced by half-baked political theories and legislative enactments. In the hurry to achieve wealth and secure pleasure the soul is often left impoverished and unhappy."

He also bequeathed some guidance to the inheritors of his dream. "If there is one firm guiding and restraining word which should be passed on to those who will be responsible for the restoration in the future," he wrote, "that one word is <u>integrity</u>. A departure from truth here and there will inevitably produce a cumulative deterioration of authenticity and consequent loss of public confidence. Loyalty demands that this principle of integrity be adhered to."

Unacquainted with the Restoration's new organizational chart or its public relations practices, people went on writing to the Father of Colonial Williamsburg about the enterprise and inquiring about its progress. Goodwin cheerfully replied. He was, after all, still a trustee and, with the Restoration's support, ranged all over the East Coast presenting slide-show lectures on Colonial Williamsburg and taking questions from the audiences. Sixteen months after the Doctor announced the end of his business connection to Colonial Williamsburg, he wrote to Chorley asking for 100 envelopes and sheets of Restoration stationary "for special letters which, from time to time, I am called upon to write relating to the work here."

Chorley answered, "You will recall that shortly after you publicly announced your resignation from the Restoration in a sermon at Bruton and by a statement to the press, which was following a readjustment of the financial arrangements with you, at which time all salary from the Restoration for your secretary ceased, you and I had a talk regarding the letters which came to your office regarding the Restoration. It was agreed at that time that, in view of the fact that the Restoration no longer made any provision for secretarial help for you, and in view of your announced resignation from the Restoration, you would simply transmit these letters to the office of the Restoration for answer. I was under the impression that this was what you had been doing. . . . In this connection, it should be remembered that, while you are a Trustee of Colonial Williamsburg Incorporated, you are not a member of the corporation's active staff anymore than Mr. Albright, or Mr. Webb or Mr. John D. Rockefeller, 3rd is. The business of the corporation is conducted not by its trustees but by its regular staff. The reason for this is obvious." It was, Chorley said, to avoid confusion about who was in authority.

"I beg to say," Goodwin replied, "that when I suggested that some of this stationary be put at my disposal there was no thought in my mind of intruding upon the official duties of the officers of Colonial Williamsburg, Inc. There are, however, certain amenities and courtesies which, by reason of my personal connection with the Restoration through past years and to some extent at the present time I am privileged to express, and it occurred to me that such expression could be more graciously communicated by using the decorative stationary of Colonial Williamsburg, Inc. . . .

"I take it that one of the great privileges of the Restoration is the opportunity which is given to us outside of contractual relationships and the routine business of an organization to show consideration and courtesy to the people who are interested in the spiritual side of the Restoration and who are appreciative of the amenities and courtesies which are extended to them here, and it was just with the thought that this might be done more fully in the name of the Restoration if the Restoration paper were used than would be the case if I used my official business stationary.

"I am coming to feel with increasing conviction that we should welcome every opportunity to do those things which will give soul and spirit and a certain gentleness of response to those who visit this place or make inquiries concerning it. This, however, I can continue to do either as an individual in no way related to the Restoration or in such official capacity as I may hold regardless of the use of Restoration stationery—but I did feel that the use of this stationery would give a bit of color and of feeling to our relationships which lie outside and above the routine official business and commercial transactions of the Restoration."

In a separate letter of the same day, the Doctor upped the ante in the negotiations for his Francis Street home. He said he intended to retire before the end of 1937. "In considering a future home for myself and my family the thought has been in my mind that if possible I would like to live in a Colonial house," he said. "You can understand, I am sure, the sentiment which prompts this desire." He wanted to purchase what is now called the Timson House, perhaps the oldest home in the city. A few days later, Goodwin went to see Chorley in person to discuss, among other things, when the Restoration could have the Francis Street place. Goodwin wanted to know, in that connection, if it would sell him the vacant lot at 200 Nassau Street, just behind the Timson House, if he could have an about-to-be-demolished Penniman bungalow to put on it; and "my future relation to the Restoration."

While waiting for a reply, the Doctor complained to Rockefeller that Chorley had begun to open the Restoration to the public on Sunday mornings. Because so many Bruton Parish congregants were employed by Colonial Williamsburg, he said, it was playing hob with early Sabbath church activities. He wondered why the Restoration couldn't stay closed until 1 p.m. Rockefeller passed the inquiry to Chorley, who prepared a memo saying there were only four Bruton parishioners among the hostesses, and the church attendance of none had been hindered by their jobs. Goodwin penciled on the memo the names of six women Chorley overlooked and filed it.

A month later, President Roosevelt returned to Williamsburg and attended a Bruton service. Perhaps as much for his Restoration colleagues in the pews as for the chief executive, Goodwin took for his text, "Men's affairs do but little prosper where God's service is neglected." Afterward, Goodwin and the President posed for a newspaper photographer at Bruton's south gate.

That summer Goodwin granted himself a few rewards for his labors. He purchased a small boat and a lot on the shore of the York River, and built a cottage. Then he took Ethel on a vacation in the Blue Ridge Mountains, where he had the leisure to think of the Restoration from a distance. When he returned to Williamsburg, he was anxious to share his thoughts with Rockefeller, vacationing in Seal Harbor, Maine. The Doctor wrote to him and asked if he could come up for a conference. Mr. David telegraphed his reply: "Letter August twenty second received greatly regret not to see you here as you suggest but quite frankly I find myself in need of every moment of these short summer weeks for rest and freedom from the cares that press upon me day and night during the balance of the year

Stop I am therefore under the necessity of arbitrarily declining to take up business or other problems shall look forward to seeing you in Williamsburg in the fall."

The last sentence of the rebuff could only have reminded the Doctor that the Rockefellers had the year before purchased Bassett Hall from the Restoration and had made it their Virginia getaway residence for Octobers and Aprils, when the weather was best. Abby had told a hostess, "Oh, I am so happy today. John has promised me we can have Bassett Hall. . . . And he says I can keep it if I promise not to take in tourists."

Goodwin was still working with the Restoration on residential arrangements, too. He agreed in November to purchase two bungalows before the Restoration wrecked them, paying $1 for each and promising to truck them away. The Doctor told Chorley he would sell the Francis Street house to the Restoration for what it cost him in 1923. "This offer was made because of my glad determination not to personally profit financially in any way whatsoever from any property dealings which I might have with Mr. Rockefeller," Goodwin said. He made an offer on the Timson House, and said he would be ready to move between June 15 and July 1.

The Doctor had no idea how to fit all his family, its effects, and his library into their new home. It would have six bedrooms, four baths, a living room, a dining room, a sun porch, and a kitchen; but the Goodwins were moving out of a three-story house so large that the Doctor rented out some of the rooms. As the packing boxes filled, he finished work on an article he was preparing on the Restoration for *National Geographic's* April issue. Rockefeller provided the introduction.

On April 28, the Doctor turned his Francis Street deed over to Vernon Geddy, the new resident officer of the Williamsburg Holding Company. In May, Goodwin ordered work on the Nassau Street property begun and submitted his resignation as a Colonial Williamsburg trustee. The Doctor decided to rent out the Timson House; he would never live in a colonial home. As wrecking crews and carpenters worked to ready the Goodwins' new place, he sat in his Wythe House study and composed a remembrance of times gone by.

"I am sitting just where ten years ago today we sat around a card table gambling on the future," he wrote to Rockefeller. "You did not probably know it but the Fates had stacked the cards. The preliminary plans showing what might be accomplished were on the table. The ghosts of the past invisibly presided over us. This morning this scene comes back to us just ten years afterwards. It is the anniversary also of the day when Lindbergh flew to Paris. So I can not resist writing to you on this anniversary day, out of my feeling of gratitude and appreciation."

Two weeks later, he sent Mr. David a less cheerful letter. "In order that my withdrawal from official connection with the Restoration may be by you entirely understood," Goodwin said, "you will permit me, I am sure, to review the connection which, through your courtesy and kindness, I have been privileged to have with the endeavor, and to explain my gradual, and it would now seem complete, official severance from the work."

Goodwin had twice before orally offered his resignation as a trustee, but had not been separated. The board accepted a written notice June 14, made him an honorary member, and asked Chorley to present him with a bronze lifetime pass to the exhibition buildings. Through an oversight, Goodwin neglected to resign from both Restoration boards, a mistake not rectified until September 14. Rockefeller telephoned and wrote in June, thanking Goodwin for his work and his explanations and offering what amounted to a pension. Goodwin accepted. "It seems only yesterday that you and I were first talking about the possibilities of restoring Williamsburg," Rockefeller said, "and now there has already been accomplished vastly more than either of us ever had the courage to dream of at that time. That you have been able and willing to stay with the enterprise until it had reached so high a degree of perfection has given us all the greatest satisfaction.

"Although it is only fair to you that you should no longer be called upon for active service in connection with the operation of the enterprise, it is most gratifying to me, as well as to my associates, to know that you have been willing to continue in an honorary relationship to the Board, which will make us all feel only the freer to come to you for counsel and advice from time to time as occasion may arise. "

He mentioned Goodwin's health, said he feared for the Doctor's well-being, and was relieved that the restoration burdens had been lifted from him. "To thank you for what you have done for and meant to the restoration of Williamsburg," Rockefeller said, "would be like thanking a mother for giving birth to her child." It must have taken some time for the letter to reach Goodwin—he had been planning to go to the Yorktown cottage—and he did not reply for nearly a month. Then he sent a wire: "Mr. David. For all your letter conveyed of gracious kindness and generous consideration and help please accept my cordial thanks and sincere appreciation."

That August the Doctor went to Norwood for what was probably the last time. He was thinking of selling the place.

Tourist Fred Cross, New England archivist, snapped this shot of Goodwin at the Wythe House of October 30, 1936.

Goodwin was dying of heart disease when, for what may have been the last time, he left his home and sickbed for a final look at Bruton Church and the Wythe House when this picture was taken.

Chapter Sixteen: **1938-1939**

Goodwin and Chorley had a lunch date December 2, 1937. Neither what they discussed nor the tenor of their conversation is mentioned in Goodwin's files. In the early afternoon, as the Doctor returned to his work, he developed a strong headache. He lay down. His stomach was troubling him. His left arm went numb, then his left leg. He could control neither limb; and when he rose, he could not walk. His local physician, Henry E. Davis, made the diagnosis. Goodwin had suffered a stroke. It didn't take a medical degree to know the cause. "His attack was brought on by years of overwork and strain," Hayes said. Goodwin's mind was clear, and, under the circumstances, his spirits were good. The next day he wrote to his Richmond physician, describing the attack in detail and asking for his services. "The fact that my good friend the undertaker has just sent me word that he will be glad to take me up to Richmond," he said, "suggests to me that it might be well for me to let him take me while I know what it is about."

The physician came to Williamsburg instead and ordered Goodwin confined to bed, where he lay for the next six weeks. Abby Rockefeller, still at Bassett Hall, sent him flowers. From New York, her husband sent a letter. "Mr. Chorley has just told me of your sudden illness following, as he put it, a luncheon which he had just had at your house and at which he said you never looked happier or better physically. While the absolute quiet and rest, which your doctor prescribes for some weeks in order to work the recovery which he so confidently predicts, will not be without their drawbacks to one so active mentally and physically as you are, I am sure you will be patient and follow the doctor's orders implicitly since that is apparently the price of a return to your usual good health."

Hayes said the physician was, in fact, "very hopeful that if he will rest he will completely recover." As Christmas vacation neared, she wrote to the Doctor's sons Howard and Bill at their boarding school, Episcopal High in Alexandria, to prepare them. "When you see him," she said, "you'll hardly know he is ill, as he looks so well, is propped up in a new hospital bed surrounded by newspapers and sucking on his pipe."

As the old year dissolved into the new, Goodwin's health did slowly improve, but he understood it was time to stand aside and relax while others carried forward his work. On January 17, 1938, the Doctor notified Bruton's vestry he would leave its pulpit July 1, or when his replacement could be found. The *Virginia Gazette* printed his resignation in full on its front page with a picture and a story on his achievements.

"I found that I was partially paralyzed, but I am making a good comeback, and I am now walking around the house," he wrote to a Rochester friend. "It was a red light signal flashed across my path. I have resigned from all compelling duties and will be able to take things more quietly." He decided to occupy himself with another book, one he would call *The Background and Beginnings of the Williamsburg Restoration.*

In late February the Doctor felt he was "only now slowly recovering." He was getting around with the aid of a cane "walking around inside and a little way outside." It was mid March, nearly four months after the stroke, before he could return to church, and it was late May before he was well enough to preach. As Bruton prepared to transfer the Wythe House to Colonial Williamsburg, the Doctor described in a long monograph called *Notes on the Wythe House* how he had acquired the property and restored it, and who had assisted him in saving the house from demolition.

Chorley, who had moved back to New York and was commuting to Williamsburg, sent the Doctor a golden pass for admission to the exhibitions with a note that said, "If you will remove it from the leather folder and look on the back, you will find something which I hope will help to meet the problem with which I know you are confronted from time to time." They had no more confrontations, and Chorley seemed to rue their earlier disputes. It looks as if the Doctor did, too. The next year, after Goodwin was gone, Chorley confidentially told Rutherfoord he had written to the Doctor, as Rutherfoord said, "some very unpleasant letters, which he had subsequently repented and regretted." Rutherfoord said Chorley asked, in view of his "devotion to and admiration for my Father to locate these letters in my Father's files and permit him to destroy them, in order that their friendship might appear undisturbed." Rutherfoord looked but could find no such correspondence. He concluded the Doctor had destroyed them himself. Be that as it may, the Doctor's feelings were still bruised. When a cousin wrote looking for Restoration work, Goodwin replied, "If you would care to chance a visit here, I will be happy to refer you to the proper parties, though, beyond that, I feel that any influence brought to bear would be detrimental rather than helpful."

To help speed his recovery, Goodwin left for the milder weather of Charleston, South Carolina, in April and stayed several weeks. When he returned he came down with the grippe but waded back into Bruton's restoration, management of the church's negotiations with Colonial Williamsburg, and his book, which he now proposed to title *The Background, Beginnings, and Spiritual Significance of the Restoration of Colonial Williamsburg.* He hoped it would "lead to a deeper understanding of the significance of the Restoration and help make the Restoration minister to spiritual enrichment."

The Wythe House was to be turned over to Colonial Williamsburg in July, and Goodwin would be without an office. He asked President Bryan for space at the college to pursue his literary project, but Bryan said none was available. Nevertheless, the Doctor had a first draft done before July was out.

The search for his successor as rector had fastened on the Reverend Francis Craighill, Jr., of St. Bartholomew's Church on Park Avenue in New York, who would take over November 1. Goodwin's resignation would not be effective until then. He felt he had to carry on in the meantime, but every day took a bigger toll on his strength. His doctors ordered him into a Richmond hospital for two days of tests. The problem was his heart. He rested, gathered his strength, and told himself he would recover.

Three days before he turned his pulpit over to Craighill, the Doctor handed a letter to Hayes. "My ministry in Bruton Parish Church can not close without the expression from my heart," he said, "which you have illumined in so many ways, of my appreciation for all you have done to help me here. You will never know the measure of the help you have given or the measure of my gratitude. Always, but especially since last December when added responsibilities fell upon you, your help has been unfailing and has made my recovery possible. . . . No person ever had a more loyal, a more faithful or a more helpful assistant." Then he wrote a letter of farewell to his congregation, delivered his final sermon October 30, and became rector emeritus. He had served Bruton for 18 years and nine months of his 45-year ministry.

Chorley sent a letter from New York the next day congratulating him on his career. A notice of the sermon had appeared in the *Herald Tribune.* "How I wish I could have been there to express personally to you my appreciation and congratulations for what you have done for Bruton, for Williamsburg, for the State of Virginia, for the country, and for mankind in general," Chorley said. "What a great joy and comfort it must be to you to know that your work is not done but that the results of your labors are going to go on indefinitely."

A compulsively industrious man with nothing to keep him busy any longer, Goodwin faced the question of what to do with himself. "I shall try to find things to do to minister to the happiness of others," he said, "because it is only in doing this that we can find happiness for ourselves." Through that fall and winter, he labored on his manuscript, sending new drafts of chapters to associates and friends for comments and corrections and working with Hayes on their revisions.

But in December his condition worsened, and he was again confined to his bed. He went on writing, raised more money for Bruton's restoration, handled the administrative details, closed the negotiations, and kept up his correspondence.

He crafted a last Christmas letter to Rockefeller. Mr. David responded that his life had been enriched by the associations that the work had developed. "Among these associations my relationship with you has been the most significant and the happiest," Rockefeller said. "As you review the past ten years from the point of view of the Restoration, you may well take boundless pride in what has resulted from the ideas which had so long been germinating in your mind and which, only as a result of your own enthusiasm and indomitable steadfastness of purpose, have at length come into such beautiful fruition. I am glad that you are now having the time to put in writing some of your thoughts and ideas in connection with the

Restoration and feel that in doing so you are adding materially to the contribution you have already made."

As the last year of his life opened, the Doctor wrote to a friend, "Old Bruton Church is now undergoing a thorough and complete restoration. . . . . Like the Church I also am seeking restoration, but not so successfully!" He told sculptor Sanford, "The climb back seems to be for me a very slow climb. I see little of my friends and then for a very little time. Except when bundled up and put in the car for a quick drive I do not go out at all. But one can stay in and think out."

The book—which in its final form would be titled *Williamsburg and the Restoration, The Story of a Dream which Survived the Dawn*—had grown from 7 chapters to 12. He sent them all out again for criticism and correction, and as he waited for their return, he dictated to Hayes his *Personal Memories*. A 33-page compilation of anecdotes, it is the musing of a man thinking back across the happy moments of a fruitful life. "Into this hallowed treasure house of cherished memories many of those living in Williamsburg today were permitted to enter," he said. "Within the charmed circle of the custodians of the history and traditions of the ghost-inhabited city we were privileged to sit and listen and to become one of the dreamers also." Bryan added to the store of life's rewards when he came to Nassau Street on Valentine's Day to present the Doctor with an honorary degree. They posed for photographs in the living room, the Doctor looking as enthusiastic as ever.

Two weeks later, Goodwin's condition went critical. He was hospitalized again in Richmond, and Rockefeller flew in a prominent heart specialist from Johns Hopkins in Baltimore to consult with Goodwin's physicians. He told Rutherfoord: "Your father may live thirty seconds. He may live thirty days. It is medically impossible for him to live longer than that with a heart muscle in the condition his is in." After a six-day stay, the physicians sent Goodwin home.

Judging from photographs, sometime before spring the Doctor talked Rutherfoord into carrying him to Bruton Parish Church to see how its restoration was going. "It was not wise for him to go to the church," Rutherfood said later, "but I continue convinced that the visit did him vastly less harm than a refusal of his wishes in the matter would have done him."

Goodwin lived more than twice the months the heart specialist had predicted, but this was his last visit to Bruton. His sexton William Baker was there. "They were fixing his vault," Baker said. "He wasn't dead, and he asked what that was for, and I told him I didn't know. I did know, but I told him I didn't know. He laughed.... He always said he hoped to live to see the church restored. The first service held in that church after it was finished was his funeral."

Rockefeller shouldered the expenses of Goodwin's illness— providing everything from two full-time nurses to an oxygen tent that Chorley helped Ethel rent. She wrote to tell Rockefeller how much the oxygen seemed to strengthen her husband, and Rockefeller came to

Son Rutherfoord drove the dying Goodwin, probably in the spring of 1939, to Bruton Church for a final look at its restoration.

see for himself. Goodwin wrote to him afterward, "This morning the relief which has come to me from the use of the oxygen has been more perceptible than at any time before. I really feel that I am living in a lighter world than perhaps you are, so if you have any extra burdens to send down for me to bear for you please let me share them. Now that relief has come from those exceedingly trying days I want to say to you that I do not see how I could have lived through the days of ten days ago had it not been for the relief that you had sent to me. Never shall I forget the strength and the joy that came to me those quiet minutes when you were last here and sat by the bedside with me, giving to me the sense of comradeship, of friendship and of deeper understanding with you than I had ever known."

Near the end of the month, Bruton, though in something of a shambles, was ready for services again. Craighill reopened the doors June 4. Goodwin couldn't go, but Ethel did. She wrote on the program, "First service in the church since the restoration started. Not nearly finished." Neither was Goodwin. The same day he secured from a Hot Springs admirer a $200,000 bequest for the Bruton Parish Church Endowment Fund, and President Bryan visited his sickroom to ask for help in approaching Rockefeller for a $1 million donation to William and Mary's law school. Goodwin's correspondence picked up. He was now giving his return address as "The Oxygen Tent, Williamsburg, Virginia." Channing Hall came by for conferences. Goodwin opened negotiations on his book with a New York publisher. He gave Bryan thorough advice on what to say and what not to say to Rockefeller. Alice Cocke, a young woman from Norfolk, came by to meet him. The Doctor's son Howard, an All-American halfback at the University of Virginia, introduced her as his fiancée. Rockefeller called twice more.

"Dr. Goodwin is showing some improvement lately," Hayes wrote. The tent gave him comfort and rest. "He comes out of the tent to talk and to smoke and has a number of short visits with friends," she said." On June 18, Goodwin celebrated his 70th birthday. He told friends and well-wishers that he had joined the patriarchs, "passing the three-score and ten mark." Rockefeller sent him a telegram two days later that said, "My heartiest congratulations to the newly arrived patriarch together with cordial thanks for his note and his blessing." It was the last telegram he got from David's Father.

Chorley collaborated with Goodwin in the law school approach to Rockefeller, for which the Doctor sent him a warm

letter of appreciation. Chorley, who was also helping to edit
Goodwin's book and had been asked to contribute an appendix,
sent roses. The Doctor began to address him as "My dear K. C."

It must have been about this time that Abby Rockefeller
asked Rutherfoord to come to Bassett Hall. As Rutherfoord recalled
their conversation, she said, "Mr. Goodwin, your father is so
desperately ill that I would not think of troubling him with the
matter—and John is so terribly busy, and is involved in so many
worries that I try to relieve him of as many burdens as I can. Mr.
Goodwin, in view of the things that I have heard and seen, and the
way things seem to be going in Williamsburg, I have been wondering
if we have the right man in charge of the Restoration in Mr. - ah - in
Mr. Chorley. I wonder what your father would think about this, if I
could ask him." Rutherfoord told her, "Mrs. Rockefeller, I think that
my father would tell you that Mr. Chorley has been improving in
recent months. He has mentioned it to me. I do not think that he
would have said this a year or so ago—but today I think that he would
say, 'He is trying. Give him a chance.'" Chorley led Colonial
Williamsburg until his retirement in 1963.

Cousin Mamie wondered if the Doctor was spending too
much energy on his Restoration history, but Hayes assured her he was
"going slowly and wisely. It is his chief interest right now . . ." In mid-
July, the Doctor told Chorley, "The days are up and down with me, but
taking it all in all I am considered to be and feel somewhat better. The
oxygen tent continues to be of invaluable help to me." But a dozen
days later, he drafted a new will. After disposing of most of his assets,
belongings, and properties among his wife and children, Goodwin
penned a provision that read, "To Mr. John D. Rockefeller Jr. I give the
old silver spoon which I dug up between Jamestown and Williamsburg
as a token of my heart's deepest gratitude for his friendship, his
example, and for his generous and gracious consummation of the
dream of the restoration of Colonial Williamsburg."

If nothing else, the gift of a silver spoon to the millionaire
son of a millionaire showed the Doctor had not lost his sense of
humor. To Colonel Woods, architect Perry, and landscape architect
Arthur Shurcliff, he gave copies of his book *Bruton Parish Church
Restored*. To Kenneth Chorley he gave a copy of Lyon G. Tyler's
Williamsburg, the Colonial Capital from his library. He provided small
cash remembrances for Christ Church in Norwood, Bruton Parish
Church, the Theological Seminary of Virginia, the Endowment

Association of the College of William and Mary for the benefit of the school of jurisprudence, to Roanoke College in Salem, and the Mother's Club of St. Paul's Church, Rochester.

Then he forgave all debts due him and bequeathed some advice on that subject to his boys: "I suggest to my SONS that they REFRAIN from endorsing notes or lending money unless they are entirely willing and ABLE to GIVE THE MONEY if the obligation should not be met, or debt repaid. I also URGE them NOT to borrow money and NEVER under any circumstances to gamble. I beg them to be temperate in all things and reverent, honest, and obedient to the law, and to their conscience and to God."

He began to put his other affairs in order, too. On August 10 he wrote what may have been his last two letters to Rockefeller. One recommended Mr. David's support of the law school. The other, which ran three pages, began: "Very constantly I have missed you this summer. The days have been distinctly lonely days. . . . It has now been over three months since I have left either my room or my bed. Not being able to read because of my eyes or to talk much because of my voice, it has consequently left me very much alone. . . . More and more during these silent spaces I have thought of the Restoration, of the College, and of you. More and more the thoughts have woven themselves into a unity of thought." The rest of the letter he devoted to his last proposal on the privatization of William and Mary. That's what he had been thinking about—fund raising. He asked Rockefeller to commission studies on the mission of William and Mary, its reorganization, and its cooperation with the Restoration. Rockefeller assured him that other people were studying the situation. "Rest assured, therefore," Mr. David said, "that you may dismiss the matter from your mind, confident in the belief that although it may take some time to find that solution, it will surely be found."

At the end of the month, on the 25th, there was a special Friday afternoon two-organ concert at Bruton Parish Church. The telephone company, with the help of Richmond radio station WRNL, transmitted it by wire to the Doctor's bedside. "It was a complete surprise," he said. "Miss Hollister Jones, the new organist, played her first program on the new organ . . . . You can well imagine how delighted I was to be able to hear the music from Bruton, on the new organ, and then on the organ of 1785."

Bentley, his former curate, returned to Williamsburg and called on his old rector for the last time. "I went to see him just before he died," Bentley said. "He was . . . not the least bit dispirited. He said, 'John, now that I have a good deal of time and can lie here and think about my sins and my friends, I've spent a good deal of time thinking about my friends.' It was that little spark of humor that was the saving grace in so many difficult situations. His zeal never flagged in any way. I think up to the very end he was still on fire with the whole thing. Physically, of course, he was dreadfully handicapped, and helpless. But mentally, when I saw him last, he was just as alert and keen as he had ever been."

On September 1–the day World War II began with the German invasion of Poland–Goodwin put aside the revisions of his book. The manuscript would never find a form that Rutherfoord, the Doctor's literary heir, thought was ready for publication, despite Rutherfoord's own efforts to perfect it.

The Doctor began to slip away. His strength and his vision began to fail. When Hayes brought his church pension check to endorse, he put his name on the wrong side. It was likely the last time he attempted the intricacies of his ornate signature. She wrote a letter for him, her last, sometime the day of the 7th. "Dr. Goodwin has not been feeling well lately," she said, "and has seemed dazed at times. Unless he shows radical improvement I don't see how he can do any more work on the book."

The Reverend Doctor William Archer Rutherfoord Goodwin died that night in his sleep at 11:30.

Rockefeller telegraphed his condolences as soon as he got Rutherfoord's telegram the next day in Seal Harbor, Maine. "He has immortalized himself in the Restoration," Mr. David said. He signed the wire, "Your father's friend–John D. Rockefeller, Jr." He told Ethel, "I shall miss him profoundly and shall always be grateful that I have had a part with him in the realization of his great vision." To Hayes he said, "We will all miss Dr. Goodwin greatly but can be but grateful that the end came so peacefully and quietly." Rockefeller tried to get back to Williamsburg to participate in the funeral, but the train connections made it impossible. John D. Rockefeller III represented the Restoration and his family at the funeral.

Craighill conducted the service with another of Goodwin's friends, the Right Reverend A. C. Thompson, retired bishop of the diocese of Southern Virginia. The *Gazette* report said the ceremony was "very simple, only a few flowers on the altar where the lighted candles reflected the shadows on the black cloth-covered bier."

They buried the Doctor in the Bruton Parish Church nave, his head toward the altar. The inscription on the slab that marks his tomb beneath the floor says merely. "Here rests the Reverend William Archer Rutherfoord Goodwin, a native of Virginia, late rector of this parish–Born 1869–Died 1939." Rockefeller later commissioned a plaque to be let into a wall near the grave. It says, "To the GLORY of God and in MEMORY of William Archer Rutherfoord Goodwin. Minister, Teacher, Man of Vision in whose Heart and Mind was conceived the Thought of restoring the Beauty of this ANCIENT CITY and who was himself the inspiration of its Fulfillment THIS TABLET is erected by his Friend and Fellow Worker JOHN DAVISON ROCKEFELLER JR. ANNO DOMINI 1941."

It is, as Goodwin might have said, a noble inscription. But the most moving lines written in his memory came from the hand of W. A. R. Goodwin, Jr.–18-year-old Billy–the day after the funeral. It was a poem titled "Father."

He spent his life in
dreaming dreams
But did not let them pass
unseen
By God or man.

His thoughts were ever
brought to light
By work and prayer and
his delight
In doing good.

His work is done; his body
stilled
He lived to see his dreams
fulfilled
Upon this earth.

How Godly and how good
does seem
That he should pass while
in a dream
Of God and Man.

Index

PHOTO CREDITS: *Colonial Williamsburg Foundation— 15, 29, 132, 152, 172, 173, 181, 198, 218, and 236;
Additional illustrations from Goodwin family and private collections*